LEARNING MATHEMATICS AT ELEMENTARY LEVEL

D.El.Ed.-504

For

Diploma in Elementary Education [D.El.Ed.]

IMPORTANT STUDY MATERIAL FOR NIOS, SCERT, B.El.Ed. (DU), DIET, JBT, IGNOU

GULLYBABA PUBLISHING HOUSE PVT. LTD.

ISO 9001 & ISO 14001 CERTIFIED CO.

Developed and Produced by:
GullyBaba Publishing House Pvt. Ltd.

Regd. Office:
2525/193, 1st Floor, Onkar Nagar-A,
Tri Nagar, Delhi-110035
(From Kanhaiya Nagar Metro Station Towards Old Bus Stand)
Ph. 011-27387998, 27384836, 27385249

Branch Office:
1A/2A, 20, Hari Sadan,
Ansari Road, Daryaganj,
New Delhi-110002
Ph. 011-23289034
011-45794768

E-mail: hello@gullybaba.com, **Website:** GullyBaba.com
First Edition: 2017

Author: Gullybaba.Com Panel
ISBN: 978-93-86276-51-3

Preface

Mathematics is recognised as one of the central strands of human intellectual activity. From the very beginning, mathematics has been a living and growing intellectual pursuit. It has its roots in everyday activities and forms the basic structure of our highly advanced technological developments. It comprises intricate and delicate structures which have a strong aesthetic appeal. It also offers opportunities for opening the mind to new lines of creative ideas and channeling thought. Undoubtedly, the mechanism of resolving an intractable problem offers the most intense of all intellectual pleasures. At the same time, it is reputed to be, and rightly so, the most hypothetical of all sciences. It exhibits connections between things, which can be visualized only through the agency of human reason.

The revised syllabus of mathematics formulated on the basis of NCF, 2005 for the elementary stage of education reflects the recent developments and trends in mathematics education. It emphasizes conceptual understanding, skill proficiencies and thinking skills in the teaching and learning of mathematics. These competencies are integral to the development of mathematical problem solving ability. Emphasis is also need to be given to reasoning, applications, and use of technology.

The present book of GPH *'Learning Mathematics at Elementary Level (Course-504)'* discusses the pedagogical skills of teaching mathematics at elementary stage. This book also describes various skills of assessing young children's learning and performance in Mathematics.

This book is written specially in question & answer format to provide students the instant gratification of a correct answer. In this book, we have tried to solve all possible questions from the exams' point of view. Solutions of previous years' questions papers have also been included to help you to understand the unique examination structure. We hope that this book would not only be a favourite study material for the students but also can be a nice resource for teaching.

An attempt has been carefully made to present this book more useful and meet the requirement and challenges of the course prescribed by University/Institution.

We wish you a successful and rewarding career ahead. Feedback in this regard is solicited.

-Gullybaba.Com Panel

Acknowledgement

Our compliments go to the **GullyBaba Publishing House Pvt. Ltd.,** and its meticulous team who have been enthusiastically working towards the perfection of the book.

Their teamwork, initiative and research have been very encouraging. Had it not been for their unflagging support, this work wouldn't have been possible. The creative freedom provided by them along with their aim of presenting the best to the reader has been a major source of inspiration in this work. Hope that this book would be successful.

– Gullybaba.Com Panel

Publisher's Note

The present book D.El.Ed.-504 is targeted for examination purpose as well as enrichment. With the advent of technology and the Internet, there has been no dearth of information available to all; however, finding the relevant and qualitative information, which is focussed, is an uphill task.

We at **GullyBaba Publishing House Pvt. Ltd.,** have taken this step to provide quality material which can accentuate in-depth knowledge about the subject. GPH books are a pioneer in the effort of providing unique and quality material to its readers. With our books, you are sure to attain success by making use of this powerful study material. Provided book is just a reference book based on the syllabus of particular University/Board. For a profound information, see the textbooks recommended by the University/Board.

Our site **gullybaba.com** is a vital resource for your examination. The publisher wishes to acknowledge the significant contribution of the Team Members and our experts in bringing out this publication and highly thankful to Almighty God, without His blessings, this endeavor wouldn't have been successful.

– Publisher

Topics Covered

Contents

Question Papers

Importance of Learning Mathematics at the Elementary Stage of Schooling

INTRODUCTION

Mathematics pervades all aspects of our lives. Each and every person, whether s/he is a farmer, daily labourer, artisan, teacher or a scientist uses the principles of mathematics in his/her day-to-day activities at different situations. Holding a key position in our life, it has also enjoyed a privileged or a sheltered position in the school curriculum. In spite of its pervasive use, mathematics is perceived as a difficult subject to master because of its abstractness. Most of us believe that mathematics is a difficult subject, beyond the understanding of common man. Most of the pupils as well as quite a significant number of teachers are literally afraid of mathematics and it is no wonder that they develop mathematics phobia.

There is a close relationship between the growth of thinking and the development of mathematical concepts. A teacher should be aware of such relationship so that s/he can develop understanding of the strength and difficulties of every child in his/her class in learning of mathematical concepts and can take appropriate facilitating steps in that direction. In accordance with the cognitive development of the child, teachers have tried to discuss the ways the children love to learn mathematics by studying the development of the mathematical concepts. Teachers on their part may also try to search for the typical problems of children in learning mathematics with their solutions.

Q1. Explain the stages of cognitive development of children as stated by Piaget.

Or

In which stage of cognitive development are the students of primary classes? Briefly discuss.

Ans. The cognitive structures are constructed and continuously reconstructed through an interaction between the student and various experiences in and out of the classroom. As a result of modification in the cognitive structure, more and more concepts will be assimilated and accommodated. Based on his studies, Piaget put forth clearly demarcated sequential stages in cognitive development in children, namely:

- Sensory motor period (Birth to 2 years)
- Pre-operational period (2-7 years)
- Concrete operational period (7-11 years)
- Formal operational period (11-15 years)

(1) **Sensory Motor Stage (Birth to 2 years):** During this stage, infants and toddlers acquire knowledge through sensory experiences and manipulating objects. It was his observations of his daughter and nephew that heavily influenced his conception of this stage. At this point in development, a child's intelligence consists of their basic motor and sensory explorations of the world. Piaget believed that developing object permanence or object constancy, the understanding that objects continue to exist even when they cannot be seen, was an important element at this point of development. By learning that objects are separate and distinct entities and that they have an existence of their own outside of individual perception, children are then able to begin to attach names and words to objects.

(2) **Pre-operational stage (Ages 2 to 7):** At this stage, kids learn through pretend play but still struggle with logic and taking the point of view of other people. They also often struggle with understanding the ideal of constancy. For example, a researcher might take a lump of clay, divide it into two equal pieces, and then give a child the choice between two pieces of clay to play with. One piece of clay is rolled into a compact ball while the other is smashed into a flat pancake shape. Since the flat shape looks larger, the preoperational child will likely choose that piece even though the two pieces are exactly the same size.

(3) **Concrete operational stage (7-11 Years):** This stage is differentiated from the pre-operational stage in terms of the development of logical thinking in the children. Piaget believes that a child is able to manipulate and organise information during this period. Concrete operational child uses written words and numbers to symbolise them. This stage is characterised by seven types of conservation (number, length, liquid, mass, weight, area and volume), intelligence is demonstrated through logical and systematic manipulation of symbols related to concrete objects.

(4) **Formal operational stage (11 Years and above):** Formal operational stage is characterised by abstract thinking and the beginning of adolescent thinking. During the formal operational stage, a child is engaged in abstract thinking. S/he does not take anything for granted. Formal operations consist of four overlapping logical abilities, namely (i) Hypothetico-Deductive Thinking; (ii) Inductive Thinking; (iii) Reflective Thinking and (iv) Inter-propositional Logic.

Q2. What are the basic mathematical concepts that are essential in all topics included in the mathematics curriculum at the elementary school level? Discuss each of them in brief.

Or

Which basic mathematical concept should be developed to the young children of elementary school level?

Or

Differentiate between cardinal aspect and ordinal aspect of numbers. [April-2016, Q.No.-19]

Ans. The basic mathematical concepts that are essential in all topics included in the mathematics curriculum at the elementary school level are as follows:

(1) **Development of Number Concepts:** Counting is considered as the first step to familiarise number concepts. And in most of the children admitted to class I, know the number names at least up to 10, mostly, through rote methods. But the children are required to acquire some preliminary concepts called the pre-number concepts, for effective learning of number concepts.

(a) **Pre-number concepts:** This can be developed in children during the preschool years, i.e. before the concrete operation stage or before attaining 7 years of age.

- **Matching:** Children can understand the concept of **one-to-one correspondence** through matching. When a child passes out cookies, each child in the room gets one cookie. Maybe there are extra cookies or maybe there is just the right amount of cookies. Matching forms the basis for our number system. When a child can create "the same", it then becomes possible to match two sets. This becomes a pre requisite skill for the more difficult tasks of conservation.
- **Sorting:** Children are required to consider the characteristics of different types of items and find characteristics that are the same. This will create a sorting attribute in them, i.e. children are able to sort things. Initially, young children begin sorting by colour instead of any other attribute.
- **Comparing:** Comparing means comparison of two or more things. This attribute can be inculcated in children by make them look at various items and them compare these items by understanding differences like hot/cold, big/little, smooth/rough, heavy/light, tall/short, etc. Using comparison terms like these is important when children are looking for a relationship between two or more quantities. Initially, children are required to construct and compare sets of concrete objects to determine more/less/same comparisons. Children should make comparisons of more, less and same by making visual comparisons at the per-school level.
- **Ordering:** This is foundational to the number system. Putting numbers into their correct places by following some rules is known as ordering of numbers. Children have to be able to put items in an order so they are counted once and only once. Putting items in order is a prerequisite to ordering numbers. **Seriation** is ordering objects by size, length or height. At the time of giving directions

to a child, we should use ordinal words like first, next, last, etc.

- **Subitising:** It refers to the ability to instantaneously recognise the number of objects in a small group without the need to count them. This can be reconstructed without knowing the amount. Subitising helps the children to see small collections as one unit. It provides an early perceptual basis for numbers, but isn't about the knowledge of numbers.

(b) **Number Concepts:** In the development of number concepts, counting, recognising and using numerals correctly, comparing numbers and operations on numbers are considered as important milestones.

- **Counting:** The numbers are applies to objects in counting, which is the common use of numbers. The process of counting involves two steps. The first one is assigning a number to a particular object which forms one of the sequence of objects is known as *ordinal* aspect of number. The second and final step of counting is of knowing that the number of objects in a collection ('manyness', or 'numerosity') i.e. the *cardinal* aspect. The order (what is the position?) of the objects in a collection whereas cardinality refers to the size (How many objects?) of the collection is called ordinality. It develops earlier at about 3 to 5 years of age after the child is able to match the objects in two collections using the method of one-to-one correspondence along with the knowledge of number names. The knowledge of numbers names from 1 to 9 develops around 2 to 3 years of age not as a matter of numerical ability, but as words in course of language development. Associating these words (one, two, three, four,....., nine) with the objects is the beginning of the development of numerical skill. The process of ordinality is establishing one-to-one correspondence between the objects and the number names in a sequential order. However, for two reasons, ordinality does not ensure knowing the size of the collection of objects, i.e. (i) child at the age of 2 to 4 years is yet to know the quantity associated with number names, and (ii) he has not yet developed the conservation of numbers.

For example, the child below 5 years of age would say that there are more objects in the second line than in the first line (Fig. 1.1). Here, the child lacks the Mathematics sense that a collection of objects when spread linearly without changing the number remains invariant. When the child acquires this sense of invariance, s/he is said to have acquired the conservation of numbers which comes around age 6.

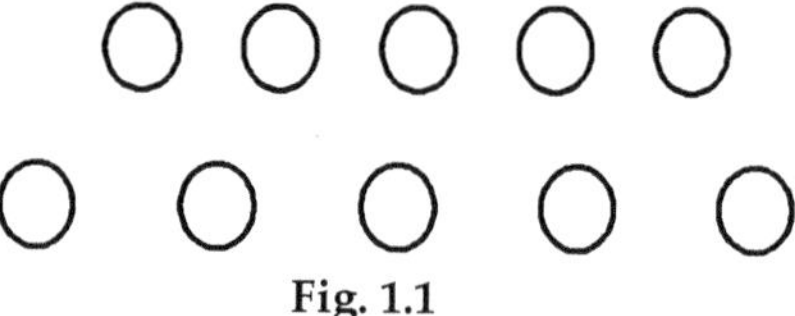

Fig. 1.1

From age 7 to 11 or 12, the child acquires the conservation of length, area, volume and mass in later years. Once the conservation of numbers is achieved around the age of 4 to 5, s/he can group the objects and within the group count to know the quantity of objects.

- **Use of numerals:** Numerals should be introduced to children only after they have had considerable experience in counting concrete objects. Numerals are the symbols used to represent numbers like 1,2, 3,... are used for the numbers one, two, three, ... and so on. While the concept of numbers is learnt through manipulation of objects and interactions with others, one has to introduce the child about the structure of numerals used for different numbers. In the decimal system of numbers, once the child becomes familiar with the numerals for the single digit numbers from 0 to 9, numerals for other numbers can be constructed by the child. The child becomes ready to understand and use the numerals by the age 7, but it is by the age 11 that s/he can write large numbers stating the place value of each number.

Using numerals in writing for numbers ten and more than ten, the knowledge of place value is essential which is developed around age 7 to 8 through process of counting in groups. It becomes easier for the child to compare the numbers. Once the knowledge of place value is developed.

- **Operations on numbers:** The addition and subtraction are observed to be performed by the children at a very early age. Adding and subtracting with concrete objects are quite familiar to those who never visit the schools. But the real understanding of the structure and operations comes around the age 9 to 11. From a developmental standpoint, children are able to learn multiplication at the same time that they are able to learn addition. But in schools, it is delayed and multiplication along with division is taught in grade III, i.e. till the children attain age 9. Again the structural properties of multiplication and division in natural numbers are introduced in the later part of the concrete operation period around age 11.

(2) **Development of Measurement Concepts:** The main aim of the concept of measurement is to help children understand what measurement is and how to go about doing it. Piaget identifies two processes, i.e. conservation and transitivity upon which the measurement process is dependent.

In the following example, the notion of transitivity is best illustrated. "Suppose a child is shown a rectangular plot of land in the school garden and was asked to create another such plot in the garden with equal measures of the sides of the given plot. Suppose the length of the given plot is say A. Then the child measured the length to be B by using a measuring stick. Then, the child carved out a plot the measure of which length was C. If he has performed the process of measurement of length correctly, we have a situation where he is displaying his grasp of the fact that if A = B and B = C, then A = C, i.e. his plot is of same length as the given one by virtue of the intermediary B (the measurement on the stick) as a comparison. Whatever the measuring situation, the meaningful use of an instrument of measure rests on the notion of transitivity."

From Piagetian studies, most of the research concerning the development of measurement concepts emanates and relates mainly to the measurement of spatial entities such as length.

Initially, in the preschool, i.e. below 6 years of age, the young child displays no grasp of conservation of length. His judgments are based primarily on a single perceptual feature. At this age, a child judges the two lines (Fig. 1.2) to be unequal because their end points are not aligned.

Fig. 1.2

The area and volume judgments are usually based on the longest linear dimension. The child uses non-standard unit of measuring length like, his hand span or his own height to measure the length, around 6 to 7 years of age. However, around 7 to 8 years of age, the child begins to understand the conservation of volume of liquid when s/he realises that the liquid poured from a wider vessel from a tall thin vessel is of same amount.

With smaller units of measure, the average child of around 8 to 10 years of age can appreciate measurement in terms of covering whatever is to be measured. Up to this stage, development of the measurement has been characterised by a trial and error approach. Now, the child is able to proceed by means of a more calculated approach. However, in terms of space, the measurements of area and volume occupied by a particular object lags behind.

To measure area and volume, the child reaches the final stage of development by calculation of linear dimensions (length, breadth and height/thickness) by the age of 10 and 11 or a few years later.

(3) **Development of Spatial Thinking:** The first impression of child's space or world in which s/he lives is a very disorganised one. Neither s/he can discriminate the figures nor s/he can hold the image of the figure for long time. When the child has passed the scribbling stage, around three and half years of age, s/he can distinguish between the closed and

open figures. But all simple closed figures are all the same for him/her and are drawn the same way such as squares, circles or triangles.

The child becomes able to differentiate between similar shapes around 7 to 8 years of age such as squares, rectangles and rhombus correctly. But it is not until the child reaches 10 years old, s/he is able to name the figures correctly and it is not until a year or two older than this that s/he could distinguish the presentation of 3D objects from those of the 2D figures.

During the later years of the concrete operation period and mostly during the formal operation period, mostly, the intricate aspects of development of spatial thinking unfold.

Q3. Explain the characteristics of nature of mathematics learning.

Ans. According to White Bread (Anghileri, 1995), following are the certain characteristics of nature of mathematics learning:

- It starts from the secure 'home learning' established in the child before s/he comes to school.
- It is based on understanding.
- It puts great emphasis on the child's own methods of calculating and solving problems and rejects the previous practice of heavy emphasis on standard written algorithms.
- It is regarded as a powerful tool for interpreting the world, and therefore, should be rooted in real experience across the whole curriculum as mathematics is brought out of the child's everyday situations.
- Mathematics with reason is rooted in action - learning through doing and puts less emphasis on representing numbers on paper as 'sums' and more emphasis on developing mental images in the child.
- The main tool for child and teacher to employ in the mastery of mathematics concepts is language, not pencil and paper exercises from textbooks. The child is encouraged to talk about what s/he is doing.
- Errors are accepted as an essential part of the learning process. The child, freed from the fear of criticism, will more readily experiment.

- Mathematics with reason emphasises the thinking processes of mathematics, and these are made explicit in the conversations between adult and child.

Q4. What are the basic ways of learning mathematics, which a teacher can facilitate in the classroom situations?

Or

What are the different ways through which children can learn mathematics? Discuss.

Ans. Some of the basic ways of learning mathematics, which a teacher can facilitate in the classroom situations, are as follows:

(1) **Placing tasks in meaningful contexts:** Young children quickly and easily develop their own informal and largely effective methods in real-life situations where the mathematics serves real-life purposes. The challenges begin when they enter the school and are expected to operate in the abstract, to use formal 'pencil and paper' routines and procedures and to do mathematics for no clear purpose. Evidence from research about the ways children learn seem to suggest that what we need to do is to start with real problems, and work from them to abstract representations, not the other way around.

In the everyday activities of young children, there are abundant opportunities to get themselves involved in rear mathematics. There are few such examples like playing games, sharing sweets, groupings in the class for performing different activities, finding out the holidays, etc.

While developing mathematical abilities in young children and understanding by tackling real problems placed within meaningful contexts, it is important that they learn to depend less upon the support on such contexts. The same process or concept needs to be presented to them in a variety of meaningful contexts. In this way, by natural processes of induction, children are able to sort out the relevant from the irrelevant and they are ultimately able to abstract for themselves the essential elements of the process or concept. All the while we must keep in mind that mathematics gains its power from abstractness, and from the real and concrete experiences, children need to be helped to become confident with drawing abstractions.

(2) **Manipulation of objects:** At the early stage, it is through the manipulation of concrete objects through which the children may acquire the mathematical skills. Acquisition of any mathematical skill at the early stage like comparison, categorisation, counting and four fundamental operations cannot be possible without manipulation of concrete objects. Provision of a variety of objects both familiar and novel, should be made available to children in the classroom for their free handling, so that to facilitate their learning of desired mathematical concepts, it would be easier.

(3) **Developing alternative strategies:** Children can also develop various approaches or ways to calculate and solve mathematical problems other than the prescribed ways given in the textbooks. That a child can evolve his/her own method of calculation, stems from the observations of totally non-schooled children performing calculations of various types required in their daily lives which are different from those given in textbooks. A major cause of young children's loss of confidence with school mathematics is the lack of relationship between formal and informal ways.

A child should be reinforced when s/he is developing new strategy and searching for alternate strategy need to be a regular feature in the classroom transaction. Children may be encouraged to think of any alternate strategy of the one discussed in the class either individually or in groups, after the discussion of any operation or procedure for solution of a problem.

The attitude of mathematics teacher about the formal methods given in the mathematics textbooks is very rigid, which does not help children to explore alternative strategies and loses interest in meaningful learning in mathematics. The mathematics teacher need to recognise the ability of the children to build alternative strategies and encourage it as much as possible.

(4) **Representation in multiple ways:** Through representation of mathematical concepts in multiple ways, children move towards abstract thinking in mathematics. Representation is the mental imagery of the object, event or process as perceived by the individual. It is now an established fact that children should be given opportunities to make their own

representations of mathematical problems, processes and procedures before they are introduced to the conventional symbols. In solving mathematical problems, if children are to become able and confident, they must be able to represent mathematics to themselves and to others in language and in mathematical symbols. Many mathematics educators now believe that it is important that children express their mathematical thinking in language, through talk, before they begin to represent it on paper and before they use mathematical symbols. James (1985) reviewing the work of Bruner and others on the inter-relationship between language and thought propounds a mathematics teaching procedure which he terms *'do, talk and record'*. This involves children in doing mathematics practically, and then following are the five-step sequence of activities towards recording. The learners:

- explain their thinking to others;
- demonstrate their mental images either with objects or by sketches;
- record in writing the 'storey' of what their sketches show;
- make successive abbreviations of the process they used; and
- can see the relevance of and adopt standard notations.

Sharing one's representation with others in the class helps to explore different approaches for elaborating the process or procedures and to develop multiple representations.

(5) **Problem solving and problem posing:** Although, solving mathematics problems and the process of problem solving, are different, but these have a lot of similarity in understanding the problem, suggesting and trying out different possible procedures of solution and solving the problem. Without providing any direct support, problem solving abilities can be developed when we encourage children in solving the problems independently or in groups. Besides promoting problem solving abilities in children, they should be encouraged to pose problems. The level of understanding of the concepts, processes and procedures of mathematics is indicated by posing relevant problems.

Q5. Why mathematics is considered as the most difficult of all the school subjects?

Or

Enumerate the four key features, inherent in the ways the school, mathematics has been designed to be taught which can create anxiety and fear among learners.

Or

Mention two reasons for developing fear for mathematics in the classroom. [April-2016, Q.No.-16]

Ans. Mathematics is considered as the most difficult of all the school subjects due to the following reasons:

(1) The mathematics at school level commonly involves the use of abstract symbolism which puts the young learners in difficulty.

(2) School mathematics is often taught as a set of prescribed procedures, without helping children really understand numbers and the ways they behave. There is often more emphasis placed on 'getting the right answer' than on understanding the processes involved. And, above all, it is the precision (accuracy) that makes mathematics more difficult.

(3) It is commonly devoid of any real, meaningful or supporting context. In the words of one, often quoted, famous mathematician, the trouble with mathematics is that 'it isn't about anything'.

(4) School mathematics often requires children to use new 'paper and pencil' strategies which are not simply written versions of the mental strategies which they have already developed for themselves.

Q6. What are the features of the human information processing system?

Ans. Following are the three main features of human information processing system:

(1) Limited 'working memory' capacity: Usually, teachers are not aware while teaching mathematics that human being has a limited capacity of processing information. For example, Miller has demonstrated from a whole range of evidence that we hold only about seven separate pieces of information in our short-term or 'working' memory. This is why as adults, we can easily process in our heads a sum such as 17×9, but have much greater difficulty with 184×596. We know the procedures we must go through to get the answer to the second sum, and we can carry out each of the separate computations involved. What we cannot do is hold all the information in our head at once. While we are working out one part, the result of the previous computation is very likely to be forgotten. With much smaller numbers and less complicated procedures, this happens all the time for children.

(2) **Development of 'meta-cognitive' awareness and control:** Another important feature of human processing system is that it is a system which not only learns but learns how to learn. When one is aware of his/her ways of thinking or learning called 'meta-cognition'; s/he acquires more ability to control over his/her actions and learning. In the prescribed ways, solving textual problems becomes monotonous and burdensome.

(3) **Learning by induction:** Humans are appeared to be very able to engage in the process of induction, but relatively less well-equipped for **deductive** reasoning. Inductive reasoning is the basic process whereby children can easily make sense of their world by classifying and categorising experience into increasingly structured conceptual structures and models. For children's learning, the overwhelming significance of inductive process has long been recognised, and has long been a strong element.

Q7. What are the various causes of mathematics phobia in learners?

Ans. The major causes of mathematics phobia in learners are as follows:

(1) **The fear of looking or feeling "stupid" in front of others:** Many learners do not clarify their doubts while doing mathematics because they are afraid of being regarded as "stupid" in front of others. In this way, they go on piling their doubts and become handicaps in mathematics learning in the long run.

(2) **The pressure of taking timed tests:** In the school, the emphasis of the examinations is so great that one feels as if the aim of all learning in schools is to perform well in the examinations. There is heavy pressure on children from the family and school to perform well in the weekly, fortnightly, monthly, quarterly, half–yearly and annually tests. Gradually, in the context of the continuous and comprehensive evaluation, the frequency of

tests is more than before. To perform better are mathematics, taking so many tests at regular intervals and expectations to perform better in mathematics than in any other subject are driving students to frustration.

(3) **Lack of preparedness:** Usually, with increasing number of tests they notice that the students are not always well-prepared for the class as well as for the tests. In just about any situation, this will cause anxiety.

(4) **Prior negative experiences with mathematics**: These may be related to one or more of the following:

- *Lack of positive role models:* It has been observed that the students belongs to higher classes or a family member with exceptional mathematics abilities do inspire the children of lower grades in mathematics learning. Towards an abstract subject like mathematics, such a role model is rare to find and the child does not find adequate inspiration.
- *Lack of encouragement from parents and/or teachers*: A child may have to face anxiety to perform well in the subject when s/he does not get any support from home and encouragement from teachers in the school. In most of the cases, it has also be observed that when parents and teachers pressurise the child for better and higher performance in mathematics, then the child develops fear for mathematics in him/her.
- *Mathematics problems being used as punishment in school:* When teachers use mathematics problems as a disciplinary measure in their classrooms, this generates fear among learners.
- *Unfavourable school climate*: Schools where extremely rigid discipline is maintained in coverage of the course with strict adherence to the textbooks without allowing freedom to children to think and to choose alternative ways to solve mathematical problems create more anxiety in learners towards the subject.
- *Ethnic and/or gender stereotypes:* There is a common feeling that girls and children from disadvantaged social groups do not perform well in mathematics. In mathematics classes, such children are looked down and are subjected to humiliating remarks.

Q8. How can a teacher reduce the mathematics phobia among learners and make classroom learning of mathematics pleasurable?

Or

State some methods to make mathematics learning pleasurable by overcoming difficulties of students.

Or

Give two measures to remove 'mathematics phobia' of a Class VIII student. [October-2016, Q.No.-36]

Ans. A teacher can reduce the mathematics phobia among learners by engaging them in activities that provide them pleasure while learning. Generally, a child loves to play games with other children and there are several games that prove to be a perfect medium for learning certain mathematical concepts. Teachers can take any familiar game children love to play and with slight modification, s/he can integrate some mathematics concepts in it so that the children can acquire those concepts while enjoying the game. In addition to these efforts, teacher can devise interesting activities specifically for the purpose. Some other methods to make mathematics learning pleasurable by overcoming difficulties of students are:

(1) **Guessing Game:** Guessing game is played between two teams (Team A and B), where the Team A decides a number between 0 to 100 and writes it in a slip of paper and gives it to the teacher or the leader conducting the game without revealing it to the other team and the Team B has to guess the number by asking questions. In a variation of this game, the team is allowed to ask definite number of questions (say 10 questions) whose answer is either 'yes' or 'no'. The score to be awarded to the team B depends on the number of questions they ask to reveal the number. If through asking one question they guess the number correctly, they are awarded 10 marks and if two questions are used to reveal the number, then 9 marks are awarded. The score goes on decreasing with increase in the number of questions. Next, it would be the turn of the team B to decide the number and the team A to guess it through questioning. The game goes on in turns and after definite number of rounds, the team aggregating higher score becomes the winner.

(2) **Number Race:** A teacher can divide the students of her class into 4 or 5 groups and let them elect a leader from among

them to act as the leader. Each group stands in a row facing the blackboard in their front. Keep a collection of pebbles in a place about 2 meters in their front. When the leader shows a numeral card, say 5, the first player in each team runs to the place where the collection of pebbles are kept and picks up 5 pebbles from it and raises his/her hand immediately after the collection. Whoever raises the hand first earns a point for his/her group after the leader ascertains the correctness of the count. The players who have completed their turn join the end of the row of their respective teams. The leader shows another card and the second player in each team races to the collection and the game continues. Towards the end, the game won by the team earning maximum points.

(3) Addition Game: This type of game is generally played between 2 or more players individually or in teams. The addition games are best suited to class II students. For this game, teachers are required a pack of playing cards without the picture cards. The players sit in a semicircle. The cards are shuffled and placed face down in the center before the players. Players/teams take turns to reveal two cards, find the sum and record this as their score. Players/teams keep a running total, checking each other's calculations. When all the cards have been used, the winner is the player/team with the greatest total.

(4) Place Value: In place value, two teams or two players can play. Each team or player has a slate or a drawing sheet with two adjacent boxes marked **Tens** and **Ones**. Numeral cards from 0 to 9 are shuffled and put face down in a pile. The first player picks a card and decides where to put the card, either in **Tens** place or **Ones** place. The next person from the other team or the other player picks a card and puts the card in the box as s/he decides to put. Next comes the turn of the first player to pick a numeral card and this time s/he has to put it in the vacant box. The player from the second group does the same. Each player has to tell the name of the number so formed. The round won by the player or the team forming the larger number.

Given the following figures:

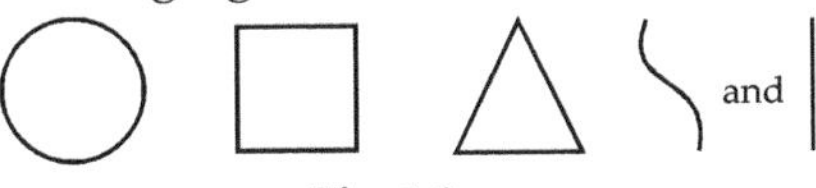

Fig. 1.3

Using these figures, a teacher may ask his/her students to draw the diagram of the objects familiar to the students. The student wins the game who draws more variety of figures within a fixed time span (say 5 to 10 minutes).

While learning mathematics, there are several other activities which are enjoyed by the children. A few such activities are creating symmetrical '**Rangolis**' on the paper using colours, introducing the children to **origami**, the art of paper folding to create various shapes of 2D and 3D objects, and familiarising with **tangrams** for producing several 2D figures.

For making mathematics learning pleasurable, while teaching learning process is going on especially when mathematics is being taught, teacher needs to create a learner friendly environment in the classroom. This is essential in building a free and joyful interaction between students and the teacher and among students in the classroom. Such a climate of trust and equality would help in removing anxiety and fear and make mathematics learning really pleasurable and more meaningful thus more effective.

Q9. State the nature of mathematics with suitable examples.

Ans. The nature of mathematics can be studied under the following heads:

(1) Mathematics is symbolic: To understand the symbolic nature of mathematics, following two examples can be considered:

(a) "Two hundred when multiplied by ten gives two thousand."

(b) "When the sum of any two natural numbers a and b is squared, it gives the sum of squares of a and b added with twice the product of the two numbers."

The above examples can be expressed in mathematical symbols, as:

$$200 \times 10 = 2000$$

and, $$(a+b)^2 = a^2 + b^2 + 2\,ab$$

The usage of symbols make mathematical expressions brief and clear. The symbols like those for numerals, four basic operations (i.e. +, –, ×, and ÷) or figures representing line, angle, triangle, quadrilateral, circles and the like are so familiar with everybody that not only these are easily understood but also widely used in our daily lives.

The core concern of mathematics in expressing complicated abstract ideas, in brief symbolic forms using common notations makes them comparatively easier to understand and communicate to others. These systems of notations add power to mathematics and allow us to visualise whether the mathematical statement is correct and valid or not.

(2) **Mathematics aims at abstraction:** Mathematics deals with abstraction. To understand this, following activity is conducted by a teacher of class-I:

Teacher made two set of people pieces, such as male and female. Some more pieces were not used. S/he gave the remaining pieces to the children and asked them to place these pieces in the set. The children did the activity. Then the teacher asked them to tell why they placed these pieces as they did.

Primarily, the children observed the properties common with all the elements in a group and on the basis of the common properties, they compared the remaining pieces. If the property of the remaining pieces is fitting to a particular group, then that piece is put in that group. This process is based on the principle of abstraction.

According to L, Bers, "The strength of mathematics is abstraction, but the abstraction is useful only if covers a large number of special cases." In mathematics, abstraction is essential as it is one of the amazing features of mathematics and this nature of mathematics gives rise to the development of new areas of mathematics like algebra. Algebra, a branch of mathematics deals with abstraction (one concept can be an abstraction in the sense that it is thought of as apart from material objects). A means of encompassing wider range of applications of mathematics is abstraction.

(3) **Mathematics is precise:** Another important nature of mathematics is precision. The term precision means 'accuracy' and 'exactness'. For example, we are familiar with the concept of a cone. The definition of cone is clear and precise. 'A cone is a 3-dimensional geometric shape that tapers smoothly from a base (usually flat and circular) to a point called the apex or vertex.' If an object is given to us, we can definitely say whether it is a cone or not.

Precision is that nature of mathematics which deals with accuracy and exactness and leaves no scope for doubt and ambiguity. According to C.J. Keyser, "The quality of mathematical thought, the certainty and correctness, its conclusion are due to the characteristics of the concepts with which it deals precision, sharpness and completeness. Such ideas admit of such precision, others do not, and the mathematician is the one who deals with those that do." While teaching mathematics, teachers have to focus on development of such qualities among their learners. Mathematics is characterised by its exactness and accuracy. The exactness in mathematics refers to the correctness in all aspects. Among the children, Mathematics helps in developing the abilities of accurate reasoning, thinking and judgments.

The learners learn the values and appreciation of accuracy during the learning of mathematics. S/he also learns to be accurate in approaching all the problems s/he faces in life and also precision in defining and as a result of studying mathematics, solving the problem becomes a habit with him/her.

(4) **Mathematics is logical:** The subject mathematics is accepted as a branch of logic, as C.G. Hempel said that mathematics can be derived from logic in the sense that all its concepts like, arithmetic, algebra and analysis can be defined in terms of logic. Thus, all the theorems of mathematics can be deduced by means of the principles of logic, and hence, mathematics truth can be established with logic. The proof of mathematical statements consists of a series of logical arguments, applied to certain accepted rules, definitions and assumptions.

There are two types of logic, i.e. inductive and deductive.

Now, consider the following mathematical statement (S1), which cannot be proved just by mere experienced observations.

S1: Two even numbers when added, it gives rise to another even number.

If we can take several examples and test them, then we can say that the statement could be correct. If we understand what even number is and the concept of addition, then we can prove the statement mathematically. Any even number can be written as 2n, where n is any natural number. Now we can take two even numbers, $2n_1$ and $2n_2$ (where n_1 and n_2

are natural numbers). The sum of these two numbers is $2n_1 + 2n_2 = 2(n_1 + n_2) = 2m$, where $m = n_1 + n_2$ is a natural number. Here, 2m is a number which is divisible by 2, and hence, is an even number. Thus, the sum of two even numbers is an even number. This kind of logic known as deductive logic, which uses known results, definitions and rules of inference to prove something.

In mathematics, use of another kind of logic is inductive logic. Following is an example:

2, 4, 6, 8, 10, 16, 36, 54, 68 and 102 are all even numbers. Now add any two of these even numbers and find out whether the sum is an even number or an odd number.

We find,

2 + 4 = 6, 6 is an even number.

12 + 8 = 20, 20 is an even number.

36 + 22 = 58, 58 is an even number and so on.

Teachers can ask their students to add any such two even numbers and in each case they will get an even number. So studying numerous such cases, s/he can conclude that any two even numbers when added the sum would be an even number. This type of logic is known as inductive logic. In mathematics, logic of induction used in several cases to prove mathematical results. Following is an example from geometry:

In a plane triangle, if the measure of the 1st angle is 80° and the measure of the 2nd angle is 60°, then what is the measure of the 3rd angle? If teacher will draw such a triangle with the given measures and measure the 3rd angle then s/he will see that it will be of 40°. Similarly, s/he can draw a number of different types of triangles and find out the measures of the three angles of each triangle s/he has drawn. The teacher will see that in each case, the sum of the measures of the three angles will be 180°. If the result is true for the 1st case, 2nd case, 3rd case and several similar cases, then we can reasonably conclude that if ABC is any plane triangle, then the sum of its three angles would be equal to 180°. This type of logical process of arriving at a generalised statement of relation observing the relation in several cases in similar conditions is known as mathematical induction. For n number of cases, if one statement is true then it will be true for n+1 number of cases.

(5) **Mathematics is study of structures:** The word structure means "arrangement, composition, configuration, form, order or system". The child is going through the concept of natural numbers, whole numbers, integers, fractional numbers, rational numbers and real numbers during the elementary stage.

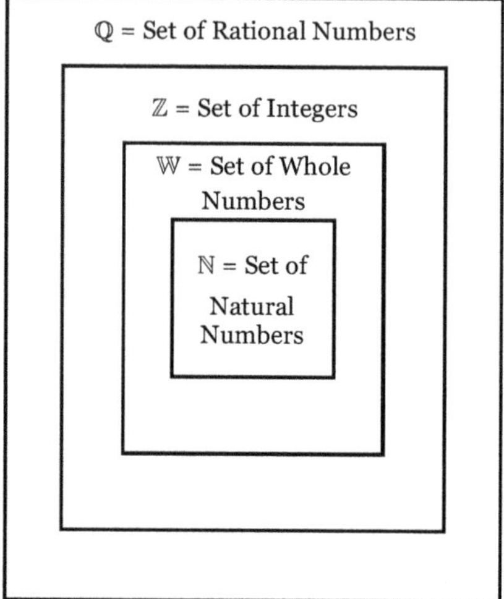

Fig. 1.4: The Hierarchy of Number system

Q10. What is the importance of mathematics in real-life situations of individuals?

Or

Discuss about the utility of mathematics in day to day life.

Or

"Mathematics is not only confined to the classroom only, rather we can see mathematics all around us." Comment over the given statement.

Ans. The subject mathematics has extensive application in our day-to-day life situations. It is an indispensable tool of precision in measure involving quantity and time. The moment one wakes up in the morning he encounters mathematics, the time, whether early or late and subsequently the entire days plan from daily chores to special works if any. Even for man's well being the financial planning tax planning everything is math.

In the field of education, be it the elementary or Ph.D. level, mathematics plays a vital role it begins with numeration exhibiting its numeral nature, then develops into the other branches as the student grows bigger in the form of Algebra, Geometry and Trigonometry and as theorems and abstractions at higher levels. It demands one to think, communicate, measure, reason and, connects, etc.

A fundamental knowledge of basic mathematics concepts is valuable for all individuals. In his day-to-day life when he calculated his wages, plans his expenses, estimates his balances, he is making use of a lot of simple mathematics.

An example can be taken that of a farmer. In this case, a farmer normally starts planning for cultivation taking into consideration of the area of land to be cultivated, amount of seeds, fertilisers and pesticides required for cultivation, number of agriculture workers required for farming, tentative amount of money required for this. Thus, it can be seen from here that a farmer uses mathematical knowledge in his day-to-day activities.

For an intellectual understanding of contemporary literature and to lead a successful life in society, a knowledge of mathematical language and symbols and their manipulations are essential. Even for a student who discontinues his education, after his primary or secondary education, the fundamental knowledge in mathematics helps him in taking up a good number of vocations such as tailoring, carpentry, etc. A knowledge of elementary mathematical concepts such as interest rate, banking, percentage, discount, ratio and proportion, variation is very essential to lead a fruitful life in the society. While teaching mathematics, the teacher of mathematics should cite examples from mathematics to stress upon the practical applications of mathematics. This will make the learning of mathematics interesting and meaningful.

Thus, mathematics is not only confined to the classroom only, rather we can see mathematics all around us. It is everything we do.

Q11. Describe the relationship of mathematics with other branches of knowledge.

Or

How does mathematics related to literature? Discuss.

Or

Name few subjects to which you can relate 'mathematics'. Discuss relation of mathematics with any two of these subjects.

[April-2016, Q.No.-35]

Or

Given an example to show the relation between 'mathematics and science'. [October-2016, Q.No.-18]

Or

How would art education be affected, if there were no mathematics? [October-2016, Q.No.-37]

Ans. Mathematics with its special features and nature seems to have a wider applications in daily life and other fields of study. There is no sphere of human knowledge which has remained unaffected by the influence of mathematics. Apart from the use of numbers, mathematical figures, formulas and processes, the subject has influenced the ways of presentation and communication of all areas of knowledge marked by coherence and mathematical precision. All this facilitates the correlation of mathematics with other fields and disciplines. A teacher of mathematics with a knowledge of the correlation of mathematics can enhance the effectiveness of his/her instructional process by relating it to other areas of interest.

(1) **Mathematics and Environment Study:** There are several topics in the curriculum of EVS at the primary grades, which require quantitative descriptions and analysis based on the quantitative data. Some such examples are, planning a school campus including school garden requires the concepts of measurement of length, area to be utilised. So also in beautifying a clean classroom environment need the mathematical concepts of symmetry along with the measurement skills. In approximating biodegradable wastes and other types of garbage produced in the school or in its near vicinity, teacher need to use of knowledge of ratio and proportions so that provisions for appropriate waste disposal system can be developed by the students.

The proportion of the different components of food for a balanced and nutritious diet, is calculated mathematically depending on the requirement of the individual. If a child is underweight and prone to infection, then proportion of proteinous food materials along with vitamins are increased based on the calculation of the degree of deficiency of these materials. Likewise, an obese (over fat) child needs less carbohydrate and fat materials in food which are calculated by the dieticians.

(2) **Mathematics and Art Education:** An individual with a mathematical background can perceive qualities such as symmetry, pattern, proportion, balance and harmony in creations of art. Shaw states, "Mathematics is engaged in fact, in the profound study of art and the expression of beauty." Therefore, mathematics itself is a piece of art, a study of harmony and of symmetry. There is beauty, symmetry, pattern and rhythm in mathematics and one could derive happiness and satisfaction from mathematics like any other piece of art. Its beauty, elegance and precision may appear sometimes to be cold or inhuman, and yet even very young children can gain great pleasure from working and solving problems within its domain. *Without mathematics, the art would look disproportionate, and hence, lose its artistic quality.* Therefore, before actually going to paint or sculpt, every artist or sculptor prepares a sketch of the art ensuring the right proportion of the parts of the figure s/he is going to develop in the final art.

The knowledge of beats or rhythm is the key to all such performances like singing, playing an instrument or dancing. For each *raga*, one sings or plays in instrument (say flute or sitar), there is definite scale of *taal* associated with it. Changing the slightest beat in the scale, may disturb the tune and may lose its musical value. The music scale, in written form using musical notations, looks like a pictorial graph with notations arranged in a specific order and specific distances among the notes indicating the definite time gap needed between producing the consecutive notes. At the beginning stage, the learners are habituated with the variations in tones and rhythms through counting the beats. Similar rhythm is maintained in different dance forms and styles through performing according *taal* produced by oral counting and then by the beating of drums or some percussion instruments. It is required to differentiate the tonal variations and the differences in *taals* through the rhythmic variations in counting.

(3) **Mathematics and Literature:** Language is the vehicle for communication and mathematics cannot be learned without the use of language. Though mathematics has its own language of symbols, they become more clear, meaningful and operational only when they are clearly explained in clear simple language.

Certain mathematical concepts especially abstract concepts can be learned only in the form of verbal statements known as definitions. Such definitions become specific and concise when stated in simple, clear language. In turn, mathematics helps the students to learn the language with clarity and exactness. The logical thinking and reasoning that the student develops through the study of mathematics can be applied to learn the language, especially in the usage of grammar and organising ideas logically and precisely.

Children are given freedom to express themselves in as many words as they can at the initial stage of language learning. But at each grade, we need to ensure their vocabulary acquisition and it is stipulated that towards the end of primary level, they should acquire around 5000 words. To have regular assessment of vocabulary acquisition, we need to use objective methods. In the upper primary grades, the children are encouraged to express within stipulated number of words, i.e. they are encouraged to be precise and comprehensive in their expression. Therefore, within specific number of words and in specific length of sentences, children are trained in precis writing and paragraph writing.

The length or meter of lines used in writing poem is also carefully chosen and meticulously adhered to throughout the poem. This helps in maintaining poetic rhythm, feeling and above all expressing the meaning. In all these, the overall structure and sense of the literature is prevailed and controlled by the mathematics sense.

(4) **Mathematics and Physical Education:** We need number wherever we desire to maintain some form of order, and physical education provide the brightest example of it. Whether it is mass drill, or individual yoga or performing aerobic exercises, we find wide use of numbers. Recording exact time for each event while performing in sports, building strategies for different games and athletics need mathematical expertise which is now being included in the training of the coaches and trainers.

(5) **Mathematics and Science:** Science is absolutely incomplete without mathematics as these two have the closest relation. All branches of science, whether biology, chemistry and physics, all use mathematics.

All chemical combinations are governed by certain mathematical laws. In chemical compounds, the constituent elements are combined in a definite ratio. In chemical reactions, the chemical equations are balanced by balancing the number of atoms on either side of the equation. In every field of physical science, like mechanics, light, sound, chemical reactions, mathematics plays vital role in explaining these phenomena.

John Perry has correctly estimated the value of mathematics in the study of Natural sciences by saying, "In these days, all men ought to study natural sciences, such a study is practically impossible without the knowledge of higher mathematical methods." The mathematical procedures of biometry are utilised for generalisations arrived from observed data. There are a few examples of use of mathematics in biological science, ascertaining the rate of growth of various species of plants and animals, the arrangement of leaves in different plants and trees, the rate of heart beat, measuring blood pressure, etc. It is difficult to enlist all the areas of science where mathematical knowledge is required to understand the concepts. Infact, in all branches of science, there is hardly any area where mathematics is not required.

(6) **Mathematics and Geography:** At every step in geography, we need mathematics. For instance, in studying landforms, we need to have clear idea of measuring larger heights and variations in temperature at different heights. In calculating the temperature, humidity and rainfall in a place, drawing graphs of their indicators and in determining their interrelationships, knowledge of corresponding mathematical concepts is essential. Trigonometry helps in estimating the height of a mountain or hill.

The knowledge of plane and solid co-ordinate geometry is required in determining the longitude and latitude of a place and in preparing maps.

(7) **Mathematics and History:** Children need to develop their chronological understanding in order to understand and explore historical events. So, as in mathematics, they need to learn the vocabulary associated with the passing of time and the relationship between units of times; this can be an element of historical study as they study specific periods. Also children need to use a range of information sources. Data

about people or events can take many forms, and mathematical skills may be needed to interpret this information, be it working out the length of a reign or analysing parallel events in history.

Q12. What is the relationship between mathematics and problem solving?

Ans. The Hilbert's Thesis on Mathematics quotes, 'Mathematics is forward looking, being more connected with solving outstanding problems and creating powerful new concepts and methods than with merely contemplating knowledge that has already been won.' According to N. J. Fine, 'A problem that is posed represents an outpost to be taken, a simple engagement in our conquest of the unknown.'

Thus, among learners learning mathematics is and developing problem solving abilities are nearly synonymous. Mathematical problem solving is used in most of the literatures, is far more than solving the word problems. George Polya, in his book *Mathematical Discovery*, defines problem solving as the conscious search for some action appropriate to attain some clearly conceived, but not immediately attainable aim.

The learner's problem solving ability is dependent on the acquisition of mathematical knowledge. Problem solving is far more useful as a guide to preparing children to be effective problem solvers in everyday life.

For example:

Mohan sold 8 boxes of candy and Gouri sold 3. How many boxes must Gouri sell in order to sell as many as Mohan?

By using mathematical knowledge, such type of problem can be solved.

If appropriate experiences are provided to the learner, then young children can learn basic problem solving processes such as:

(1) The problem should have few abstract concepts and the child must be able to make connection among the data given in the problem.

(2) The problem requires several steps to arrive at a solution. This causes the children to organise, reflect and record intermediate solutions.

(3) The ideal problem has multiple answers rather than one correct answer. The children should be allowed to search those multiple answers.

(4) The problem requires analysis and synthesis of information. Complex problems help the children to solve life-related problems.

The processes involved in problem solving include observing, inferring, comparing, copying patterns with objects, using trial and error, classification of objects and data and using appropriate strategies. These processes can be well-developed through learning of mathematics. Thus, mathematics learning is important to not only solve the mathematical problems but also the problems we confront in our day-to-day situations.

Q13. Define mathematical thinking. How can you understand the learner's ability to think mathematically?

Or

What is the process of mathematical thinking for problem posing and problem solving? [April-2016, Q.No.-36]

Ans. H. Weyl stated, "By the mathematical thinking, I mean first that form of reasoning through which mathematics penetrates into the sciences of the external world and even into our every day thoughts about human affairs." Thus, mental abilities like thinking precisely, articulating clearly, think logically and systematically and generalising from patterns help us immensely in our real life situations.

Learning mathematics serves both as a means and an end. It is a means to develop logical and quantitative thinking abilities. Children's learning of mathematics should be a natural outgrowth from children themselves at the early grades. Such experiences must be interesting and should challenge their imagination, so they can think mathematically while observing any natural phenomena.

Among the learners, intuitive thinking and reflective thinking develop mathematical thinking. Intuitive thinking means learning by experimenting with concrete materials, through experiencing ideas in various concrete ways, and by visualising ideas relying on analytical thought processes. But reflective thinking comes later. Reflective thinking means being able to reason with ideas without needing concrete material. Reflecting, inventing, imagining and playing (dealing) with ideas, problem solving, theory building and generalising are included in the process of reflective thinking.

To understand the learner's ability to think mathematically, let us take an example in which we have to find out the relationship between HCF and LCM of any two natural numbers.

The problem here is to find out the relationship between the HCF and LCM of any two natural numbers.

Table 1.1

Number Pair	HCF	LCM	Remarks
(4, 6)	2	12	HCF < LCM
(3, 8)	1	24	HCF < LCM
(6, 6)	6	6	HCF = LCM
(3, 7)	1	21	HCF < LCM

By observing the chart, we may arrive at the general rule which are as follows:

- The HCF of any two numbers is either less than both the numbers or equal with them, but it should not greater than each of the numbers.
- The HCF of two prime numbers is always 1 and the LCM of them is the product of the numbers.
- The product of the two numbers is equal to the product of the HCF and LCM.

Whether these general rules are applicable to three different numbers? Are these rules applicable to numbers more than 10,000? In this case, we are posing a problem. Once we pose a problem, we will definitely test our conjecture, and prove it. In case it cannot be proved, we may go back and make modifications in our conjecture and generalisations and try to prove it again or otherwise reject it. So during the process of problem posing and problem solving, the mathematics thinking goes in this line:

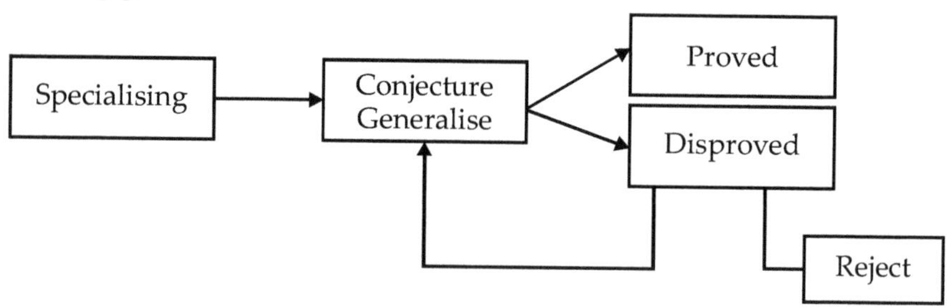

Fig. 1.5: Thinking Mathematically

Q14. What are the various goals of mathematics education according to George Polya? Discuss in detail.

Or

State broader and narrower aims of teaching and learning mathematics education.

Or

What is the broader aim of mathematics education? Discuss.

[April-2016, Q.No.-34]

Ans. According to George Polya, a Hungarian mathematician, also known as "The Father of Problem Solving in Mathematics Education", there are two kinds of goals of education, i.e. good and narrow aims; and higher aims.

(1) The Good and Narrow Aims of Mathematics Education: This aim of mathematics education is turning out employable adults who (eventually) contribute to social and economic development. With regard to school mathematics, this is specifically related to numeracy. Primary schools teach numbers and operations on them, measurement of quantities, fractions, percentages and ratios; all these are important for numeracy.

According to Polya, "The good and narrow aim of the primary school is to teach the arithmetical skills – addition, subtraction, multiplication, division, perhaps a little more. Also to teach fractions, percentages, rates, and perhaps even a little more. ... Arithmetical skills, some idea about fractions and percentages, some idea about lengths, areas, volumes, everybody must know this. This is a good and narrow aim of the primary schools, to transmit this knowledge, and we shouldn't forget it."

However, considering the broader and narrower aims of education, some of the major aims of mathematics education are to:

(i) develop in the child the power for invention;

(ii) understand and acquainted with the environment and culture;

(iii) develop the powers of thinking and reasoning;

(iv) prepare the child for various technical and general future professions;

(v) solve mathematical problems of daily life; and

(vi) prepare the child for higher study.

(2) The Higher Aims of Mathematics Education: The higher aims of mathematics education are to developing a child's inner resources, the role that mathematics plays is mostly about thinking. Clarity of thought and pursuing assumptions to logical conclusions is central to the mathematical enterprise. There are many ways of thinking, and the kind of thinking one learns in mathematics is an ability to handle abstractions. Even more importantly, what mathematics offers is a way of doing things: to be able to solve mathematical problems, and more generally, to have the right attitude for problem solving and to be able to attack all kinds of problems in a systematic manner. Following are the various abilities included in the higher aims of mathematics education:

(i) **Use of patterns:** Students to recognise, describe and generalise patterns to arrive at rules and formulae are required by study of patterns. If children are made to identify regularities in events, shapes, designs and sets of numbers then they will realise that regularity is the essence of mathematics. It provides the basis for inductive learning too. Exploring patterns is both fascinating and interesting and for children, can be made also a fun activity.

(ii) **Optimisation:** The utilisation of available conditions and resources to the fullest extent which is never included in the school mathematics curriculum is referred to optimisation. The skill of optimisation helps to examine whether the conditions provided for the solution of a problem are sufficient and whether all the conditions provided can be utilised in solving the problem.

For optimisation, considerations may not be always easy, but intelligent choice based on best use of available information is a mathematical skill that can be taught even at primary school stage.

Proofs of geometric deductions, constructions of geometric figures, algebraic equations or identities, or solving any arithmetic problem and skills of optimisation can be developed which have immense relevance for solving the real life problems are several problems in all sections of school mathematics.

(iii) **Reasoning and proof:** Mathematics is based on reasoning and proof. Two persons may have same answer to a particular question, in different ways. In mathematics, the process of reasoning and proof is important. So school mathematics should encourage proof as a systematic way of argumentation. The aim should be to develop arguments, evaluate arguments, make and investigate conjectures, and understand that there are various methods of reasoning.

(iv) **Problem solving:** Problem solving means that an individual has learned the skills and acquired relevant information necessary to solve problems that are not only curricular, but also related to everyday life. Various skills required for problem solving can be enhanced by providing opportunities to students to ask questions, think aloud, look for alternative explanations and procedures, isolate and control variables, keep record, apply reasoning and analogy, make models and apply process skills in teaching-learning of mathematics. Students can explore such potentiality while working on the problem. They feel a sense of achievement on getting success and develop self-confidence. Thus, the main goal in teaching mathematics is problem solving that students develop a generic ability to solve real life problems and apply mathematics in real-life situations. The basic purpose of education is to enable the child to adopt herself/himself to life in the society which is full of problems. To be successful, one must be adequately equipped with proper reasoning and critical thinking. Therefore, it is very important that problem solving must be encouraged in school life. Learners often learn facts and procedures with few tries to the context and application of knowledge. The problem solving skills include skills of observation, experimentation, estimation, reasoning and verification. Abstraction, quantification, analogy, case analysis, reduction to simpler situations, even guesses and verification are useful in many problem contexts.

Successful mathematical problem solving depends upon many factors and contents is important but is not enough students how to use these facts to develop their thinking skills and solve problems. It involves defining clearly, the problem to be solved, gathering relevant information, analysing the information and being aware of and evaluating the anticipated outcomes.

(v) **Mathematical communication:** Important characteristics of mathematics education are precise expression and unambiguous use of language. Using mathematical symbols, language, operations, etc. makes mathematics more meaningful and systematic. X is two times and 52 more than Y, and if Y is 75 what is X? Can precisely express as $X = 2Y + 52 = 2 \times 75 + 52 = 202$. It helps the persons in a precise manner, to communicate their experience and views.

(vi) **Use of heuristics:** Heuristics is the study of means and methods of problem solving and refers to experience-based techniques for problem solving, learning and discovery that would enhance one's ability to solve problems. A heuristic is a generic rule that often helps in solving a range of non-routine problems. Heuristics such as think of a similar problem, draw a diagram or a picture, working backward, and guess and check can serve different purposes such as helping the student to understand and represent the problem, simplify the problem, identify similarities with other problems, and to identify possible solutions. These heuristics often used in combinations can be used to solve different types of problems, though there is no guarantee that applying these heuristics will be successful.

Heuristics are an important aspect of mathematical problem solving, especially if we refer to them as the capabilities for mathematical reasoning that enable insightful problem solving. Beyond those proposed by Polya, the appropriate inclusion of more general heuristics like spatial visualisation, diagrammatic and symbolic representations in complex novel problems, and the recognition of mathematical structures in the teaching and learning of problem solving might result in enhanced student problem-solving behaviour.

However, when an individual solves a problem in a way different from the one given in the textbooks thought to be the only way, s/he feels a sense of discovering the alternative. This encourages the learner to try different hunches for solving the problems. One who uses such heuristics becomes, in the long run, efficient in solving real life problems.

(vii) **Making connection:** The subject mathematics is making correlation or connection between mathematics and other subjects of study and within mathematics. Children learn to draw graphs in mathematics class, but fail to think of drawing such a graphs in their project work, or in solving problems in physics and in other subject areas. Mathematical symbols and logic have wide implications in solving problems in science and presenting facts effectively. The skill of connecting mathematical knowledge with other areas of curriculum and with the problems of real life needs to be initiated from an early age.

(viii) **Representation:** The best use of mathematics is modeling situations using quantities, shapes and forms. Such representations aid visualisation, clarify essentials, help us discard irrelevant information. For example, a fraction can be well understood through an object and its cut pieces but can also be visualised as a point on the number line. Both representations are useful and appropriate in different context. Learning this about fractions is far more useful than arithmetic of fractions.

(ix) **Estimation and approximation:** When exact ones are not available, estimating quantities and approximate solutions are considered essential skills required for scientific investigations. When we estimate the total expenditure in organising a cultural function, or approximate time for completing a task, we may not get the right answer but surely gain advantage of reaching nearer to the solution. In many cases, students use this skill to employ these approximations in solving more complex problems. Therefore, in developing and refining such useful skills which is not found in the textbooks and in our classroom transactions, school mathematics can play a significant role.

Generally, the broader aims of learning mathematics have been grossly neglected in curricular and co-curricular activities at the school level. NCF-2005 is explicit in stating that "the narrow aim of school mathematics is to develop 'useful' capabilities, particularly those relating to numeracy- numbers, number operations, measurements, decimals and percentages". While the acquisition of basic content knowledge is necessary, learning content for content sake only encourages rote learning without developing proper understanding and skill in using to achieve the broader aims of mathematics education. The curriculum as well as classroom transactions need to synchronise the two aspects.

Q15. What are the specific aims of mathematics education? Why do we need to state such aims?

Or

State some reasons for stating specific aims for teaching and learning mathematics concept.

Ans. The specific aims of mathematics education are to:

- prepare them for mathematical exhibitions;
- develop appreciation for accuracy;
- develop in them the habits like regularity, practice, patience, self reliance and hard work;
- acquaint them with the relation of mathematics with their present as well as future life;
- ensure a good start to the students in learning mathematics;
- apply mathematics in other subjects;
- create love, faith and interest for learning mathematics;
- give clarity on fundamental concepts and processes of the subject;
- acquaint them with mathematical language and symbolism;
- develop in them a taste and confidence in mathematics;
- see aesthetics in mathematics; and
- prepare them for the learning of mathematics of higher classes.

The specific aims for teaching and learning mathematics concept are required to be stated because it helps to design suitable methods for planning effective classroom learning process, curriculum, guide to prepare TLMs, prepare evaluation procedures, etc. Thus, it is desirable to write the specific aims in action verbs, pin pointed, short, achievable, etc.

Q16. What are the visions of elementary school mathematics as provided by NCF-2005?

Or

Mention two points of vision for school mathematics as stated by NCF, 2005. [April-2016, Q.No.-20] [October-2016, Q.No.-38]

Ans. In the vision provided by NCF-2005, school mathematics takes place in a situation where:

- Children learn to enjoy mathematics rather than fear it.
- Children learn the importance of mathematics because the subject is more than formulae and mechanical procedures.
- Children see mathematics as something to talk about, to communicate, to discuss among themselves and to work together on.
- Children pose and solve meaningful problems in school mathematics.
- Children use abstractions to perceive relationships to see structure, to reason out things, to argue the truth or falsity of statements.
- Children understand the basic structure of mathematics: arithmetic, algebra, geometry and trigonometry, the basic content areas of school mathematics, all offer a methodology for abstraction, structuring and generalisation.
- Teachers engage every child in class with the conviction that everyone can learn mathematics.

Q17. What are the problems in teaching and learning of mathematics?

Ans. Following are some of the major problems in teaching and learning of mathematics:

- A sense of fear and failure regarding mathematics among a majority of children.
- A curriculum that disappoints both a talented minority as well as the non-participating majority at the same time.
- Crude methods of assessment that encourage perception of mathematics as mechanical computation.
- Lack of teacher preparation and support in the teaching of mathematics.
- Inadequate learning materials create problems in teaching and learning of mathematics, through which students find very little scope for pleasure and fun in learning mathematics from the textbooks; and in rural and remote areas, there is hardly any other material.
- Learning of mathematics seems to be difficult for learners and lose their confidence, lack their interest and attitude.

Q18. How can child learn mathematics beyond classroom? Discuss the scope of connecting knowledge to life outside the school.

Or

How can you as a teacher go beyond the textbook for teaching and learning mathematics concepts?

Ans. Children learn not only from the teacher, but also from interaction with other children as well as environment around them. They learn easily if the teaching-learning process is interesting, activity-based, allows for active participation and thinking at their level, joyful and relevant to the child's immediate environment. Children learn through their senses like smell, touch, taste, hearing and vision, also. The activities involving more than one sense will help children learn better. Usually, it is in nature of each and every child to learn at all time, everywhere inside or outside the classroom, i.e. home, playground, market, etc. Thus, teachers are required to make learning in school a happy experience breaking the boundary between learning within and outside the classrooms.

Scope of connecting knowledge to life outside the school can be seen under the following heads:

- **Real life:** A frog climbs 30 meters on a pole in a day and slides back 20 meters in a night. If the pole is 70 meters high, then how many days the frog will take to climb to the top of the pole? Most of our students of upper primary classes may calculate the answer as 7. One student told the answer is 5 as the frog climbs 40 meters in 4 days and in the fifth day it reached on the top, i.e. 70 meters. Students get opportunities to work in a natural setting, they work according to their own perceptions. So their real life experience must take into consideration.
- **Market:** Children, when went to market with their family, though indirectly, may have observe and participate in the way of buying and selling of goods and also the approach of the buyer and seller. Teachers must take the advantage of real situations and utilised the experience of the students in calculation of profit and loss, preparation of bills, process of weighting, counting of money, amount and price, etc.
- **Playground:** Children, while playing games like kabaddi, football, cricket, volley ball, basket ball and indoor games, usually frame the rules of the game of their own. Thus, teachers may prepare playground in a group. Students construct Circles, Rectangles, Squares, triangles, etc. in their playground without knowing the rules of construction. They count individual and group scores through their own strategies.

- **Garden:** Students prepare plots in home, schools and also in playing with peers. During that time, they may not know counting, measurement, construction of angles, different types of geometrical figures, areas, different lines, average, etc. but they may do it using their perception. How can one prepare a plot of two meters each side? We may share the experience of the students in these activities and it will be amazing to find out that they have already acquired a lot of mathematical concepts which requires slight refinement for acquiring formal knowledge and understanding of the concepts.
- **Festival:** We celebrate many festivals in our homes as well as in our schools. Students heartily involved on the Independence day, Republic day, Teacher's day, Children's day, Saraswati puja, Ganesh puja, Eid, Christmas, etc. They involve themselves in different activities to make these special occasions memorable. They go to market to buy various materials, decorate the school, distribute sweets, calculate expenditure, etc. at that time they also learn mathematics.
- **Making designs:** Students covered their note books, paint pictures, decorate their houses, plants trees in garden, design their playing kits, etc. At that time, are they using mathematics? How many match sticks are required to design your name? Teacher must observe the process of making design and utilised it in classroom.

Q19. State the ways for joyful mathematics learning.

Ans. The ways for joyful mathematics learning are:

- Developing Mathematics magic makes the mathematics learning interesting.
- Reduce wide gaps between mathematical theory and practice.
- Asked the students to collect local games, songs, dramas, etc. and convert it to mathematics learning.
- Children will learn more mathematics if the mathematics learning is joyful.
- Organise mathematical quiz, debate, seminar, etc.
- Each child's learning experience must be taken into consideration.
- Use diverse materials like flash cards, stones, sticks, objects, pictures, cutouts, charts, calendars, playing cards, cartoons, etc.

- Establish linkage between concrete objects and abstract concepts in mathematics learning.
- Do not impose adult's views on the students as it restricts the child's creative expression.
- Take students to outside the classroom to observe the nature.
- Collections of photographs of great mathematicians.
- Use Mathematical games, puzzles and stories to create curiosity among the students.
- Linking mathematics with life situation.
- Ensure opportunities for learning by discovery.
- Allow the child to take independent decision.

Q20. Give some suggestions to create conducive learning environment in the school for mathematisation.

Or

Give suggestions for learner friendly environment.

Ans. Some suggestions to create learner friendly environment are as follows:

- **School environment:** The environment of school should be developed in such a way that the child may be motivated to learn mathematics. Walls of the classrooms and schools should be designed with mathematical concepts. Innovative ideas on mathematics might be written on the walls. In prayer class also we may read the history of some mathematicians. It is necessary to bright classrooms with display of children's work and other interesting materials.
- **Knowing the children:** In learning of mathematics, a teacher should know every individual child in the class, praise children when they attempt to the mathematical problems, do not except children to do tasks which we ourselves do not do, know merits and demerits of every child in solving the problems in mathematics, provide sufficient time to solve the mathematical problems, etc.
- **Teaching learning equipments:** Teacher should collect mathematics textbooks, mathematics reference books, magazines, mathematics magic, story and puzzle books, project books, books related to history of mathematics and mathematicians, etc. Teacher should talk to the students, parents and community members to collect/prepare mathematical equipments.

- **Learning corner:** Basic facilities such as flash cards, stones, sticks, objects, pictures, cutouts, charts, calendars, playing cards, cartoons, etc. must be available in the classroom. Teacher should be prepared/collected different activities on mathematics and kept these in the learning corner. Teacher should use the learning corner when and where necessary.
- **Teaching learning programmes:** Students consider mathematics as a borrowing subject. Teacher should adopt interesting teaching learning programmes, which will create positive attitude among the students towards learning mathematics. The mathematics teacher should i) greet the children every day with a mathematical joke, story and puzzle, etc. ii) go beyond the mathematics textbooks, iii) not to devote excessively long time on practice of exercises on mathematics, iv) use flash cards, pictures, diagrams, flow charts, graphs, objects, etc. for better understanding of mathematics concepts.
- **Recreational Activities:** The recreational activities which are almost ignored in our schools should be given importance as it motivates the students and develops positive attitude among the students. Activities like organisation of mathematics club, mathematics quiz, competition on mental arithmetic, etc. development of question bank (oral, written and performance), activity bank with competencies, answer to Olympiad questions, and enrichment and remedial materials are recreational activities.
- **Assessment:** Learners must have opportunities to evaluate their own achievement in practice sessions. When children wrongly answer the questions, do not put them to shame. Master the required competencies before proceed to next competency. Practice sessions definitely must not destroy interest in learning. It is important that pupils enjoy practice sessions devoted to mathematics so that positive attitudes are developed. Avoid physical punishment and the school should be "Punishment free zone".

Q21. What are inductive and deductive methods of teaching and learning mathematics? Discuss the steps involved in the two processes.

Or

Mention the steps that a teacher follows in deductive approach for effective learning. [October-2016, Q.No.-39]

Ans. Inductive method: Inductive method is advocated by Pestalaozzi and Francis Bacon, which is a method of constructing a formula with the help of a sufficient number of concrete examples. Induction means to provide a universal truth by showing, that if it is true for a particular case. It is true for all such cases. Inductive approach is psychological in nature. The children follow the subject matter with great interest and understanding. This method is more useful in arithmetic teaching and learning.

Inductive approach proceeds from:

- particular cases to general rules of formulae
- concrete instances to abstract rules
- known to unknown
- simple to complex

Steps in inductive method: Inductive method follows clear and specific steps as follows:

- selection of a number cases;
- observation of the cases under given conditions;
- investigation and analysis for common properties and analysis;
- finding common relations;
- arriving at generalisation; and
- verification.

Example 1: Square of an odd number is odd and square of an even number is even.

Solution:

Particular concept:

(i) $1^2 = 1$ $3^2 = 9$ $5^2 = 25$

(ii) $2^2 = 4$ $4^2 = 16$ $6^2 = 36$

From (i) we get, 'Square of an odd number is odd'.

And from (ii) we get, 'Square of an even number is even'.

Example 2: Law of indices $a^m \times a^n = a^{m+n}$

Solution:

(i) $a^2 \times a^3 = (a \times a) \times (a \times a \times a) = a^5 = a^{2+3}$

(ii) $a^3 \times a^4 = (a \times a \times a) \times (a \times a \times a \times a) = a^7 = a^{3+4}$

(iii) $a^3 \times a^6 = (a \times a \times a) \times (a \times a \times a \times a \times a \times a) = a^9 = a^{3+6}$ and so on.

Therefore,

$a^m \times a^n = (a \times a \times \ldots \text{ m times}) \times (a \times a \ldots \text{n times})$

$= a \times a \times \ldots\ldots (m+n) \text{ times}$

$= a^{m+n}$

Thus, $\mathbf{a^m \times a^n = a^{m+n}}$

Deductive method: In deductive method, learners proceed from general to particular and from abstract and concrete. At first, the rules are given and then learners are asked to apply these rules to solve more problems. This approach is mainly used in Algebra, Geometry and Trigonometry because different relations, laws and formulae are used in these sub branches of mathematics. In this approach, help is taken from assumptions, postulates and axioms of mathematics. It is used for teaching mathematics in higher classes.

Deductive approach proceeds from:

- general rule to specific instances
- unknown to known
- abstract rule to concrete instance
- complex to simple

Steps: Deductive approach of teaching follows the steps given below for effective teaching. They are:

- clear recognition of the problem;
- search for a tentative hypothesis;
- formulating of a tentative hypothesis;
- solving the problem; and
- verification.

Example 1: Find $a^2 \times a^{10}$ =?

Solution:

General: $a^m \times a^n = a^{m+n}$

Particular: $a^2 \times a^{10} = a^{2+10} = a^{12}$

Example 2: Find $(102)^2$ =?

Solution:

General: $(a+b)^2 = a^2+b^2+2ab$

Particular: $(100+2)^2 = 100^2 + 2^2 + (2 \times 100 \times 2)$

$= 10000+4+400= 10404$

We can also multiply 102 with itself to get the same result.

Induction and deduction are not opposite modes of thought. Inductive and deductive method is the combination of two approaches of teaching mathematics at the elementary level. In essence, the inductive method begins with presentation of specific examples and ends with the formation of generalised principles. In contrast, the deductive approach begins with presentation of generalised principles ends with the generalisation of specific examples. Inductive method helps the learner in developing the ability to reason by observing common elements in the similar instances and arriving at the generalised statement or rule.

Deductive method is all about applying the established rules and formulae in solving various mathematical problems. Through the application of deductive method, almost all the problems in mathematics textbooks can be solved.

Q22. Discuss analytic and synthetic methods with example.

Or

In which method the proof of a geometric theorem proceeds just the reverse way of the proof given in the textbooks?

Or

Differentiate between analytic and synthetic methods.

Ans. Analytic method: The word "analytic" is derived from the word "analysis" which means "breaking up" or resolving a thing into its constituent elements. The original meaning of the word analysis is to unloose or to separate things that are together. In this method, we break up the unknown problem into simpler parts and then see how these can be recombined to find the solution. So we start with what is to be found out and then think of further steps or possibilities that may connect the unknown, which built the known and find out the desired result. It is believed that all the highest intellectual performance of the mind is analysis. The nature of the analytic method is that it leads to:

- conclusion to hypothesis
- unknown to known
- abstract to concrete

Example: If $\frac{a}{b}=\frac{c}{d}$, prove that $\frac{ac-2b^2}{b}=\frac{c^2-2bd}{d}$

Solution: Following analytic method, we start with what is to be proved and proceeded as follows: If

$$\frac{ac-2b^2}{b}=\frac{c^2-2bd}{d}$$

$\Rightarrow d(ac-2b^2)=b(c^2-2bd)$ (by cross multiplication)

$\Rightarrow acd-2b^2d=bc^2-2b^2d$ (multiplying and simplifying)

$\Rightarrow acd=bc^2$ (by cancelling '$-2b^2d$' from both the sides)

$\Rightarrow ad=bc$ (dividing both sides by '*c*' supposed to be a non-zero term)

$\Rightarrow \frac{a}{b}=\frac{c}{d}$ (dividing both the sides by '*bd*')

Since, this condition is given to be valid, then

$\frac{ac-2b^2}{b}=\frac{c^2-2bd}{d}$ is also valid as per the above analysis.

Analytic statements are not considered as the statements of proofs for the problem. Rather analysis is considered as the means of discovering the proof.

Synthetic method: Synthetic is derived from the word "synthesis". Synthesis is the complement of analysis. To synthesis is to combine the elements to produce something new. Actually, it is reverse of analytic method. In this method, we proceed "from known to unknown". So in it, we combine together a number of facts, perform certain mathematical operations and arrive at a solution. That is we start with the known data and connect it with the unknown part.

Example : If $\frac{a}{b}=\frac{c}{d}$, prove that:

$$\frac{ac-2b^2}{b}=\frac{c^2-2bd}{d}$$

Solution : Given $\frac{a}{b}=\frac{c}{d} \Rightarrow ad = bc$ (by cross multiplication)

$\Rightarrow acd = bc^2$ (by multiplying a non-zero quantity *'c'* to both the sides)

$\Rightarrow acd - 2b^2d = bc^2 - 2b^2d$ (adding '$-2b^2d$' to both the sides)

$\Rightarrow d\left(ac-2b^2\right) = b\left(c^2-2bd\right)$ (taking common elements from both the sides)

$\Rightarrow \frac{ac-2b^2}{b}=\frac{c^2-2bd}{d}$ (dividing both the sides by *'bd'*)

This is the type of proof we come across in nearly all mathematics textbooks. This is precise, logically arranged in proper sequence and easy for reading and communicating.

Analytical proofs look somewhat disorderly which they actually are not. Many are of the opinion that through synthetic method we get the proof, while analytic method provides the way to discover the proof. In that sense, methods of analysis and synthesis in mathematics are complementary to each other.

Method of analysis and synthesis is applied for such problems in mathematics where 'if – then' type of logic is needed (***If*** a triangle is isosceles, ***then*** prove that the measures of the angles opposite to the sides of equal length are equal). In such problems, some conditions (hypotheses) are given and under those conditions some relationships have to be proved. In proving geometric relationships, and algebraic identities and in solving algebraic problems, this method can be effectively used.

Q23. What is project method of teaching and learning mathematics? Discuss.

Or

Identify the basic characteristics of the project in mathematics.

Ans. In classroom, there are number of students who are good in solving the problems from the mathematics textbook. But most of the students are unable to solve the real life problems where the solution remains similar. For example, students are familiar to solve the problems on profit and loss from the textbook, but they fail to apply the same knowledge during marketing. It is because of the way of teaching mathematics in the classroom. Students are made to spend many hours of the day in learning and repeating subjects from textbooks without understanding their value in daily life. In reality, learning mathematics prepares a child for life by making him/her live in reality and provide him/her opportunities where s/he can exercise his/her ability of thinking and skills of doing. Therefore, learning through project is an important aspect for getting real experiences.

This type of learning is an approach to learning focusing on developing a product or creation. The project may or may not be student-centered, problem-based or inquiry-based. Project-based learning is a teaching method in which students gain knowledge and skills by working for an extended period of time to investigate and respond to a complex question, problem or challenge. Project-based learning is an individual or group activity that goes on over a period of time, resulting in a product, presentation or performance. It typically has a timeline and milestones, and other aspects of formative evaluation as the project proceeds. As the project progresses, the learner or group of learners goes on picking up any piece of knowledge that may happen to be relevant, necessary and useful. So to complete any project, there are different stages in actual practice.

(a) Providing the situations
(b) Choosing and purchasing
(c) Planning for the project
(d) Executing the project
(e) Judging of evaluating the project
(f) Recording the project

Q24. What is problem solving method and what are its steps?

Ans. Problem solving means engaging in a task for which the solution method is not known in advance. In order to find a solution, students must draw on their knowledge, and through this process, they will often develop new mathematical understandings. Solving problems is not only a goal of learning mathematics, but also a major means of doing so. Problem solving gives students a context to help them make sense out of the mathematics they are learning. Problems can be used to introduce new concepts and extend previously learned knowledge.

Teachers have experience that the solution of a problem in mathematics, at the elementary level is considered to be unique, but there are more than one way to reach at the solution.

For example, the students of class-II in a school are given to find the results of 75+29 in as many ways as possible:

(i) By direct method: $75 + 29 = 104$

(ii) $75 + 29 = 75 + (30 - 1) = (75 + 30) - 1 = 105 - 1 = 104$

(iii) $75 + 29 = 74 + 1 + 29 = 74 + 30 = 104$

(iv) $75 + 29 = 75 + 25 + 4 = 100 + 4 = 104$, so on.

Therefore, while teachers are teaching to solve any mathematics problem, they need to recognise the ways it can be solved. Each student should be made aware of the fact that each mathematics problem can be solved in several ways and they should be encouraged to look for alternative methods for solving any problem. Searching for alternative solutions requires reflective and creative thinking abilities on the part of the learners. The main objective of problem-solving method is, therefore, to stimulate the reflective and creative thinking of the learners. In order to solve a problem in mathematics, a learner needs to proceed along the following steps:

(a) **Recognising the problem:** The students should be able to recognise or identify the problem before they attempt to solve it.

(b) **Defining the problem:** The second step is to define the problem as it helps in understanding the problem in terms of what is given what are to find out in a problem?

(c) **Collecting relevant information:** The students will collect related information which is required to solve the problem. Recall of previous learned knowledge, facts, skills, theorems, processes, etc. the students may learn to ask what I know that is related to this problem. For an example, in height and distance problem, one needs to recollect the trigonometric ratio.

(d) **Formulating tentative hypothesis:** The focus of this stage is on hypothesising searching for a tentative solution to the problem. For example, when students are going to find out the total surface area of cone, they may formulate the hypothesis as total surface area is the sum of the curved surface and the base area of the cone.

(e) **Testing the hypothesis:** Appropriate methods should be selected to test the validity of the tentative hypothesis as a solution to the problem. If it is not proved to be the solution, the students are asked to formulate alternative hypothesis and proceed.

(f) **Construct physical models:** Some problems need physical model for finding the solution. For example, how many 1×1 squares are there in 8×8 chess board? Children may be provided with chess board for finding the solution of the above question.

(g) **Verification of the result:** At last, the students are asked to determine their results and substantiate the expected solution. The students should be able to make generalisation and apply it to their daily life.

Q25. Explain problem posing method with suitable example. What are the benefits of problem posing for learning?

Or

What are the benefits of 'problem posing' for learning?

[April-2016, Q.No.-31]

Ans. Problem posing method has a strong relationship with problem solving method. Brown and Walter (2005) stated that one of the important consequences of mathematics education is to provide opportunities to the students in mathematics lessons for developing their problem posing skills. Because problem posing is not only to generate new problems from given situations but also reformulate given problem and generalise for the solution.

Problem posing has too much interest because of its effect in creativity and mathematical ability. Problem posing in contrast to traditional problem solving methods reduces anxiety and common fears about mathematics and increases positive attitudes towards mathematics. Problem posing improves not only students but also teachers' attitudes; alleviate misunderstanding about the nature of mathematics. Problem posing activities gives more responsibility to the students who are motivated for the problems during the mathematics class. Problem posing methods of learning bring up the students for the future as social an individual that meets the expectation of modern society.

For example, in statement $4 \times 5 = 20$

The first step of problem posing is to look closely or observe the statement critically. In the above statement, following are some of the observations we can make:

- There are two multipliers.
- The difference between the multipliers is 1.
- One is a multiple of 2 and other is multiple of 5.
- The two multipliers are two consecutive natural numbers.
- The product is 4 more than a square number (16) and 5 less than another square number (25).
- One of the multipliers is even and other is odd.

After making the observation on the statement $4 \times 5 = 20$, there are some of the examples of problem posing method:

(1) What if we tried adding two numbers to equal 20? How many ways could we do so? What do we notice about odd and even numbers when adding to make 20?

(2) What if we continued to multiply by multiples of 2 and multiples of 5? What patterns might we see?

(3) What if we tried using multipliers that are the same to make 20? Is this result possible? What products are possible using multipliers that are the same?

(4) What do we find if we multiply an odd number by an odd number? An even number by an even number? What if we multiply three odd numbers or three even numbers?

(5) Do we always get an even product when multiplying an odd number by an even number?

(6) Why, when we add an odd and an even number, do we get an odd number, but when we multiply an odd number by an even number we get an even number?

The benefits of problem posing for learning are as follows :

(1) It develops the spirit of inquiry. The more learner observes, the more learner wants to find out.

(2) The other benefit is that problem posing involves searching for patterns.

(3) It supports learners in asking the perennial question that mathematicians pose: Is this always true? That is, did this relationship occur fortuitously, or does a pattern lurk behind these numbers?

(4) Uncovering patterns is certainly joyful, but even more rewarding is discovering why those patterns are occurring. Let's see what learners notice about our original problem: $4\times 5 = 20$. Learner's see that 20 is 4 away from the nearest smaller square, i.e. 16, and is 5 away from the nearest larger square, i.e. 25. Why? They notice that 4×5 is $4 \times (4+1)$ or $(5-1) \times 5$.

(5) It leads the learner into unknown territory.

(6) It requires and promotes reflective thinking especially during posing the problems.

Q26. Describe the phases of 5E's learning model.

Or

In which phase of 5E's learning model, the learners get a chance to reflect on their knowledge? Also explain that phase briefly.

Or

Discuss 'exploration phase' of 5E's learning model.

[October-2016, Q.No.-40]

Ans. The 5E's learning model is a kind of learning cycle, used in lesson plans, follows Bybee's five steps of engagement, exploration, explanation, elaboration and evaluation. As in any cycle, there is no end to the process. After elaboration ends, the engagement of the next learning cycle begins. Evaluation is not the last step. *Evaluation occurs in all four parts of the model.*

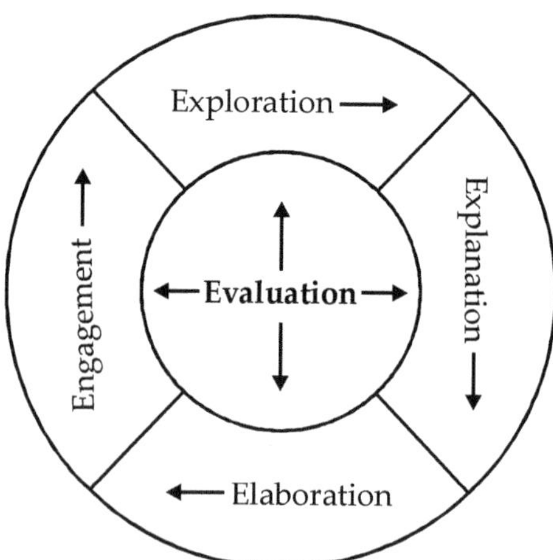

Fig. 1.6: The 5E's Learning Model (The learning cycle)

(1) **Engagement Phase:** It is the time when the teacher is on center-stage. The teacher poses the problem, pre-assesses the learners, helps them make connections and informs them about where they are heading. The purpose of engagement is to:

- focus learners' attention on the concept or topic;
- Pre-assess learners' prior knowledge;
- Inform the learners about the lesson's objectives;
- Remind learners of what they already know that they will need to apply to learning the concept or topic at hand;
- Pose a problem for the learners to explore in the next phase of the learning cycle.

Evaluation of Engagement: Evaluation's role in engagement revolves around pre-assessment that is funding out what the learners already know about the topic at hand. The teacher could ask questions and have the learners respond orally and/or in writing.

(2) **Exploration Phase:** Now, the learners are at the centre of the action as they collect data to solve the problem. The teacher makes sure the learners collect and organise their data in order to solve the problem. The learners need to be active. The purpose of exploration is to have learners collect data that they can use to solve the problem that was posed.

Evaluation of exploration: In this portion of the learning cycle, evaluation should primarily focus on process, i.e. on the learners' data collection. Teachers ask themselves questions like:

- How well are the learners collecting data?
- Are they carrying out the procedures correctly?
- How do they record the data?
- Is it in a logical form or is it haphazard?

(3) **Explanation Phase:** In this phase of the model, the learners use the data they have collected to solve the problem and report what they did and try to figure out the answer to the problem that was presented. The teacher also introduces new vocabulary, phrases or sentences to label what the learners have already figured out.

Evaluation of explanation: Here, evaluation focuses on the process the learners are using that how well can learners use the information they have collected, plus that what they already know to come up with new ideas? Using questions, the teacher can assess the learners' comprehension of the new vocabulary and new concepts.

(4) **Elaboration Phase:** The teacher provides learners new information that extends ehat they have been learning in the earlier parts of the learning cycle. At this stage, the teacher also poses problems that learners solve by applying what they have learned. The problems include both examples and non-examples. However, the *learners get a chance to reflect on their knowledge in this phase only.*

Evaluation of elaboration: The evaluation that occurs during elaboration is what teachers usually think of as evaluation. Sometime, teachers equate evaluation with "the test at the end of the chapter". When teachers have the learners do the application problems as part of elaboration, these application problems are "the test".

Methods teachers use to support the learning model should:

- create interest;
- generate inquisitiveness'
- raise questions and elicit responses;
- facilitate cooperative learning;
- refer to and include previous learning experiences as they relate to new learnings; and
- incorporate alternate assessments.

(5) **Evaluation Phase**: This is the fifth 'E' and is an on-going diagnostic process that allows teachers to determine, whether the learner has attained understanding of concepts and knowledge. Teachers may use different techniques of assessment in the classroom like portfolio, assignment, observation, concept mapping, peer assessment, etc.

Q27. State various steps involved in Interpretation Construction (Icon) Design Model.

Ans. The Interpretation Construction (Icon) model contains seven stages which are as follows:

(1) **Observation:** Students make observations of authentic artifacts anchored in authentic situations.

(2) **Contextualisation:** Students access background and contextual materials of various sorts to aid interpretation and argumentation.

(3) **Cognitive Apprenticeship:** Students serve as apprentices to teachers to master observation, interpretation and contextualisation. Teachers need to guide them how to

analyse and interpret the problem at this stage. Teachers will find their students are having several alternative conceptions or misconceptions.

(4) **Collaboration:** Students collaborate in observation, interpretation and contextualisation. They discuss freely about their alternative conceptions/misconceptions and are able to communicate with their peers.

(5) **Interpretation and Construction:** Students construct interpretations of observations and construct arguments for the validity of their interpretations.

(6) **Multiple Interpretations:** Students gain cognitive flexibility by being exposed to multiple interpretations. They are able to interpret the knowledge in different ways and different manner and form several possible interpretations of the problem situation as well as problem solution.

(7) **Multiple Manifestations:** Students gain transferability by seeing multiple manifestations of the same interpretations.

Teachers can realise in such a method which require total involvement of the learners along with s/he in a pursuit of innovation. Teachers major role is to facilitate the group interaction and keep the participants focussed on the problem. This requires a lot of imagination and patience on their part to mobilise the learners' capabilities, their willingness and enthusiasm and overall their pool of previous knowledge enabling them for multiple interpretation of the problem and going for multiple manifestations.

In the classroom situation, this method when applied in mathematics teaching – learning processes help both the learners and the teacher in successfully formulating multiple ways of solving a problem which was thought to be possessing only one correct method of solution.

Q28. What is concept mapping? Discuss with the help of an example.

Or

Define and explain concept map with example.

[April-2016, Q.No.-33]

Ans. The graphic tools in the form of drawings or diagrams that can be used to visually describe relationships between and among concepts as well as show the mental connections students make between new concepts and prior knowledge is known as concept mapping. It requires critical thinking, knowledge and an understanding of the interrelationships between concepts. Furthermore, concept mapping reflects the inherent cognitive hierarchical processes between new learning and prior knowledge.

In the subject mathematics and others, students have learnt various concepts, but gradually, they are unable to interlink the relationships between these concepts. As no concept in mathematics is isolated; a particular concept of mathematics is interlinked with different branches of mathematics and with other subjects like science and social science in different ways and different manners. Thus, it is very important to use concept maps in the process of assessment. A concept map on quadrilateral is exemplified below:

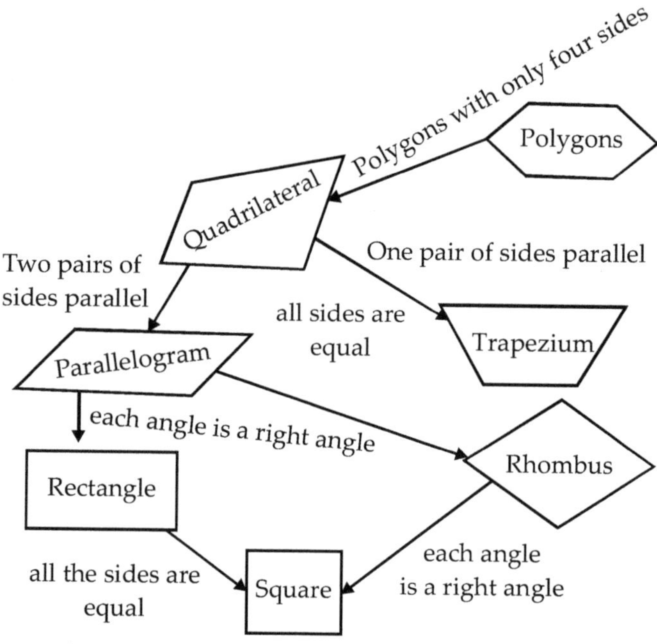

Fig. 1.7: Concept map of quadrilaterals (An Example)

Students, on their part, can form different ways/types of concept maps on a particular concept, depending upon the number of sub-concept and linking words they want to include. Therefore, the number of connections and depth of understanding can be assessed by the number of linking lines and used by the student's concept map. Hence, a concept map provides a concrete record of the connections perceived by the students, and thus, it indicates how the student's knowledge is organised and interconnected. More specifically, concept mapping can furnish valuable insight into the depth of students' understanding because it reflects the accuracy and strength of their connections. Even Venn Diagram of some concepts can play a role of concept mapping.

Q29. What is activity-based learning? Discuss with the help of an example.

Or

Discuss activity-based approach in the context of learning-centred approaches of teaching mathematics.

Ans. The activity-based learning is increasingly adopted across the nation particularly in lower grades. Activity-Based Learning (ABL) is essentially a form of learner-centered approach. Activity or a learning activity is one in which the learner willingly and spontaneously participates with delight and acquires the desired learning outcomes. Both the process of learning and learning outcomes are taken care of in this approach.

The activity-based approach makes learning interesting and it will be helpful for the students to remember content for a longtime as every student is involved in teaching-learning process, "Mathematics learning should be imparted through activities from the very beginning of school education, i.e. from the primary stage itself. These activities may involve the use of concrete materials, models, charts, patterns, pictures, posters, games, puzzles and experiments. The importance of using learning aids needs to be stressed. This may be done by involving students and teachers by mobilising community resources to this end."

For example, a teacher is going to teach the algebraic identity:

$$(a+b)^2 = a^2 + 2ab + b^2$$

S/he proves it numerically on the blackboard, but when s/he talks about to learn the same algebraic identity using activity, students may prepare a model using thermocol sheet, adhesive, thermocol cutter, glaze paper and sketch pen. During their preparation, s/he may guide them and also demonstrates it (Fig. 1.8) to prove this identity.

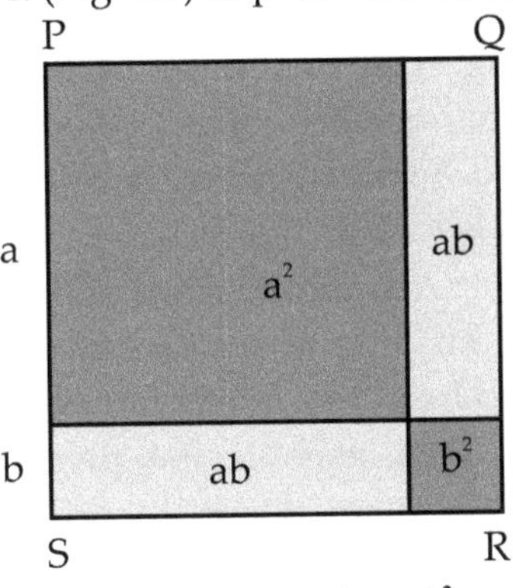

Fig. 1.8: Model of $(a+b)^2$

Q30. What is experiential learning? Discuss the steps involved in it that pave the way to meaningful learning.

Or

Explain the steps included in experiential Learning Cycle.

Ans. Experiential learning occurs when a person engages in some activity, looks back at the activity critically, draws some useful insight from this analysis, and puts the result to work. Learning which is developed experientially is "owned" by the learner and becomes an effective and integral aspect of behavioural change. Skill development occurs through Experiential Learning.

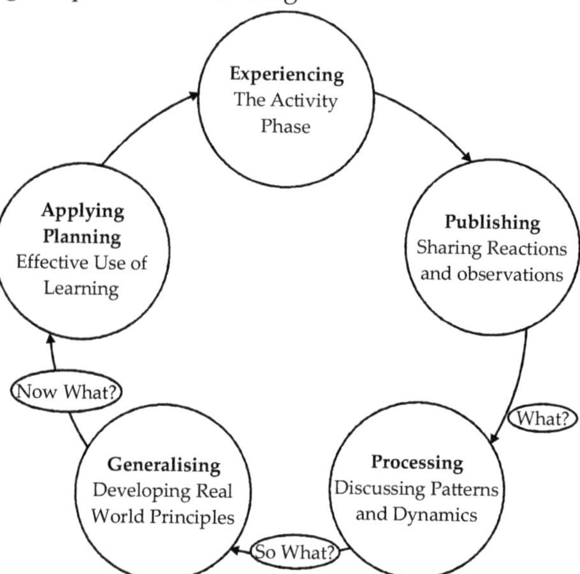

Fig. 1.9: Experiential Learning Cycle

The experiential learning cycle consists of five important stages that pave the way to meaningful learning, given as follows:

(1) **Experiencing:** The first stage of the cycle is experiencing. Almost any activity that involves self-assessment or interpersonal interaction may be used as the "doing" part of experiential learning.

(2) **Publishing:** In this second stage of the cycle, people that have experienced an activity are presumably ready to share what they saw and how they felt during the activity.

(3) **Processing:** This stage is the pivotal step in experiential learning. Group members systematically examine their common shared experience. This is the group dynamics phase of the cycle where group members essentially analyse what

happened. Group members try to determine why it happened the way it did. This talking through part of the cycle is critical.

(4) **Generalising:** In this stage, the members of the group begin to focus on their awareness of situations in their personal or work lives that are similar to those that they experienced in the group.

(5) **Applying:** In this final stage, the facilitator helps participants apply generalisations to actual situations in which they are involved.

Q31. How can you as a teacher develop creative abilities among learners? Also discuss the various points which should be addressed by learning approaches to develop creativity among learners.

Ans. The ways of solving a mathematical problem or developing any kind of activities in mathematics are unique and innovative. These abilities of the learners called as creativity or creative abilities. The important task of teaching mathematics is how to develop such abilities among the learners. The development of learners' creative abilities more or less depends on the nature of learning task and the approaches followed by the teachers in the classroom. The nature of the learning task that impacts on students' creativity can be identified under the following heads:

(1) ***Divergent solutions:*** Unlike most of the mathematical problems each of which has only correct answer, tasks encouraging creativity need to have several possible solutions. This encourages learners to search for innovative solutions.

(2) ***Logical and problem oriented:*** Unlike problems in other areas, mathematical problems have a distinct logical structure and all mathematical tasks are problem oriented. Once the learner becomes familiar with the logical structure, s/he tries to decipher the logic and in the process tries to employ several innovative processes to solve the problem consistent with the logical structure. The problem orientation of the tasks poses challenging situations for the learner to evolve new approaches for solution.

(3) ***Pictorial/graphic representation:*** Representing mathematical data and relations in various pictorial and graphic forms encourages creative talents.

(4) ***Activity based***: Tasks would be designed in such a manner that the students are attracted to it and participate in it spontaneously.

(5) ***Challenging***: The task should neither be too easy nor too difficult but must be mentally challenging for the learner so that s/he attends to it employing his/her full potential and solving the task is mentally satisfying.

Similarly the approaches of learning must have to address the following for the development of creativity among the learners:

(1) Freedom to students for questioning and expressing ideas.

(2) Encouragement for divergent thinking.

(3) Active learning and process based assessment.

(4) More scope for brainstorming and reflective thinking.

(5) More scope and freedom for fluent expression and elaboration of ideas.

(6) Motivation and accepting views/suggestions.

(7) Recognition of alternative ideas/methods of solutions proposed by students.

(8) More scope for problem posing and problem solving.

(9) Collaboration, both students and teachers search for alternatives.

Q32. What is mathematics laboratory and library? Discuss its use for learners.

Ans. A mathematics laboratory is a room which would accommodate about 25 to 30 students at a time. It should be spacious enough so that students can perform the activities with ease and may move freely in case they need to interact with fellow friends or the teacher. However, a mathematics library is the one which contains numerous books on mathematical learning.

For instance, while teaching the area of the circle to grade-VII students, teachers just give the formula of the area of circle and solve the numbers of problem on blackboard in a routine way. This way of teaching is product based on product, focuses on computational skill among the learners. Students may not come to know why and how the formula of the area of circle is πr^2. Therefore, process of learning mathematics is vital for the construction of knowledge and use of mathematics laboratory and library facilitates the process based learning.

Learning mathematics is both a creative and explorative process, and at the school level use of child resources in the process is more important. Every student of mathematics needs to learn the mathematics process.

The best way to learn the process is to practice it. However, in the classroom, students are given little chance to experience the full process of creating and exploring mathematics. Instead, they are taught merely about the products of the process. Therefore, the best way to learn mathematics is to use mathematics laboratory as it can act like a concomitant between teacher and students and provides an opportunity to understand and discover the beauty, importance and relevance of mathematics as a discipline. It can be expected to enhance the pupil's understanding of the subject as taught at the school and can also provide a pleasure to learn mathematics.

A mathematics laboratory is a place where some of the mathematical activities are carried out and the students get hands-on experience for new innovations. Further, mathematics laboratory can foster mathematical awareness, skill building, positive attitude and learning by doing in different branches of mathematics. It is the place where students can learn certain concepts using concrete objects and verify many mathematical facts and properties using models, measurements and other activities.

Nowadays, the mathematics library has different journals, magazines, reference books and CDs are available, containing the innovative ideas, experimentations, critical use of formula and life story of different mathematicians. Students are required to learn these materials regularly to get different ideas in the world of mathematics. Therefore, use of mathematics library is an important aspect in the process based learning. Teachers also used the library and motivated the students to learn from mathematics library. Thus, the mathematics library is an important place of resources for collection, dissemination of mathematical concepts, themes, story, references, articles puzzles and games. The main aim of GPH book is to provide knowledge as well as good marks in exam.

Objective Type Questions

Q1. In which stage of cognitive development, abstract mathematical concepts are likely to develop?

(a) Concrete Operation Period

(b) Formal Operation Period

(c) Pre-operation Period

(d) Sensory-motor Period

Ans. (b) Formal Operation Period

Q2. Which of the pre-number concepts are used for classification of objects?

(a) Matching and sorting

(b) Matching and comparing

(c) Ordering and subitising

(d) Sorting and comparing

Ans. (a) Matching and sorting

Q3. Which of the following are instructional objectives of mathematics?

(a) To develop in the child the power of thinking and reasoning

(b) To develop in the child a scientific and realistic attitude towards life

(c) To apply addition of two digit numbers in solving problems of daily life

(d) To perform computations with speed and accuracy

Ans. (c) To apply addition of two digits numbers in solving problems of daily life

Q4. Which method focused on application or use of formula directly on problem?

(a) Inductive method

(b) Deductive method

(c) Both (a) and (b)

(d) None of the above

Ans. (b) Deductive method

Q5. In which of the following steps of ICON design model, students are able to relate their previous knowledge?

(a) Observation

(b) Collaboration

(c) Cognitive apprenticeship

(d) Contextualisation

Ans. (d) Contextualisation

Q6. The project based learning is a ___________.

(a) learner-centred method

(b) teacher-centred method

(c) Both (a) and (b)

(d) None of the above

Ans. (a) learner-centred method

Q7. The students will able to:

(a) divide a collection of objects into two equal parts

(b) identify even and odd numbers of three digit numbers

(c) differentiate between even and odd numbers

(d) All of the above

Ans. (d) All of the above

Q8. How many stages or periods of cognitive development have been categorised by Piaget?

(a) Two

(b) Four

(c) Six

(d) Eight

Ans. (b) Four

Q9. Instant recognition of a number pattern without counting is ___________.

(a) Matching

(b) Counting

(c) Ordering

(d) Subitising

Ans. (d) Subitising

Q10. First step in process of problem solving is to ___________.

(a) design a solution

(b) identify/recognise a problem

(c) practicing solution

(d) organising data

Ans. (b) identify/recognise a problem

Q11. According to Piaget, in which development stage, "Object permanence" develops?

(a) Concrete operation period

(b) Sensory-motor Period

(c) Pre-operational Period

(d) Formal operation period

Ans. (b) Sensory-motor Period

Q12. In which phase of 5E'S learning model, students get chance to reflect on their knowledge?

(a) Elaboration

(b) Exploration

(c) Explanation

(d) Evaluation

Ans. (a) Elaboration

Q13. Choose the incorrect statement.

(a) Mathematics is precise.

(b) Mathematics is problem.

(c) Mathematics is symbolic.

(d) Mathematics is logical.

Ans. (b) Mathematics is problem.

Q14. From abstract to concrete is related to:

(a) inductive method

(b) deductive method

(c) analytic method

(d) synthetic method

Ans. (b) deductive method

Q15. New innovations in mathematics with hands on experience can be done in:

(a) mathematics classroom

(b) mathematics library

(c) mathematics laboratory

(d) mathematics teacher's room

Ans. (c) mathematics laboratory

Q16. Providing mathematics learning beyond classroom is:

(a) dull

(b) difficult

(c) boring

(d) joyful

Ans. (d) joyful

Q17. Optimisation means:

(a) utilisation of available conditions and resources to the fullest extent

(b) increase the availability of resources

(c) demand for good conditions and resources

(d) form good conditions and construct good resources

Ans. (a) utilisation of available conditions and resources to the fullest extent

Q18. Matching, sorting, comparing, ordering are:

(a) number concepts

(b) pre-number concepts

(c) counting process

(d) measurement concepts

Ans. (b) pre-number concepts

Q19. Nature of mathematics is:

(a) good

(b) positive

(c) exact

(d) problem solving

Ans. (c) exact

Q20. The method based on the principle of generalisation or establishment of formula/laws/principle from the observation of concrete examples is the __________ method.

(a) analytic

(b) project

(c) problem posing

(d) inductive

Ans. (d) inductive

Q21. In which phase the students have an opportunity to get directly involved with the phenomena and materials?

(a) engagement phase

(b) exploration phase

(c) explanation phase

(d) elaboration phase

Ans. (b) exploration phase

Q22. What is ordering objects by size, length or height?

(a) seriation

(b) equilibrium

(c) comparing

(d) sorting

Ans. (a) seriation

Q23. The mathematical structures are __________.

(a) easy and comfortable

(b) elegant and precise

(c) difficult and complex

(d) dull and boring

Ans. (b) elegant and precise

Q24. Mathematics is based on:

(a) use of patterns

(b) representation

(c) reasoning and proof

(d) making connection

Ans. (c) reasoning and proof

Q25. Children learn not only from the teacher, but also from interaction:

(a) with their parents

(b) with other children

(c) with their peers

(d) with their teachers

Ans. (b) with other children

2 Enriching Contents and Methodology

INTRODUCTION

Mathematics is useful in everyday life and it develops many mathematical concepts and skills. Mathematics makes our life orderly and prevents chaos. Certain qualities that are nurtured by mathematics are power of reasoning, creativity, abstract or spatial thinking, critical thinking, problem-solving ability and even effective communication skills. In our daily life, we are required to measure something or other. Measurement is quantification of the size or some definite aspects of the size of an object like length, area and volume. Collecting data, arranging or processing them and drawing inferences from these data and using those to solve different problems have been regular features in the management of all developmental activities including school education. Children too are often engaged in activities that require basic knowledge of handling data. They also often generate data through their own games and activities. Thus, we need to help children acquire some techniques which will be useful in handling data.

Q1. Describe the different sets of numbers. Briefly discuss the representation of rational numbers on a number line.

Ans. Different sets of numbers are are as follows:

(1) Natural numbers: Natural numbers are those who from the beginning of time have been used to count. These are the first numbers we learn about as a child, perhaps we can count the number of apples in a bag (1, 2, 3, 4, 6, ...). So the natural numbers are called counting numbers also.

The set of natural numbers is denoted as $\mathbb{N}$;

$\mathbb{N} = \{1, 2, 3, 4, 5, 6, ...\}$

Natural numbers are characterized by two properties:

(i) The number 1 is the first natural number; and

(ii) Each natural number is formed by adding 1 to the previous one.

(2) Whole numbers: This is just the number zero included with the counting numbers.

When a natural number is subtracted from itself, we cannot say what is the left out number. To remove this difficulty, the natural numbers were extended by the number zero (0).

In short, the set formed by the number zero and the natural numbers is called the set of whole numbers .The set of whole numbers is denoted as $\mathbb{W}$;

$\mathbb{W} = \{0, 1, 2, 3, 4, ...\}$

So, there is no greatest whole number.

(3) Integers: Integers are the natural numbers and their negatives. The set of integers is demoted by the symbol $\mathbb{Z}$.

These are some of the integers:

$\mathbb{Z} = \{..., -2, -1, 0, 1, 2, ...\}$

Zero is also an integer but it is not positive nor negative. An integer is a rational number with no "fraction", or part. An integer is a decimal number with all zeros after the decimal separator. (For example, the integer 17 is the same as the decimal 17.0 or 17.0000.)

An integer has a next smaller number and a next larger number. There is no smallest integer. There is no largest integer. Each integer is either larger than, equal to, or smaller than any integer. Consecutive integers are integers that come after each other, like 3, 4, 5, 6.

(4) **Rational numbers:** Rational numbers are those numbers which can be expressed as a division between two integers. The set of rational numbers is denoted as $\mathbb{Q}$, so

$$\mathbb{Q} = \left\{ \frac{p}{q} \mid p, q \in \mathbb{Z} \right\}$$

where, q is not equal to zero.

The result of a rational number can be an integer $\left(-\frac{8}{4} = -2\right)$ or a decimal $\left(\frac{6}{5} = 1.2\right)$ number, positive or negative.

It should be noted that every integer is a rational number, since, for example, $5 - \frac{5}{1}$; therefore, $\mathbb{Z}$ is a subset of $\mathbb{Q}$. In the same way, every natural number is also an integer number, specifically positive integer number.

A rational number $\frac{a}{b}$ is said to be in the standard form if b is positive, and the integers a and b have no common divisor other than 1.

Representation of rational numbers on the number line: Let us consider the following examples on representation of rational numbers on the number line:

Example 1: Let we have to represent $\frac{1}{2}$ and $-\frac{1}{2}$ on the number line.

Solution: Draw a line. Take a point O on it. Let the point O represent 0. Set off unit lengths OA to the right side of O and OA' to the left side of O.

Then, A represents the integer 1 and A' represents the integer -1.

A′	P′	O	P	A
–1	–1/2	0	1/2	1

Fig. 2.1

Now, divide the segment OA into two equal parts. Let P be the mid-point of segment

OP is the first part of OA. Thus, OP = PA = $\frac{1}{2}$. Since, O represents 0 and A represents 1, therefore P represents the rational number $\frac{1}{2}$. Again, divide OA' into two equal parts. Let OP' be the first part out of these two parts. Thus, OP' = PA' $= -\frac{1}{2}$. Since, O represents 0 and A' represents -1, therefore P' represents the rational number $-\frac{1}{2}$.

Example 2: Represent $\frac{13}{5}$ and $-\frac{13}{5}$ on the number line.

Solution: Draw a line. Take a point O on it. Let it represent 0.

Now, $\frac{13}{5} = 2\frac{3}{5} = 2 + \frac{3}{5}$

From O, set off unit distances OA, AB and BC to the right of O. Clearly, the points A, B and C represent the integers 1, 2 and 3 respectively. Now, take 2 units OA and AB, and divide the third unit BC into 5 equal parts. Take 3 parts out of these 5 parts to reach at a point P. Then the point P represents the rational number $\frac{13}{5}$.

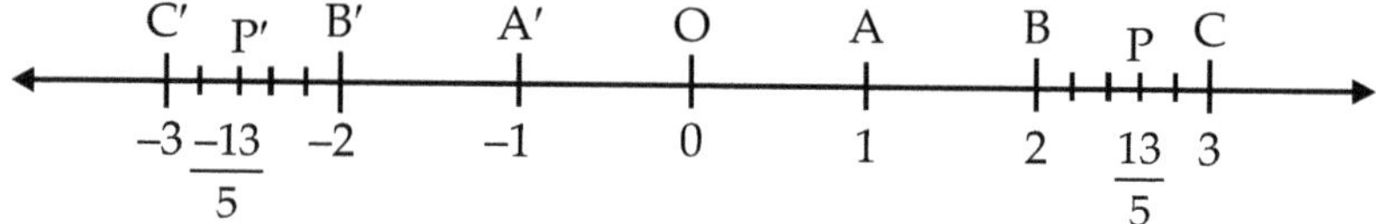

Fig. 2.2

Again, from the point O, set off unit distances to the left. Let these segments be OA', A'B', B′C′, etc. Then, clearly the points A′, B′ and C′ represent the integers -1, -2, -3 respectively.

Now, $= -\frac{13}{5} = -\left(2+\frac{3}{5}\right)$ Take 2 full unit lengths to the left of O.

Divide the third unit B′C′ into 5 equal parts. Take 3 parts out of these 5 parts to reach a point P′.

Then, the point P′ represents the rational number $\left(-\frac{13}{5}\right)$. Thus, we can represent every rational number by a point on the number line.

Q2. Explain the concept of fractional numbers.

Or

Every fraction is a rational number but a rational number need not be a fraction. Briefly discuss.

Ans. The numbers that are found to have been constructed to measure different parts of a complete object are known as fractional numbers. Fractions of a whole numbers are explained here with two following examples.

Example 1:

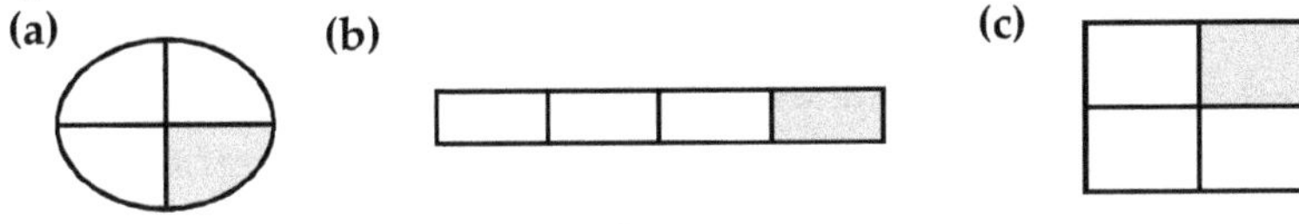

Fig. 2.3

In figure, each one is divided into 4 equal parts. One part is shaded, i.e., one-fourth of the shape is shaded and three parts of the shape is unshaded. We say that, $\frac{1}{4}$ of the shape is shaded and $\frac{3}{4}$ of the shape is unshaded.

This $\frac{1}{4}$ or $\frac{3}{4}$ is a **fraction** or a **fractional number**.

$\frac{1}{4}$ = Out of 4 equal parts of a whole, one part is taken.

$\frac{3}{4}$ = Out of 4 equal parts of a whole, 3 parts are taken.

Example 2: The rectangular shape is divided into 5 equal parts. 2 parts of this rectangle are shaded. The total parts of a whole are 5. Each equal part of the whole shape is $\frac{1}{5}$. Two equal parts (shaded part) of the whole is $\frac{2}{5}$. Three equal parts (unshaded parts) of the whole is $\frac{3}{5}$.

Fig. 2.4

$\frac{2}{5}$ means 2 parts out of 5 equal parts. We read it two-fifths or two by five.

In a simple fraction, there is a horizontal line. Above this line, we write a number which is called the **numerator,** which denotes total number of equal parts, a whole is divided into. Below this line, we write another number which is called the ***denominator***, which denotes total number of equal parts of the whole being considered.

The various types of fractions are:

(1) **Equivalent Fractions:** The fractions having the same value are called equivalent fractions. Their numerator and denominator can be different but, they represent the same part of a whole.

For example, $\frac{1}{2} = \frac{2}{4} = \frac{4}{8} = \frac{8}{16} = \frac{5}{10} = \frac{10}{20} = \frac{6}{12} = \frac{3}{6} = \frac{1}{2}$.

(2) The same Numerator Fractions: The factors having the same numerators are called the ***same numerator fractions.*** Fractions such as $\frac{2}{5}, \frac{2}{7}, \frac{2}{9}, \frac{2}{11}$, ..., etc., are same numerator fractions.

(3) Unit Fractions: The fractions having one (1) as their numerator are called ***unit fractions.***

$\frac{1}{3}, \frac{1}{5}, \frac{1}{7}, \frac{1}{9}$, ..., etc., are unit fractions.

(4) Proper Fractions: A fraction in which the denominator is greater than the numerator is called a ***proper fraction.*** We can also say that a fraction with its numerator less than the denominator is known as a proper fraction.

$\frac{1}{2}, \frac{2}{3}, \frac{4}{5}, \frac{5}{6}, \frac{7}{10}, \frac{9}{11}, \frac{11}{21}, \frac{35}{45}$, ..., etc., are proper fractions.

(5) Improper Fractions: A fraction in which the denominator is smaller than or equal to its numerator is called an ***improper fraction.***

$\frac{5}{3}, \frac{9}{5}, \frac{11}{7}, \frac{17}{8}, \frac{21}{14}, \frac{19}{15}$, ..., etc. are improper fractions.

(6) Mixed Fractions: When an improper fraction is written as a combination of a whole number and a proper number, it becomes a ***mixed fraction*** or ***mixed number.*** $2\frac{1}{3}, 3\frac{2}{7}$ etc. are mixed numbers and each of them can be changed into an improper fraction and an improper fraction can be changed into a mixed numbers, such as

$2\frac{1}{3} = \frac{7}{3}, \quad 3\frac{2}{7} = \frac{23}{7}$

(7) Like and Unlike Fractions: Like and Unlike Fractions are the two groups of fractions:

(i) $\frac{1}{5}, \frac{3}{5}, \frac{2}{5}, \frac{4}{5}, \frac{6}{5}$

(ii) $\frac{3}{4}, \frac{5}{6}, \frac{1}{3}, \frac{4}{7}, \frac{9}{9}$

In group (i), the denominator of each fraction is 5, i.e., the denominators of the fractions are equal. The fractions with the same denominators are called ***like fractions***.

In group (ii), the denominator of each fraction is different, i.e., the denominators of all the fractions are different. The fractions with different denominators are called ***unlike fractions***.

Every fraction is a rational number but a rational number need not be a fraction: Let $\frac{a}{b}$ be any fraction. Then, a and b are natural numbers. Since every natural number is an integer. Therefore, a and b are integers. Thus, the fraction a/b is the quotient of two integers such that $b \neq 0$. Hence, $\frac{a}{b}$ is a rational number. We know that 2/(-3) is a rational number but it is not a fraction because its denominator is not a natural number. $\frac{0}{1}$ is not a fraction, because the numerator is 0 and which is not a natural number. Since every mixed fraction consisting of an integer part and a fractional part can be expressed as an improper fraction, which is quotient of two integers. Thus, every mixed fraction is also a rational number. Hence, every fraction is also a rational number but a rational number need not be a fraction.

Q3. Explain four operations on natural numbers and whole numbers with the help of examples.

Ans. There are 4 operational function:

(1) Addition: Addition represents the idea of finding a total count, or summing up, of values. Since we use only ten digits in our system (remember base 10), it is often necessary to use place value to "carry" digits.

For example, 3 monkeys and 1 monkey are 4 monkeys.

Thus, 3 +1 = 4

Some properties of addition in natural and whole numbers:

(i) ***Closure property*:** Sum of two natural/whole numbers is also a natural/whole number.

(ii) ***Commutative Property*:** $p + q = q + p$ where p and q are any two natural/whole numbers.

(iii) ***Associative property*:** $(p + q) + r = p + (q + r) = p + q + r$. This property provides the process for adding 3 (or more) natural/whole numbers.

(iv) ***Additive Identity in Whole Numbers:*** In the set of whole numbers, $4 + 0 = 0 + 4 = 4$. Similarly, $p + 0 = 0 + p = p$ (where p is any whole number).

Hence, 0 is called the *additive identity* of the whole numbers.

(2) **Subtraction:** Subtraction is a mathematical operation that represents the operation of removing objects from a collection. It is signified by the minus sign (–).

Given the addition statement $6 + 4 = 10$, there are two associated subtraction statements: $10 - 6 = 4$ and $10 - 4 = 6$ Thus subtraction represents the idea of "undoing" addition. In general, if $a + b = c$, then $c - a = b$ and $c - b = a$

(3) **Multiplication:** The multiplication of whole numbers may be thought as a repeated addition; that is, the multiplication of two numbers is equivalent to adding as many copies of one of them, the ***multiplicand,*** as the value of the other one, the ***multiplier***.

For example: $4 \times 5 = 5 + 5 + 5 + 5 = 20$

$5 \times 4 = 4 + 4 + 4 + 4 + 4 = 20$

Table 2.1: Properties of Multiplication

Property Name	Property	Example
Commutative Property	$a \times b = b \times a$	$5 \times 4 = 4 \times 5$
Associative Property	$a \times (b \times c) = (a \times b) \times c$	$5 \times (2 \times 3) = (5 \times 2) \times 3$
Identity Property	$a \times 1 = 1 \times a = a$	$12 \times 1 = 1 \times 12 = 12$
Multiplication Property of 0	$a \times 0 = 0 \times a = 0$	$8 \times 0 = 0 \times 8 = 0$
Zero Factor Property	If $a \times b = 0, a = 0$ or $b = 0$	If $5 \times x = 0, x = 0$

(4) **Division:** Division of numbers represents the idea of repeated subtraction.

For example, $36 \div 12 = 3$ since $36 - 12 - 12 - 12 = 0$

$15 \div 3 = 5$ since $15 - 3 - 3 - 3 - 3 - 3 = 0$

Division is more commonly thought of as the inverse operation for multiplication.

For example: $36 \div 12 = 3$ since $3 \times 12 = 36$

$36 \div 3 = 12$ since $12 \times 3 = 36$

$15 \div 3 = 5$ since $5 \times 3 = 15$

$15 \div 5 = 3$ since $3 \times 5 = 15$

In general, if $a \times b = c$, then $c \div a = b$ and $c \div b = a$.

Q4. What is prime number?

Ans. A prime number is a whole number greater than 1, whose only two whole-number factors are 1 and itself. The first few prime numbers are 2, 3, 5, 7, 11, 13, 17, 19, 23, and 29.

Some terms related to primes:

(1) Co-Primes (or Mutually Primes): Two natural numbers are *co-primes* if those do not have a common factor. Following are the examples:

(i) 8 and 27 are co-primes (even if each of them is composite).

(ii) 17 and 20 are co-primes.

(2) Twin Primes: Two prime numbers, the difference between is 2, are known as twin primes.

3 and 5, 5 and 7, 11 and 13, 17 and 19 are examples of twin primes.

(3) Even Prime: 2 is the only prime which is even. It is also the *Smallest Prime*.

Q5. How would you identify the prime numbers within a certain range?

Ans. The following is the process to find the prime numbers between 1 and 100.

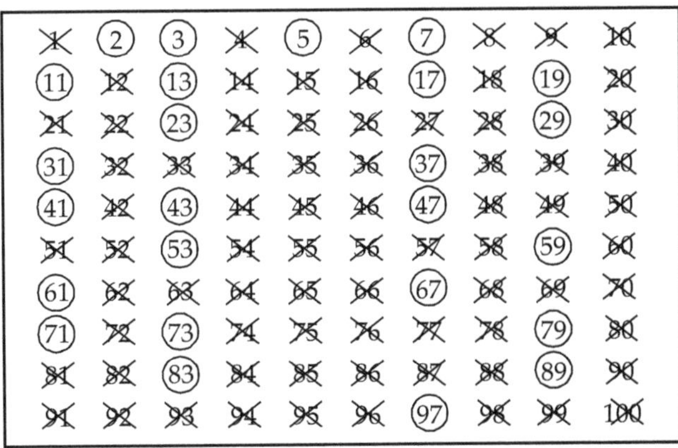

Fig. 2.5

[The Sieve of Eratosthenes. Eratosthenes was Greek Mathematician]

Procedure:

(i) Strike out all multiples of 2 greater than 2.

(ii) Strike out all multiples of 3 greater than 3.

(iii) Strike out all multiples of 5 greater than 5.

(iv) Strike out all multiples of 7 greater than 7.

All numbers (except 1) that are not struck off are prime numbers. Why the process stops at 7?

Square root of 100 is 10.

Prime number just less than 10 is 7. Hence, the process continues up to 7.

Thus, the prime numbers between 1 and 100 are:

2, 3, 5, 7, 11, 13, 17, 19, 23, 29, 31, 37, 41, 43, 47, 53, 59, 61, 67, 71, 73, 79, 83, 89, 97.

Q6. Elucidate four operations and their properties on integers.

Ans. Four operations and their properties on integers are as follows:

(1) Addition of integers

(i) **Addition of two positive integers:**

(+1) + (+4)

(+1) + (+4) = +5

(ii) **Addition of two negative integers:**

(-1) + (-4)

(-1) + (-4) = -5

(ii) **Addition of a positive integer and a negative integer:**

(a) (+5) + (-3)

(+5) + (-3) = +2

(b) (-4) + (+2)

(-4) + (+2) = -2

Observations:

(i) The sum of two positive integers is positive.

(ii) The sum of two negative integers is negative.

(iii) The sum of a positive integer and a negative integer is positive if the +ve integer is greater than the absolute value of the –ve integer.

(iv) The sum of a positive integer and a negative integer is negative if the absolute value of the -ve integer is greater than the +ve integer.

Addition of Numbers using Number Line: Addition of numbers can be well understood with the help of the number line. We keep in mind the following rules of movements on the number line:

(i) In order to add a positive number, we move the same number of steps to the right on the number line as the value of the number.

(ii) In order to add a negative number, we move the same number of steps to the left on the number line as the value of the number.

Addition of numbers using number line in different situation:

(i) Addition of a positive number to a positive number,

For example: (+2) + (+3)

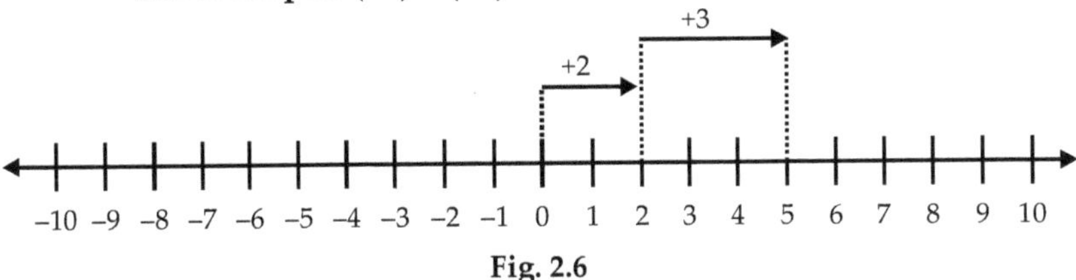

Fig. 2.6

First of all, for +2, count 2 units to the right of zero (because right side is for the positive sign). Then for +3 move three units to the right of +2. Thus, we reach at +5.

Therefore, (+2) + (+3) = +5 or simply we can write, 5.

(ii) Addition of a positive number to a negative number,

For example: (+3) + (-4).

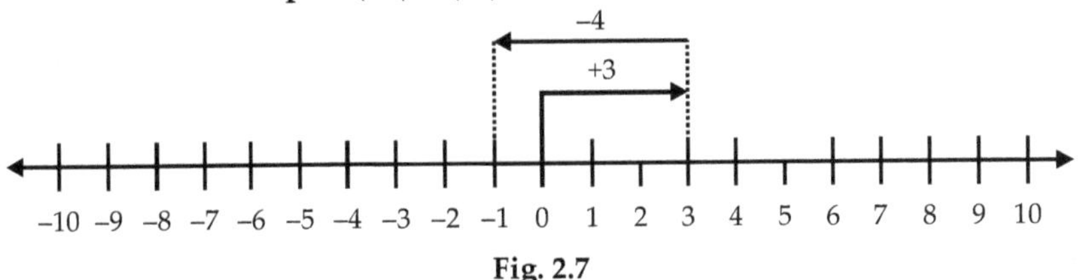

Fig. 2.7

For +3, move 3 units to the right of zero and then for -4, move 4 units to the left of 3.

Thus, we reach at -1.

Therefore (+3) + (-4) = -1.

(iii) Addition of a negative number to a positive number,

For example: (-4) + (+3)

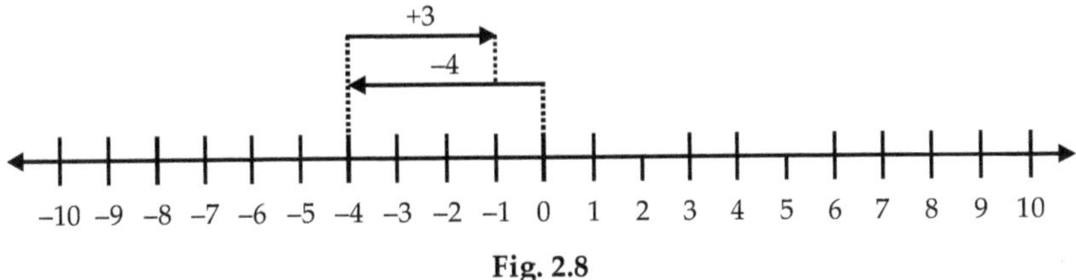

Fig. 2.8

For (-4), move 4 units to the left of zero and then for +3, move 3 units to the right of (-4).

Thus, we reach at -1.

Therefore, (-4) + (+3) = -1.

(iv) Addition of a negative number to a negative number,

For example: (-2) + (-4)

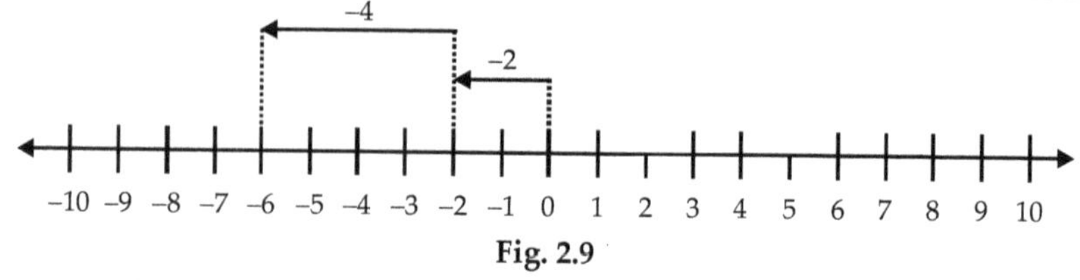

Fig. 2.9

For (-2), start from zero and move two units to the left and then again for (-4), move 4 units to the left of (-2). Thus, we reach at (-6). Therefore, (-2) + (-4) = -6.

(2) Subtraction of integers: Subtraction in integers is the addition of the opposite numbers (i.e., additive inverse). Thus, if 'p' and 'q' are two integers, then $p - q = p + (-q)$

For example, $(-5) - (7) = (-5) + (-7)$

In Natural numbers $p - q$ was a meaningful operation, if $q < p$. But in integers, $p - q$ is also meaningful when $q < p$, $q = p$ or $q > p$ as well.

Subtraction of Numbers using Number Line:

(i) $-8-(-5) = -8 + 5 = -3$

+5

–10 –9 –8 –7 –6 –5 –4 –3 –2 –1 0 1 2 3 4 5 6 7 8 9 10

Fig. 2.10

(ii) $6-2 = 4$

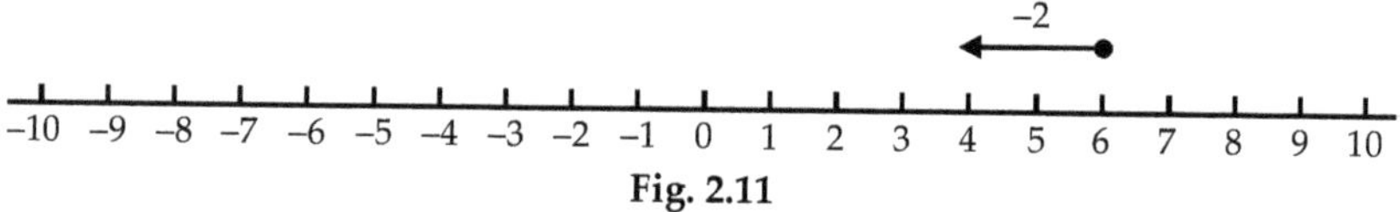

Fig. 2.11

(3) Multiplication of integers: Multiplication of two integers is the addition if one of integer is a non-negative integer.

Such as:

(i) $(+5)+(+5)+(+5)+(+5)=(+5)\times 4$

Thus $(+5)\times(+4)=+20$ [as was done with natural numbers]

(ii) $(-3)+(-3)+(-3)+(-3)+(-3)=(-3)\times 5$

Thus $(-3)\times 5=(-3)+(-3)+(-3)+(-3)+(-3)=-15$

Table 2.2: Sign rules for multiplication of Integers

Sign of Multiplicand 1	Sign of Multiplicand 2	Sign of Product
+	+	+
–	–	+
+	–	–
–	+	–

Applying the sing rules to multiply two integers means following a two-step process:

(i) Ignore any signs and solve the related whole number multiplication problem.

(ii) Adjust the signs, as necessary. If the two factors have the same sign, then the product is positive; if the two factors have different signs, then the product is negative.

Properties of Multiplication of Integers

- Commutative Property of Multiplication of Integers
  Let *a* and *b* be any integers. Then $a \times b = b \times a$.
- Associative Property of Multiplication of Integers
  Let *a, b* and *c* be any integers. Then $(a \times b) \times c = a \times (b \times c)$.
- Zero Multiplication Property of Multiplication of Integers
  Let *a* and *b* be any integers. If $a \times b = 0$, then $a = 0, b = 0$, or both.
- Identity Property of Multiplication of Integers
  Let *a* be any integer. Then $a \times 1 = 1 \times a = a$.
- Distributive property of Multiplication of Integers
  Let *a, b* and *c* be any integers. Then $a \times (b + c) = a \times b + a \times c$.

(4) Division: Division of integers is the opposite operation of multiplying integers.

If 'p' and 'q' are non-zero integers and p ×q = r, then we say

(i) $r \div p = q$

(ii) $r \div q = p$

Thus,

(i) (+5) × (+3) = +15 ∴ (+15) ÷ (+5) = +3
and (+15) ÷ (+3) = +5

(ii) (+4) ×(-6) = - 24 ∴ (-24) ÷ (+4) = -6
and (-24) ÷ (-6) = +4

(iii) (-3) × (-5) = +15 ∴ (+15) ÷ (-3) = -5
and (+15) ÷ (-5) = - 3

Table 2. 3: Sign rules for division of Integers

Sign of Multiplicand 1	Sign of Multiplicand 2	Sign of Product
+	+	+
–	–	+
+	–	–
–	+	–

Applying the sing rules to divide two integers means following a two-step process:

(i) Ignore any signs and solve the related whole number division problem.

(ii) Adjust the signs, as necessary. If the two integers have the same sign, then the quotient is positive; if the two integers have different signs, then the quotient is negative.

Q7. Discuss the operations and their properties on rational numbers.

Or

Write properties of 'addition in rational numbers'.

[April-2016, Q.No.-40]

Ans. Operations on rational numbers with their properties are as follows:

(1) Addition of Rational Numbers: The addition of rational numbers is carried out in the same way as that of addition of fractions.

(a) Consider the addition of rational numbers like $\frac{p}{q}, \frac{r}{q}$

$$\frac{p}{q}+\frac{r}{q}=\frac{p+r}{q}$$

For example:

(i) $\frac{2}{3}+\frac{5}{3}=\frac{2+5}{3}=\frac{7}{3}$

(ii) $\frac{3}{17}+\frac{9}{17}=\frac{3+9}{17}=\frac{12}{17}$

(iii) $\frac{14}{3}+\left(\frac{-5}{3}\right)=\frac{14-5}{3}=\frac{9}{3}=3$

(b) Let us consider the two rational numbers like $\frac{p}{q}$ and $\frac{r}{s}$

$$\frac{p}{q}+\frac{r}{s}=\frac{ps}{qs}+\frac{rq}{sq}=\frac{ps+rq}{qs}$$

For example:

(i) $\frac{3}{4}+\frac{2}{3}=\frac{3\times3+4\times2}{4\times3}=\frac{9+8}{12}=\frac{17}{12}$

(ii) $-\frac{4}{5}+\frac{7}{8}=\frac{-4\times8+5\times7}{5\times8}=\frac{35-32}{40}=\frac{3}{40}$

From the above two cases, we generalise the following rule:

(a) The addition of two rational numbers with common denominator is the rational number with common denominator and numerator as the sum of the numerators of the two rational numbers.

(b) The sum of two rational numbers with different denominators is a rational number with the denominator equal to the product of the denominators of two rational numbers and the numerator equal to sum of the product of the numerator of first rational number with the denominator of second and the product of numerator of second rational number and the denominator of the first rational number.

Properties of addition of rational numbers:

(i) **Closure property of addition of rational numbers:** The sum of two rational numbers is always a rational number.

If $\frac{a}{b}$ and $\frac{c}{d}$ are any two rational numbers, then $(\frac{a}{b}+\frac{c}{d})$ is also a rational number.

For example: Consider the rational numbers $\frac{1}{3}$ and $\frac{3}{4}$ Then

$\left(\frac{1}{3}+\frac{3}{4}\right)=\frac{4+9}{12}=\frac{13}{12}$, is a rational number.

Then, we say that set of rational numbers satisfies closure property with respect to addition.

(ii) **Commutative property of addition of rational numbers:** Two rational numbers can be added in any order.

Thus, for any two rational numbers $\frac{a}{b}$ and $\frac{c}{d}$, we have

$$\left(\frac{a}{b}+\frac{c}{d}\right)=\left(\frac{c}{d}+\frac{a}{b}\right)$$

For example:

$$\left(\frac{1}{2}+\frac{3}{4}\right)=\frac{(2+3)}{4}=\frac{5}{4} \text{ and } \left(\frac{3}{4}+\frac{1}{2}\right)=\frac{(3+2)}{4}=\frac{5}{4}$$

Therefore, $\left(\frac{1}{2}+\frac{3}{4}\right)=\left(\frac{3}{4}+\frac{1}{2}\right)$

Then, we say that set of rational numbers satisfies Commutative property with respect to addition.

(iii) **Associative property of addition of rational numbers:** While adding three rational numbers, they can be grouped in any order. Thus, for any three rational numbers $\frac{a}{b},\frac{c}{d}$ and $\frac{e}{f}$, we have $\left(\frac{a}{b}+\frac{c}{d}\right)+\frac{e}{f}=\frac{a}{b}+\left(\frac{c}{d}+\frac{e}{f}\right)$

For example:

Consider three rational numbers $\frac{-2}{3}, \frac{5}{7}$ and $\frac{1}{6}$

Then, $\left\{\left(-\frac{2}{3}+\frac{5}{7}\right)+\frac{1}{6}\right\}=\left\{\left(\frac{-14+15}{21}\right)+\frac{1}{6}\right\}=\left(\frac{1}{21}+\frac{1}{6}\right)=\left(\frac{2+7}{42}\right)$

$=\frac{9}{42}=\frac{3}{14}$

and $\left\{\frac{-2}{3}+\left(\frac{5}{7}+\frac{1}{6}\right)\right\}=\left\{\left(-\frac{2}{3}\right)+\left(\frac{5}{7}+\frac{1}{6}\right)\right\}=\left\{-\frac{2}{3}+\left(\frac{30+7}{42}\right)\right\}=\left(-\frac{2}{3}+\frac{37}{42}\right)$

$=\frac{(-28+37)}{42}=\frac{9}{42}=\frac{3}{14}$

Since, $\left\{\left(-\frac{2}{3}+\frac{5}{7}\right)+\frac{1}{6}\right\}=\left\{-\frac{2}{3}+\left(\frac{5}{7}+\frac{1}{6}\right)\right\}$

Then, we say that set of rational numbers satisfies Associative property with respect to addition.

(iv) **Existence of additive identity property of addition of rational numbers:** 0 is a rational number such that the sum of any rational number and 0 is the rational number itself. Thus, $\left(\frac{a}{b}+0\right)=\left(0+\frac{a}{b}\right)=\frac{a}{b}$, for every rational number $\frac{a}{b}$

For example: $\left(\frac{3}{5}+0\right)=\left(\frac{3}{5}+\frac{0}{5}\right)=\frac{(3+0)}{5}=\frac{3}{5}$ and similarly, $\left(0+\frac{3}{5}\right)=\frac{3}{5}$

Therefore, $\left(\frac{3}{5}+0\right)=\left(0+\frac{3}{5}\right)=\frac{3}{5}$

Hence, '0' is called the ***additive identity*** for rational.

(v) **Existence of additive inverse property of addition of rational numbers:** For every rational number $\frac{a}{b}$, there exists a rational number $-\frac{a}{b}$

such that $\frac{a}{b}+\left(-\frac{a}{b}\right)=\left\{a+\frac{(-a)}{b}\right\}=\frac{0}{b}=0$

and similarly, $\left(-\frac{a}{b}\right)+\frac{a}{b}=0$

Thus, $\frac{a}{b}+\left(-\frac{a}{b}\right)=\left(-\frac{a}{b}\right)+\frac{a}{b}=0.$

$-\frac{a}{b}$ is called the ***additive inverse*** of $\frac{a}{b}$

(2) Subtraction of rational numbers: If $\frac{p}{q}$ and $\frac{r}{s}$ are two rational numbers, then subtracting $\frac{r}{s}$ from $\frac{p}{q}$ means adding additive inverse (negative) of $\frac{r}{s}$ to $\frac{p}{q}$. The subtracting of $\frac{r}{s}$ from $\frac{p}{q}$ is written as $\frac{p}{q}-\frac{r}{s}$.

Below is two rules for subtraction of rational numbers:

(a) $\frac{p}{q}-\frac{r}{q}=\frac{p-r}{q}$

(b) $\frac{p}{q}-\frac{r}{s}=\frac{ps-qr}{qs}$

For example:

(i) $\frac{7}{4}-\frac{1}{4}=\frac{7-1}{4}=\frac{6}{4}=\frac{2\times3}{2\times2}=\frac{3}{2}$

(ii) $\frac{3}{5}-\frac{2}{12}=\frac{3\times12}{5\times12}-\frac{2\times5}{12\times5}$

$=\frac{36}{60}-\frac{10}{60}=\frac{36-10}{60}$

$=\frac{26}{60}=\frac{13\times2}{30\times2}=\frac{13}{30}$

The rational numbers are closed not only under addition, but also subtraction.

(3) Multiplication of Rational Numbers: Multiplication of two rational number $\left(\frac{p}{q}\right)$ and $\left(\frac{r}{s}\right), q\neq0, s\neq0$ is the rational number $\frac{pr}{qs}$.Where, $qs\neq0$

$=\frac{\text{Product of numerators}}{\text{Product of denominators}}$

For example, $\frac{3}{7}$ and $\frac{2}{9}$

$=\frac{3\times2}{7\times9}=\frac{3\times2}{7\times3\times3}=\frac{2}{21}$

Properties of rational numbers of multiplication

(i) **Closure property of multiplication of rational numbers:** The product of two rational numbers is always a rational number.

If $\frac{a}{b}$ and $\frac{c}{d}$ are any two rational numbers then $\left(\frac{a}{b}\times\frac{c}{d}\right)$ is also a rational number.

(ii) **Commutative property of multiplication of rational numbers:** Two rational numbers can be multiplied in any order.

Thus, for any rational numbers $\frac{a}{b}$ and $\frac{c}{d}$, we have: $\frac{a}{b}\times\frac{c}{d}=\frac{c}{d}\times\frac{a}{b}$

(iii) **Associative property of multiplication of rational numbers:** While multiplying three or more rational numbers, they can be grouped in any order.

Thus, for any rationals $\frac{a}{b}$, $\frac{c}{d}$, and $\frac{e}{f}$ we have: $\left(\frac{a}{b}\times\frac{c}{d}\right)\times\frac{e}{f}=\frac{a}{b}\times\left(\frac{c}{d}\times\frac{e}{f}\right)$

(iv) **Existence of multiplicative identity:** For any rational number $\frac{a}{b}$, we have $\left(\frac{a}{b}\times 1\right)=\left(1\times\frac{a}{b}\right)=\frac{a}{b}$

(v) **Existence of multiplicative inverse property:** Every nonzero rational number $\frac{a}{b}$ has its multiplicative inverse $\frac{b}{a}$.

Thus, $\left(\frac{a}{b}\times\frac{b}{a}\right)=\left(\frac{b}{a}\times\frac{a}{b}\right)=1$

$\frac{b}{a}$ is called the **reciprocal** of $\frac{a}{b}$.

Clearly, zero has no reciprocal. Reciprocal of 1 is 1 and the reciprocal of (-1) is (-1)

(vi) **Distributive property of multiplication over addition:** For any three rational numbers $\frac{a}{b}$, $\frac{c}{d}$ and $\frac{e}{f}$, we have: $\left(\frac{c}{d}+\frac{e}{f}\right)=\left(\frac{a}{b}\times\frac{c}{d}\right)+\left(\frac{a}{b}\times\frac{e}{f}\right)$

(vii) **Multiplicative property of 0:** Every rational number multiplied with 0 gives 0.

Thus, for any rational number a/b, we have $\left(\frac{a}{b}\times 0\right)=\left(0\times\frac{a}{b}\right)=0$

(4) Division of Rational Numbers: Division of two rational numbers $\frac{p}{q}$ and $\frac{r}{s}$, such that $q \neq 0, s \neq 0$, is the rational numbers $\frac{ps}{qr}$ where $qr \neq 0$

In other words $\left(\frac{p}{q}\right) \div \left(\frac{r}{s}\right) = \frac{p}{q} \times \left(\frac{s}{r}\right)$

Or (First rational number) × (Reciprocal of the second rational number)

For example:

$\frac{5}{6}$ and $\left(\frac{-2}{19}\right)$

$\frac{5}{6} \div \left(\frac{-2}{19}\right) = \frac{5 \times 19}{6 \times (-2)}$

$= -\frac{5 \times 19}{2 \times 3 \times 2} = -\frac{95}{12}$

$\therefore \left(\frac{3}{4}\right) \div \left(\frac{7}{12}\right) = \frac{9}{7}$

Properties of Division of Rational Numbers

(i) If $\frac{a}{b}$ and $\frac{c}{d}$ are any two rational numbers such that $\frac{c}{d} \neq 0$ then

$\left(\frac{a}{b} \div \frac{c}{d}\right)$ is also a rational number.

(ii) For every rational number a/b we have:

$\left(\frac{a}{b} \div 1\right) = ab$

(iii) For every nonzero rational number $\frac{a}{b}$, we have:

$\left(\frac{a}{b} \div \frac{a}{b}\right) = 1$

Q8. How the decimal equivalence of a rational number can be done? How many types of decimals are there? Illustrate them with examples.

Or

Define irrational numbers with example of terminating, non-terminating and repeating decimal.

Or

How to express decimal expansion of a rational number in p/q form?

Ans. The process of expressing a rational number into decimal form is to carry out the process of long division using decimal notation.

Following are some examples:

Represent each one of the following into a decimal number.

(i) $\frac{12}{5}$ (ii) $\frac{-27}{25}$

Solution:

(i) Using long division, we get

$$\begin{array}{r} 2.4 \\ 5\overline{)12.0} \\ 10 \\ \hline 20 \\ 20 \\ \hline \times \end{array}$$

Hence, $\frac{12}{5} = 2.4$

(ii)

$$\begin{array}{r} -1.08 \\ 25\overline{)-27} \\ 25 \\ \hline 200 \\ 200 \\ \hline \times \end{array}$$

Hence, $\frac{-27}{25} = -1.08$

It can be seen that the division process stops after a finite number of steps, when the remainder becomes zero and the resulting decimal number has a finite number of decimal places. Such decimals are known as ***terminating decimals***.

In the above division, the denominators of the rational numbers had only 2 or 5 or both as the only prime factors.

Alternatively, we could have written $\frac{12}{5}$ as $\frac{12 \times 2}{5 \times 2} = \frac{24}{10} = 2.4$ and similarly for the others $\frac{1}{2} = \frac{1 \times 5}{2 \times 5} = \frac{5}{10} = 0.5$

Thus, we see from above examples that the decimal representation of a rational number is

(i) either a terminating decimal (and the remainder is zero after a finite number of steps)

(ii) or a non-terminating repeating decimal (where the division will never end)

Thus, a rational number is either a terminating decimal or a non-terminating repeating decimal.

Expressing Decimal Expansion of a Rational Number in $\frac{p}{q}$ form

We can understand it through examples:

Example 1: Express 0.1357 in $\frac{p}{q}$ form

Solution: $0.1375 = \frac{1375}{10000} = \frac{55}{400} = \frac{11}{80}$

Example 2: Express 0.666... in $\frac{p}{q}$ form

Solution: Let x = 0.666... ... (A)

∴ 10x = 6.666... ...(B)

Subtracting eq. (A) in eq. (B)

10x – x=6.666...–0.666...

9x = 6

x=6/9=2/3

The above example illustrates that:

A terminating decimal or a non-terminating recurring decimal represents a rational number.

We can consider the following decimal to know about it:

0.10 100 1000 10000 1 ...(i)

The above decimal has a definite pattern and it can be written indefinitely, and there is no block of digits which is repeating. Thus, it is an example of a ***non-terminating*** and ***non-repeating decimal***. A similar decimal is given as under:

0.1 2 3 4 5 6 7 8 9 10 11 12 13 ...(ii)

Such decimals as in (i) and (ii) represent irrational numbers.

Thus, a decimal expansion which is neither terminating nor repeating, represents an ***irrational number***.

Q9. Give answers of the following:

(i) Define common factor and highest common factor.

Ans. A ***common factor*** of two or more numbers is a number which divides each of them exactly.

For example,

$8 = 2 \times 2 \times 2 = 4 \times 2$

$12 = 2 \times 2 \times 3 = 4 \times 3$

We see that 2 is a common factor in both 8 and 12.

Highest common factor of two or more numbers is the greatest number that divides each one of them exactly.

For example,

$12 = 2 \times 2 \times 3 = 6 \times 2$

$18 = 2 \times 3 \times 3 = 6 \times 3$

$24 = 2 \times 2 \times 2 \times 3 = 6 \times 4$

We see that 6 is the highest common factor of 12, 18 and 24.

Highest common factor is also called ***Greatest Common Divisor*** or ***Greatest common Measure***.

Symbolically, these can be written as HCF

(ii) Write down the methods for determining HCF.

Ans. Following are the methods for determining HCF:

Process (i): After writing the list of factors of each of the numbers the HCF can be determined (as was done for 12 and 18 above).

Process (ii): Prime Factorization Method:

$12 = 2 \times 2 \times 3 = 2^2 \times 3^1$

$18 = 2 \times 3 \times 3 = 2^1 \times 3^2$

HCF is the product of the lowest powers of each of the prime factors that commonly occurs in both the numbers.

$\therefore$ HCF of 12 and 18 $= 2^1 \times 3^1 = 6$

Process (iii): Continued division method:

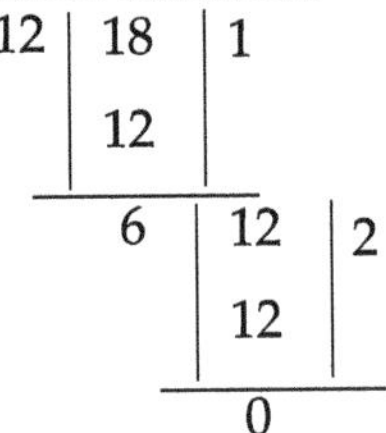

Step 1: Larger of the 2 numbers is divided by the smaller and the remainder is determined.

Step 2: Division of the previous division is taken as the dividend and it is divided by the remainder of the previous division.

This process continues till the remainder becomes zero.

Divisor of the last division, where the remainder is zero, becomes the required HCF.

(iii) Explain the application of HCF by example.

Ans. HCF is very helpful in solving the word problems. To understand the application of HCF, we go through the following example:

Problem: There are 24 boys and 30 girls in a class. Separate lines of girls and boys are to be prepared with *equal number* of students in each line. What should be the greatest number of boys (or girls) with which the lines are to be made so that all girls and all boys get accommodated?

Solution: The greatest no. of children (boys or girls) in each row is the HCF of 24 and 30.

We then find the HCF of 24 and 30 as given below:

$$\begin{array}{r|l|l} 24 & 30 & 1 \\ & 24 & \\ \hline \end{array}$$

$$\begin{array}{r|l|l} 6 & 24 & 4 \\ & 24 & \\ \hline & 0 & \end{array}$$

This shows that the HCF of 24 and 30 is 6. Thus, we get the answer.

Q10. Do as written:

(i) While discussing common multiples, define the lowest common multiples.

Ans. Common multiples of a number are the numbers which are divisible by the number.

Let us take the number 8.

Multiple of 8 is a number which is divisible by 8.

Hence, $8\times1, 8\times2\ 8\times3, 8\times4$ and so on are the multiples of it.

Thus, the multiples of 8 are: 8, 16, 24, 32, 40, 48, 56, 64, 72.............. (and it is a non-ending list)

Definition of Lowest Common Multiple (LCM): LCM is the product of the maximum number of each prime factor that occurs in either of the numbers.

(ii) Write down the methods for determining LCM.

Ans. LCM can be determined in following ways:

Process (i): After writing the lists of multiples of each of the numbers, the common multiples and the lowest common multiple (LCM) can be determined.

Example: Find the LCM of 8 & 12.

Solution: Multiples of 8 = 8, 16, 24, 32

Multiples of 12 = 12, 24, 36

Now, we can see that 24 is the lowest common multiple (LCM) of 8 and 12.

Process (ii): Prime Factorization Method: Suppose we want to determine the

LCM of 12 and 18.

$12 = 2\times2\times3 = 2^2 \times 3^1$

$18 = 2\times3\times3 = 2^1 \times 3^2$

Thus, the LCM $= 2^2 \times 3^2 = 2\times2\times3\times3 = 36$

In these prime factorisations, the maximum number of times the prime factor 2 occurs is two; this happens for 12. Similarly, the maximum number of times the factor 3 occurs is two; this happens for 18. The LCM of the two numbers is the product of the prime factors counted the maximum number of times they occur in any of the numbers. Thus, in this case LCM = 2 × 2 × 3 × 3 = 36.

Process (iii): Common Division Method: Let we have to find the LCM of 20, 25 and 30, then we write the numbers in a line, as given below and then find the LCM:

2	20	25	30
2	10	25	15
3	5	25	15
5	5	25	5
5	1	5	1
	1	1	1

Hence, the LCM is 2×2 ×3 ×5× 5 = 300

In finding LCM, we followed the following steps:

Step 1: Divide by the least prime number which divides atleast one of the given numbers. Here, it is 2. The numbers like 25 are not divisible by 2 so they are written as such in the next row.

Step 2: Again divide by 2. Continue this till we have no multiples of 2.

Step 3: Divide by next prime number which is 3.

Step 4: Divide by next prime number which is 5.

Step 5: Again divide by 5.

(iii) Explain the application of LCM with example.

Ans. LCM is used to solve the word problems and problems related to fractions, etc.

Example: Six bells commence tolling together and toll at intervals of 2, 4, 6, 8, 10, 12 seconds respectively. When will they next toll together and how often will they toll together in 30 minutes?

Solution: Six bells toll at intervals of 2, 4, 6, 8, 10 and 12 seconds respectively.

The timings of tolling for each bell separately will have to be the multiples of their respective intervals. Hence, the timing of their tolling together is the LCM of 2, 4, 6, 8, 10 and 12.

i.e. $2\times2\times2\times3\times5=120$

Thus, LCM = 120 seconds

Now, 120 seconds = 2 minutes

Hence, no. of times they will toll together in 30 minutes

$= \frac{30}{2} + 1 = 16$ times

1 is added to the no. of times the bells will toll together because they will toll 15 times after the initial toll.

That's why they toll 15+1 = 16 times in 30 minutes.

Q11. With the help of example, show the relation between the LCM and HCF of two numbers.

Ans. Relation between the LCM and HCF of Two Numbers:

Let us observe the following examples:

Table 2.4

Numbers	Product of the numbers	HCF	LCM	Product of HCF and LCM
12 & 18	216	6	36	216

Thus, we see that product of two positive numbers = Product of their HCF and LCM

Q12. What is unitary method? Discuss the applications of percentage.

Or

Briefly discuss the application of unitary method in work and time.

Or

What is percentage? Discuss its application.

Ans. The **unitary method** is a technique, which is used for solving a problem by finding the value of a single unit, i.e., 1, (by dividing) and then finding the necessary value by multiplication the single unit value. In essence, the **unitary method** is used to find the value of a unit from the value of a multiple, and thence the value of a multiple .In unitary method it is not always necessary to find the value of single unit.

For example, to solve the problem: 'A man walks 7 miles in 2 hours. How far does he walk in 7 hours?', one would first calculate how far the man walks in 1 hour. One can safely assume that he would walk half the distance in half the time. Therefore, dividing by 2, the man walks 3.5 miles in 1 hour. Multiplying by 7 for 7 hours, the man walks $7 \times 3.5 = 24.5$ miles or let us consider the distance travelled by man be X then divide it given distance that is 7 (X/7) it is equal to time take to travel X distance that is 7 hours divided time taken to travel 7 miles that is 2 hours (7/2) therefore X/7=7/2 hence X=24.5 miles.

Thus,

- while knowing for many and we calculate for one, we divide.

- While knowing for one and we calculate for many, we multiply.

Such pairs of variables between which, as many times becomes one, so many times becomes the other, are said to have ***direct variation*** between them.

Application of unitary method in work and time:

Example: A can complete a work in 24 days and B can complete the same work in 18 days. A and B started doing the work together. After 4 days, A discontinued working. How many days would the work take to be completed?

Solution: A can do the work in 24 days

$\therefore$ The work done by A in 1 day = $\frac{1}{24}$

B can do the work in 18 days

$\therefore$ The work done by B in 1 day $=\frac{1}{18}$

Work done by A and B together in 1 day $=\frac{1}{24}+\frac{1}{18}=\frac{3+4}{72}=\frac{7}{72}$

Work done by A and B in 4 days = $\frac{7}{72}\times 4=\frac{7}{18}$

Work left incomplete $1-\frac{7}{18}=\frac{18-7}{18}=\frac{11}{18}$

Work done by B in 1 day $=\frac{1}{18}$

The time required by B to complete $\frac{11}{18}$ of the work $=\frac{11}{18}\div\frac{1}{18}=\frac{11}{18}\times\frac{18}{1}=11$

Total time taken = 4 + 11 = 15 days

In course of calculation by unitary method, the following generalization is required to be done.

(i) Work done in unit time = $\frac{\text{work done}}{\text{time taken to do the work}}$

(ii) Time required = $\frac{\text{work to be done}}{\text{work done in unit time}}$

Percentage: A percentage is a number or ratio expressed as a fraction of 100. It is often denoted using the percent sign, "%".

Let us see a situation: A and B are two students. A appeared in an examination with total mark 80 and he secured 64. B appeared another examination with total mark 75 and he secured 63.

Whose performance is better, 64 out of 80 or 63 out of 75?

Solution: We think of the total mark as 100.

$\because$ Out of the total of 80, A gets 64

$\therefore$ Out of 100, A gets $\frac{64}{80}\times 100 = 80$

Now we say, A's marks are 80 out of 100, i.e. 80 percent or 80%.

Similarly, out of 75, B gets 63

$\therefore$ Out of 100, B gets $\frac{63}{75}\times 100 = 84$

Now we say, B's mark is 84 out of 100 i.e. 84 percent or 84%

$\therefore$ B's performance is better than A.

Thus, percentage is a comparison of one number with another. In other words we can say that, while comparing, we treat the 2nd number as 100, i.e. while comparing 'p' with 'q', we get $\frac{p}{q}\times$ *100%.*

Application of Percentage: The following are the occasions when application of percentage is made:

(i) Profit and Loss: In a business, **profit** or **loss** is expressed as a percentage of the cost price.

In a business:

Profit = Selling Price (S.P.) – Cost Price (C.P.)

Loss = C.P. – S. P.

Profit % = Profit as a percentage of C.P.

$= \frac{\text{Profit}}{\text{C.P.}}\times 100$

$= \frac{\text{S.P.} - \text{C.P.}}{\text{C.P.}}\times 100$

Loss % = Loss as a percentage of C.P.

$= \frac{\text{Loss}}{\text{C.P.}}\times 100$

$= \frac{\text{C.P.} - \text{S.P.}}{\text{C.P.}}\times 100$

Note: If after buying the article, some money is spent on transportation or for some other purpose, then the net cost = C.P. + Other expenditure. For calculating the profit or loss, net-cost is to be utilized instead of C.P.

For convenience of calculation of S. P. or C.P. the following rules may be used:

$$\frac{\text{S.P.}}{100 + \text{Profit\%}} = \frac{\text{C.P.}}{100}$$

$$\frac{\text{S.P.}}{100 - \text{Loss\%}} = \frac{\text{C.P.}}{100}$$

(ii) Calculation of interest: To calculate interest, following example is used:

$$\text{Interest (I)} = \frac{Prt}{100}$$

Total money to be refunded at the end the loan period is,

A = P+I or

$$A = P\left(1 + \frac{rt}{100}\right)$$

where, A = Total amount

P = Principal amount

r = interest rate

t = time

I= interest

Example: P borrowed a sum of 80,000.00 from a bank at 8% simple interest. How much has he to pay after 3 years if he is to clear his debt completely.

Solution: r = 8%, P = 80, 000.00, t = 3

$$\text{Therefore, } I = \frac{Prt}{100}$$

$$= \frac{80{,}000 \times 8 \times 3}{100}$$

$$= 19200$$

$$\text{And, } A = P + I$$

$$= 80{,}000 + 19{,}200$$

$$= 99{,}200$$

Hence, after 3 years he will pay `99,200.

Or, we can solve directly, as

$$A = 80{,}000\left(1 + \frac{8 \times 3}{100}\right) \text{ or}$$

$$= 80{,}000 \times 1.24 = \grave{}\ 99{,}200$$

Q13. What is the difference between the place value and face value of 8 when it occupies:

(i) Unit's place

(ii) Ten's place

(iii) Hundred's place

Ans. (i) Place value of 8 = 8

Face value of 8 = 8

Difference = 8-8 = 0

(ii) Place value of 8 = 80

Face value of 8 = 8

Difference = 80 – 8 = 72

(iii) Place value of 8 = 800

Face value of 8 = 8

Difference = 800 –8 = 792

Q14. Identify from the numbers given below, which are:

(i) not natural numbers

(ii) not whole numbers

(iii) not integers

(iv) not rational numbers

$\frac{-7}{3},\frac{-3}{7},-15,0,\frac{5}{17},\frac{3}{-4},-\frac{4}{3}$

Ans. (i) $\frac{-7}{3},\frac{-3}{7},-15,0,\frac{5}{17},\frac{3}{-4},-\frac{4}{3}$ are not natural numbers.

(ii) $\frac{-7}{4},\frac{-3}{7},-15,\frac{5}{17},\frac{3}{-4},-\frac{4}{3}$ are not whole numbers

(iii) $\frac{-7}{4},\frac{-3}{7},\frac{5}{17},\frac{3}{-4},-\frac{4}{3}$ are not integers.

(iv) All the numbers can be written in the form $\frac{p}{q}$,

Therefore, all the given numbers are rational numbers.

Q15. Write the following in the form of $\frac{p}{q}$

(i) 0.48, (ii) 0.1375, (iii) 0.2727…

Ans. (i) $0.48 = \frac{48}{100} = \frac{12}{25}$

(ii) $0.1375 = \frac{1375}{10000} = \frac{55}{400} = \frac{11}{80}$

(iii) Let x = 0.2727… …(i)

Multiplying both side by 100

100x = 27.2727… …(ii)

Subtracting eq. (i) from eq. (ii)

99x = 27

$x = \frac{27}{99}$

Thus, 0.2727… is $\frac{27}{99}$

Q16. Find all the factors of 36.

Ans. $36 = 1\times36$, $36 = 2\times18$, $36 = 3\times12$, $36 = 4\times9$, $36 = 6\times6$

Thus, all the factors of 36 = 1, 2, 3,4,6, 9,12, 18, 36.

Q17. Find first five multiples of '6'.

Ans. Required multiples are

$6\times1=6, 6\times2=12, 6\times3=18, 6\times4=24$ and $6\times5=30$

Q18. Prove that

$$(-5)\times[(-4)-(6)]=[(-5)\times(-4)]-[(-5)\times(-6)]$$

Ans. L.H.S. $(-5)\times[(-4)-(-6)]=(-5)\times2=-10$

R.H.S. $[(-5)\times(-4)]-[(-5)\times(-6)]=20-30=-10$

LHS = RHS

Hence, $(-5)\times[(-4)-(6)]=[(-5)\times(-4)]-[(-5)\times(-6)]$

Q19. Express $0.\overline{51}$ in $\frac{p}{q}$ form.

Ans. Suppose that

$0.\overline{51}=x$

$\Rightarrow 0.515151...=x$ .....(i)

$\Rightarrow 0.515151...\times100=x\times100$

$\Rightarrow 51.515151...=100x$ .....(ii)

Subtracting (i) from (ii)

$51 = 99x$

$\Rightarrow x=\frac{51}{99}$

Q20. Write the decimal representation of $\frac{7}{3}$.

Ans.

$$\begin{array}{r} 2.33 \\ 3\overline{)7.00} \\ \underline{6} \\ 10 \\ \underline{9} \\ 10 \\ \underline{9} \\ 1 \end{array}$$

Hence, the remainder 1 repeats.

$\therefore$ The decimal is non terminating decimal or $\frac{7}{3}=2.333=2.\overline{3}$

Q21. Find the HCF and LCM of 72, 288, and 1080.

Ans. $72=2^3\times3^2$

$288=2^5\times3^2$

$1080=2^3\times3^3\times5$

(i) The prime factors common to all the numbers are 2 and 3. The lowest indices of 2 and 3 in the given numbers are 3 and 2 respectively.

Hence, HCF = $2^3 \times 3^2 = 72$

(ii) The prime numbers present are 2, 3 and 5. The highest indices (powers) of 2, 3 and 5 are 5, 3 and 1, respectively.

Hence the LCM $= 2^5 \times 3^3 \times 5 = 4320$

Q22. A's income is 25% more than of B. B's income is 8% more than that of C. If A's income is `20250, then find the income of C.

Ans. Let income of C be `x

Income of B $= x + 8\% \text{ of } x$

$= x + \frac{8x}{100} = \frac{108x}{100}$

Income of A $= \frac{108x}{100} + 25\% \text{ of } \frac{108x}{100}$

$= \frac{108x}{100} \times \frac{125}{100}$

Now,

$\frac{108x}{100} \times \frac{125}{100} = 20250$

so, $x = 20250 \times \frac{100}{108} \times \frac{100}{125} = 15000$

$\therefore$ Income of C is ₹15, 000

Q23. A textbook of mathematics cost 2 rupees more than a textbook of literature. If 5 literature books cost 38 rupees more than 3 mathematics books, what is the cost of each literature book.

Ans. Let the cost of a literature book = `x

$\therefore$ the cost of mathematics book = `(x+2)

Now, the cost of 5 literature books = `5x

Therefore, 5x = 3 (x+2) + 38

= 5x = 3x+6+38

= 5x = 3x + 44

= 2x = 44

= x= 22

Hence, each literature book costs `22

Q24. Three persons completed half of a work in 8 days. If one of them discontinues working, how many days would they take to do the remaining half.

Ans. $\frac{1}{2}$ of the work done by 3 persons in 8 days

1 work done by 3 persons in $\frac{8 \times 2}{1} = 16$ days

The work done by 3 persons in 1 day = $\frac{1}{16}$

The work done by 1 person in 1 day $= \frac{1}{48}$

The work done by 2 persons in 1 day $= \frac{1}{16} - \frac{1}{48}$

$= \frac{3}{48} - \frac{1}{48} = \frac{3-1}{48} = \frac{2}{48} = \frac{1}{24}$

Therefore, 2 persons can do 1 work = 24 days

$\therefore$ 2 persons can do $\frac{1}{2}$ of the work in $\frac{24}{2}$ = 12 days

Thus, the required no. of days to remaining work done by 2 persons = 12 days

Q25. Write basic 'Axioms' of geometry?

Ans. Some undefined terms of geometry are– Point, Line, Plane. Some Axioms are being given below to use these three terms rightly:

(1) Through one point innumerable lines can be drawn.

(2) Through two different points one and only one straight line can be drawn.

(3) Every line (i.e. straight line) and plane is a set of points.

(4) The line drawn through two given points in a plane also lies in the plane.

(5) If two planes intersect, their intersection is a straight line.

(6) There exists only one plane containing three points not lying in a line.

The above axioms provide us with the inter-relations connecting the three undefined terms.

Q26. What are the Basic figures of geometry? Describe them briefly.

Or

Define–Line segment, Ray, Parallel Lines and Intersecting Lines.

Ans. Basic figures of geometry and their definitions are as follows:

Point: If we press the tip of a pen or pencil on a piece of paper, we get a fine dot, which is called a point.

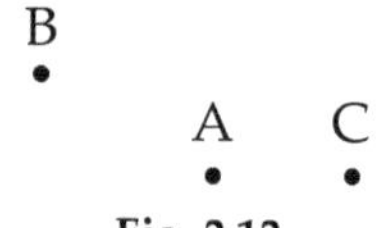

B •

A • C •

Fig. 2.12

A point is used to show the location and is represented by capital letters A, B, C etc.

Line: In geometry, a line is extended infinitely on both sides and is marked with arrows to give this idea. A line is named using any two points on it, viz, AB or by a single small letter l, m etc.

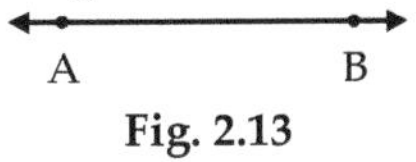

Fig. 2.13

Distance between two Points: If A and B are two points, then the distance between them is a unique non-negative real numbers and is denoted by the symbol AB.

Betweenness: If A, B and C are 3 distinct points, that lie in a straight line and AB + BC = AC, then B is said to lie between A and C and in symbol we write it as A - B - C or C - B - A.

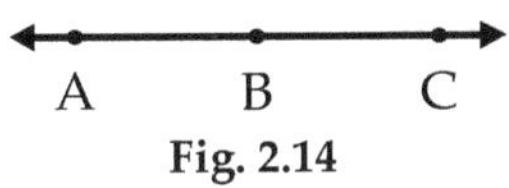

Fig. 2.14

The diagram above shows 3 points A, B and C such that A - B - C (i.e. B lies between A and C).

Parallel Lines: Parallel lines are two lines that are always the same distance apart and never touch.

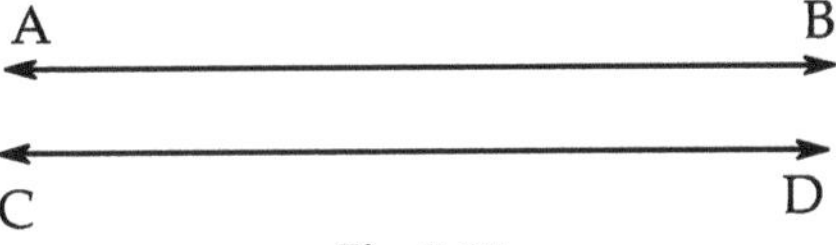

Fig. 2.15

Line Segment: The part of the line between two points A and B is called a line segment and will be named AB.

A line segment is the shortest path between two points A and B.

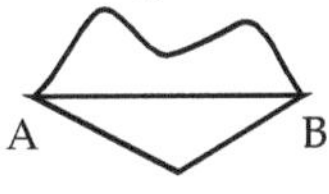

Fig. 2.16

Ray: If we mark a point X and draw a line, starting from it extending infinitely in one direction only, then we get a ray XY.

X Y

Fig. 2.17

X is called the initial point of the ray XY.

Opposite Rays: Fig. 2.18 show a line AB, OA and OB are two rays both of which are parts of AB. O is the only point common to both the rays OA and OB. In such a case, OA and OB are known as two opposite rays. Obviously two opposite rays together form a line.

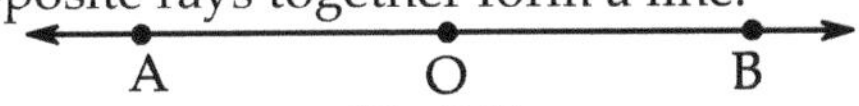

A O B

Fig. 2.18

Plane: If we move our palm on the top of a table, we get an idea of a plane.

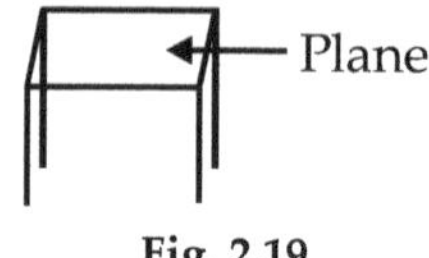

Fig. 2.19

Similarly, floor of a room also gives the idea of part of a plane.

Plane also extends infinitely lengthwise and breadth wise.

Intersecting Lines: If two lines intersect each other at a point, they are called intersecting lines.

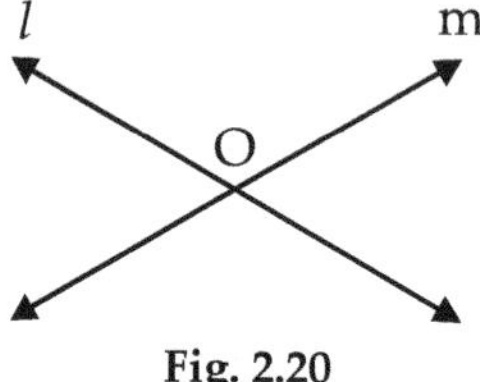

Fig. 2.20

Angle: An angle can be defined as two rays or two line segments having a common end point. An *angle* occurs when two rays meet or unite at the same endpoint.

The angles pictured below can be identified as $\angle PQR$ or $\angle RQP$.

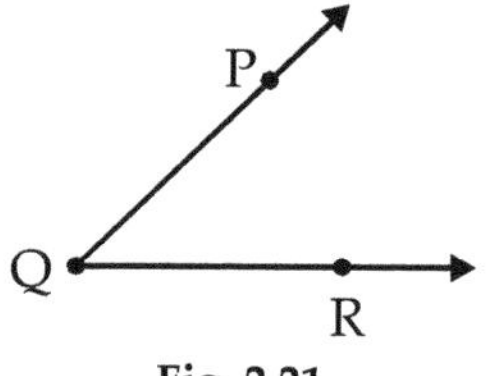

Fig. 2.21

Measurement of angle and classification of angles on the basis of measurement: An angle is measured in degrees. If we take any point O and draw two rays starting from it in opposite directions then the measure of this angle is taken to be $180°$ degrees, which is known as straight angle.

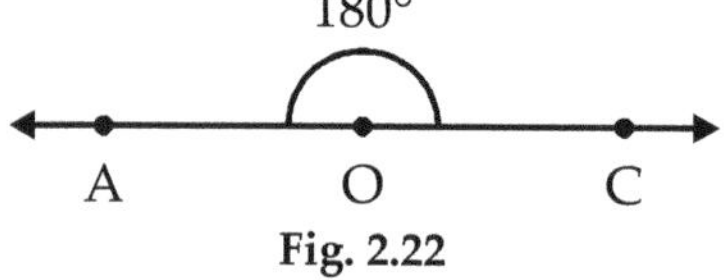

Fig. 2.22

This measure divided into 180 equal parts is called one degree (written as $1°$).

Angle obtained by two opposite rays is called a **straight angle.**

An angle of $90°$ is called a **right angle**, for example $\angle BOA$ or $\angle BOC$ is a right angle.

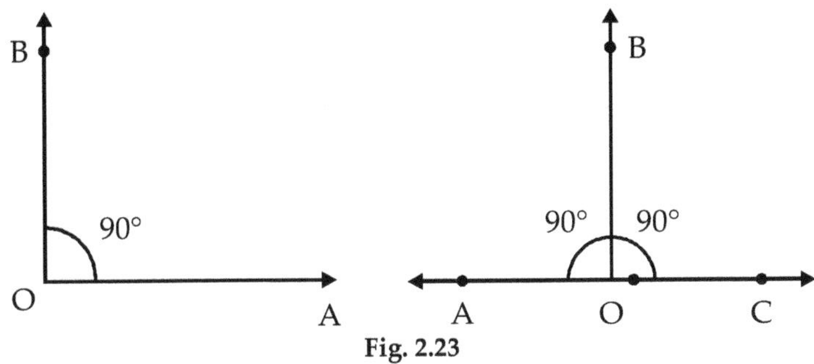

Fig. 2.23

Two lines or rays making a right angle with each other are called **perpendicular lines**.

An angle less than 90° is called an **acute angle**. For example ∠POQ is an acute angle.

An angle greater than 90° but less than 180° is called an **obtuse angle**. For example, ∠XOY is an obtuse angle.

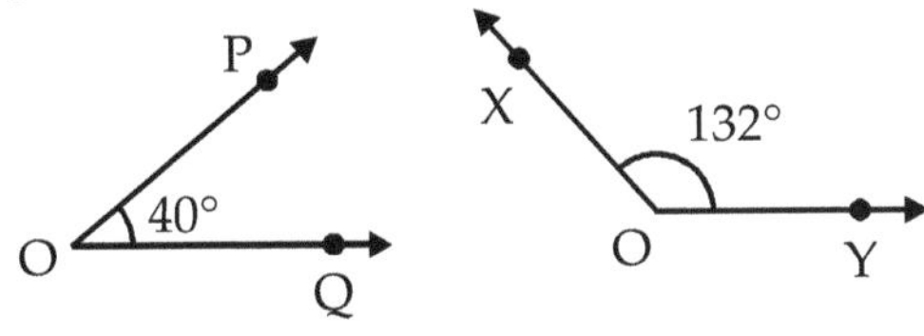

Fig. 2.24

Q27. What are the characteristics of Parallel Lines?

Ans. Following are the characteristics of parallel lines:

(i) The distance between two parallel lines always remains the same at every point.

(ii) They never intersect each other at any point. When a transversal intersects two parallel lines, then;

(iii) The pairs of corresponding angles are equal.

(iv) The pairs of alternate angles are equal.

(v) The sum of two interior angles on the same side of transversal is equal to 180°.

(vi) vertically opposite angles are equal.

For example: Given are two parallel lines AB and CD interacted by a transversal PQ.

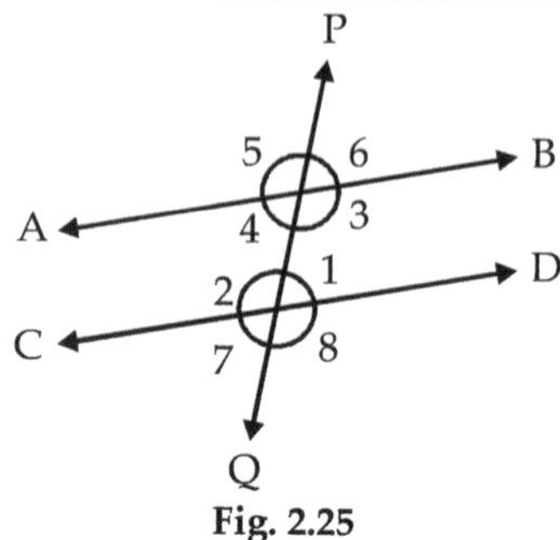

Fig. 2.25

In figure,

$\angle 1 = \angle 4$ and $\angle 2 = \angle 3$

$\angle 1 + \angle 3 = \angle 2 + \angle 4 = 180°$

In a similar way, we can verify the truth of the other two converses.

Hence, we conclude that when a transversal intersects two lines in such a way that angles in

(i) any pair of corresponding angles are equal or

(ii) any pair of alternate angles are equal or

(iii) any pair of interior angles on the same side of transversal are supplementary then the two lines are parallel.

Q28. Explain perpendicular lines with the help of a figure.

Ans. Perpendicular lines are lines that intersect at a right (90 degrees) angle. For example, in the given figure lines AB and CD intersect each other at point Q, such that; $\angle AOC = \angle BOC = \angle AOD = \angle BOD = 90°$

Thus, we can say that $AB \perp CD$

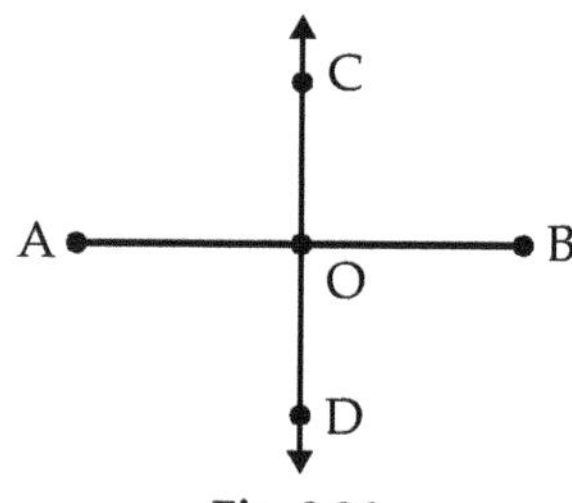

Fig. 2.26

Q29. Explain the concept of Angle Bisector with the help of a figure.

Ans. If P is a point in the interior of $\angle BAC$ and m $\angle BAP$ = m$\angle PAC$ then $\overrightarrow{AP}$ is known as the bisector of $\angle BAC$.

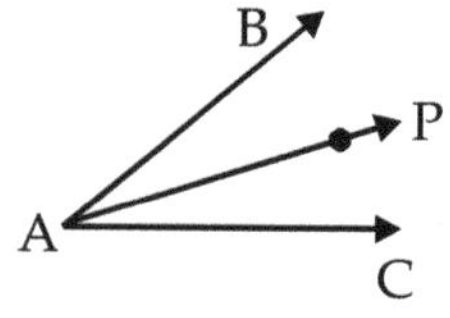

Fig. 2.27

Q30. Discuss various types of pairs of Angles.

Or

Which angles are known as–Adjacent Angles, Complementary Angles, Supplementary Angles and Vertically Opposite Angles? Describe.

Or

Name the angles that are formed when two lines are cut by a transversal and what are their characteristics in the context of parallel lines?

Or

Define complementary angles. [April-2016, Q.No.-25]

Ans. Various types of pairs of Angles are as follows:

(1) Adjacent Angles:

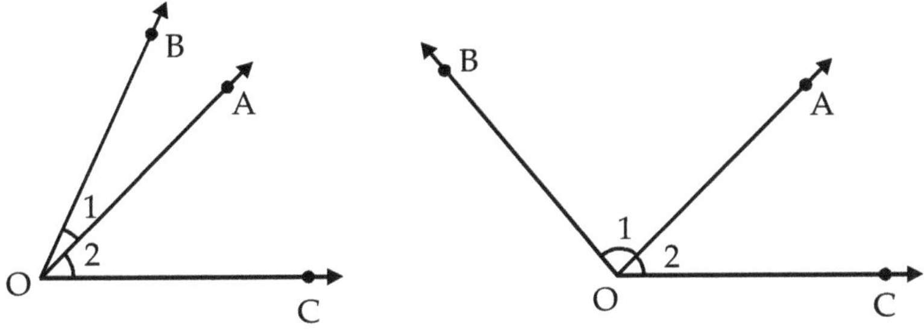

Fig. 2.28

Observe the two angles $\angle 1$ and $\angle 2$ in each of the figures. Each pair has a common vertex O and a common side OA in between OB and OC. Such a pair of angles is called a **'pair of adjacent angles'**.

(2) Complementary Angles: A pair of angles, whose sum is 90°, is called a pair of complementary angles. Each angle is called the complement of the other.

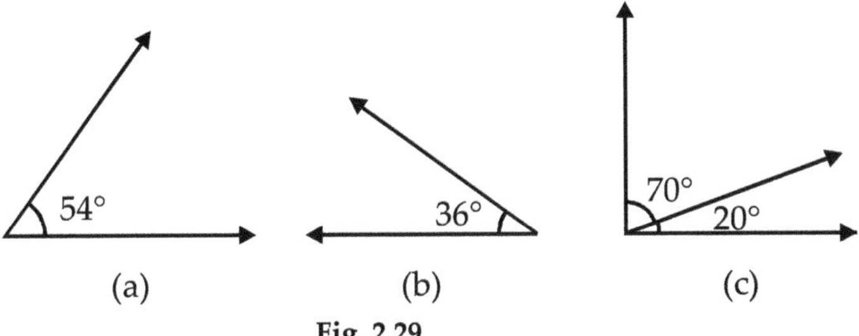

Fig. 2.29

Observe the angles in each pair. They add up to make a total of 90°.

(3) Supplementary Angles: A pair of angles whose sum is 180°, is called a pair of supplementary angles. Each such angle is called the supplement of the other.

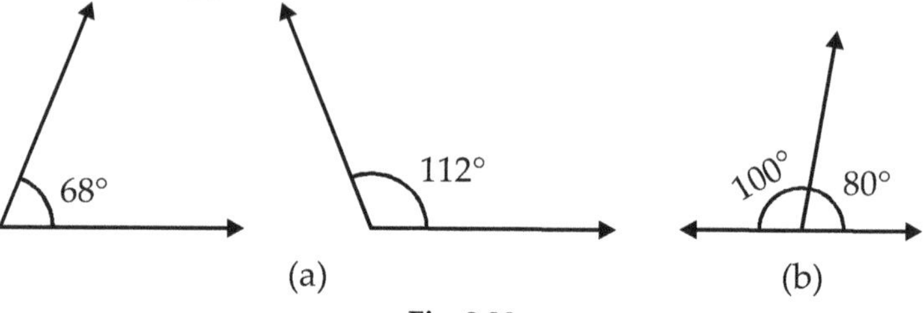

Fig. 2.30

Again observe the angles in each pair.

These add up to make a total of 180°.

(4) Linear Pair of Angles:

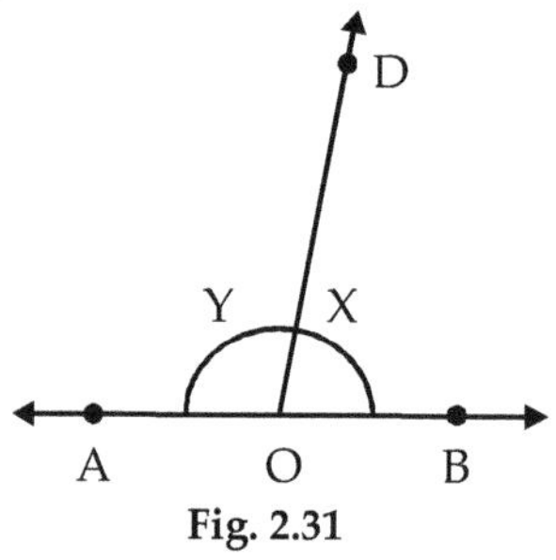

Fig. 2.31

If we measure $\angle X$ and $\angle Y$ and add, we will always find the sum to be 180°, whatever be the position of the ray OD.

If a ray stands on a line then the sum of the two adjacent angles so formed is 180°. The pair of angles so formed as is called a linear pair of angles.

Note that they also make a pair of supplementary angles.

(5) Vertically Opposite Angles: Vertically opposite angles are the angles opposite each other when two lines cross.

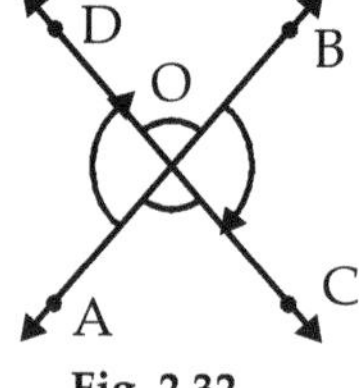

Fig. 2.32

$\angle AOC$ and $\angle DOB$ are angles opposite to each other. These make a pair of **vertically opposite angles**. Measuring them, We will always find that $\angle AOC = \angle DOB$.

$\angle AOD$ and $\angle BOC$ is another pair of vertically opposite angles.

Q31. Define a triangle and clarify the exterior and interior of a triangle?

Ans. Triangle is the simplest polygon of all the closed figures formed in a plane by three line segments. It is a closed figure formed by three line segments having six elements, namely three angles

(i) ∠ABC or ∠B

(ii) ∠ACB or ∠C

(iii) ∠CAB or ∠A and three sides:

(iv) AB

(v) BC

(vi) CA

It is named as Δ ABC or Δ BAC or Δ CBA and read as triangle ABC or triangle BAC or triangle CBA.

Interior and Exterior of a Triangle

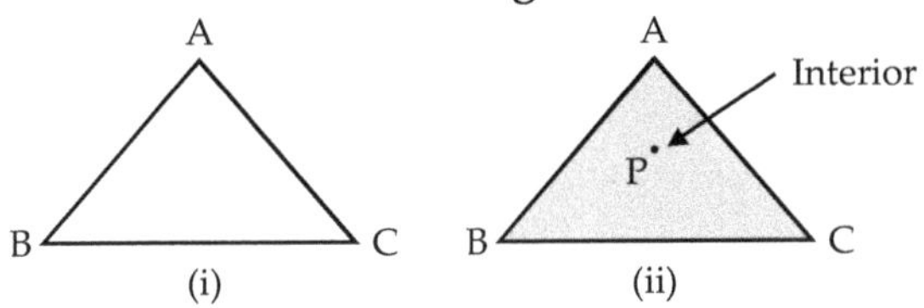

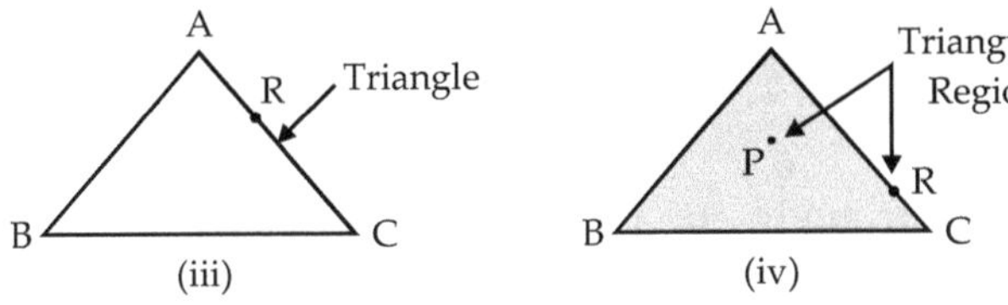

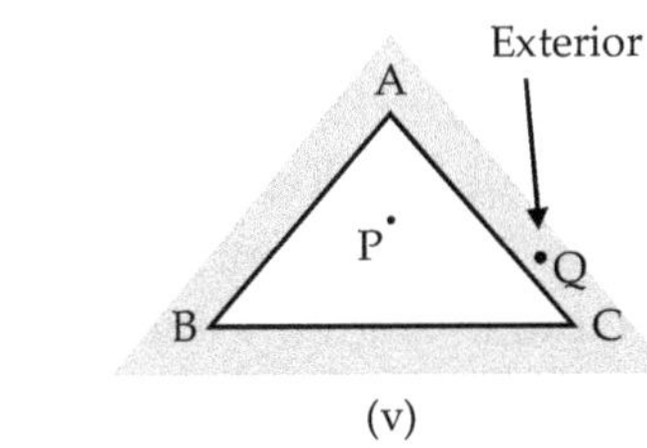

Fig. 2.33

The part of the plane, which consists of all points such as P, is called the interior of the triangle [fig. 2.33 (ii)]. The part of the plane which consists of all points such as R, forms the triangle itself [fig. 2.33 (iii)]. The interior of the ΔABC, together with the triangle, is called the triangular region ABC [fig. 2.33 (iv)]. The part of the plane which consists of all points such as Q, is called the exterior of the triangle [fig.

2.33 (v)]. In Fig. 2.33 (v), we observe that we cannot go from P to Q or from Q to P without crossing a side of the triangle.

Q32. Classify Triangles on the basis of sides and angles?

Ans. Triangles can be classified into different types in two ways:

On the basis of sides: Triangles can be classified according to the relative lengths of their sides:

- In an ***Equilateral Triangle***, all sides have the same length. An Equilateral Triangle is also a regular polygon with all angles measuring 60°.
- In an ***Isosceles Triangle***, two sides are equal in length. An Isosceles Triangle also has two angles of the same measure; namely, the angles opposite to the two sides of the same length.
- In a ***Scalene Triangle***, all sides and angles are different from one another.

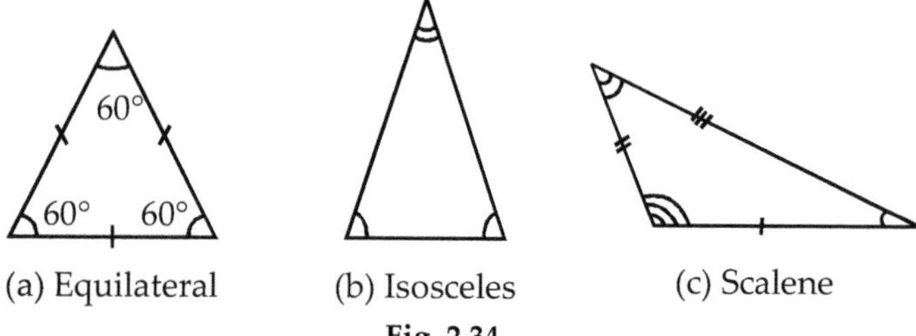

(a) Equilateral (b) Isosceles (c) Scalene

Fig. 2.34

On the basis of angles: Triangles can also be classified according to their internal angles:

- A **right triangle** (or Right-angled triangle, formerly called a **Rectangled triangle**) has one of its interior angles measuring 90° (a right angle). The side opposite to the right angle is the hypotenuse; it is the longest side in the Right Triangle.
- A triangle that has all interior angles measuring less than 90° is an **Acute Triangle** or Acute-angled Triangle.
- A triangle that has one angle that measures more than 90° is an Obtuse Triangle or **Obtuse-angled Triangle**.

Q33. Clarify the concept of Quadrilateral.

Ans. If A, B, C and D are four points in a plane such that no three of them are collinear and the line segments AB, BC, CD and DA do not intersect except at their end points, then the closed figure made up of these four line segments is called a quadrilateral with vertices A, B, C and D. A quadrilateral with vertices A, B, C and D is generally denoted by quad. ABCD. In Fig. 2.35 (i) and (ii), both the quadrilaterals can be named as quad. ABCD or simply ABCD.

In quadrilateral ABCD,

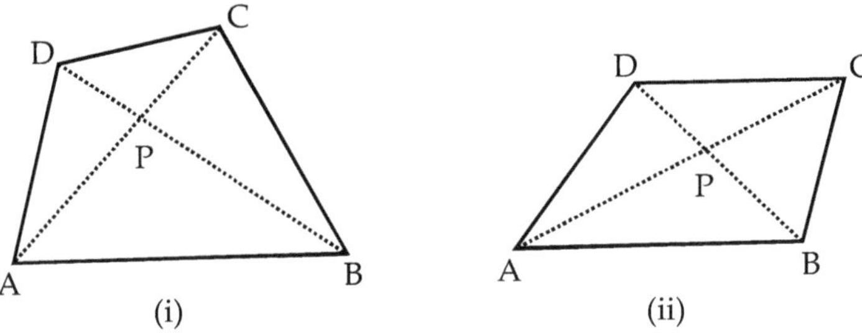

Fig. 2.35

(i) AB and DC; BC and AD are two pairs of opposite sides.

(ii) ∠A and ∠C; ∠B and ∠D are two pairs of opposite angles.

(iii) AB and BC; BC and CD are two pairs of consecutive or adjacent sides.

(iv) ∠A and ∠B; ∠B and ∠C are two pairs of consecutive or adjacent angles.

(v) AC and BD are the two diagonals.

Q34. Make a flow chart of all kinds of quadrilaterals showing inter-relation among them and define each of them with the help of a figure.

Or

Make a Flow-Chart showing inter-relations among different kinds of quadrilaterals.

Or

Draw a flowchart showing the interrelation connecting different types of quadrilaterals. [October-2016, Q.No.-32]

Ans. A family tree of quadrilaterals is given in Fig. below:

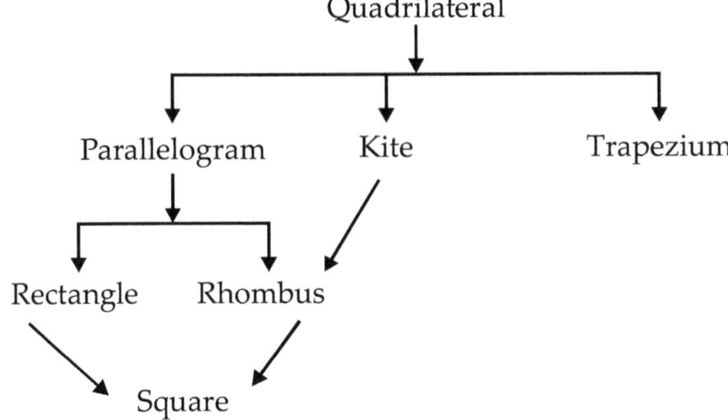

Fig. 2.36

Categories of quadrilaterals:

(1) Trapezium: A quadrilateral which has only one pair of opposite sides parallel is called a trapezium. In following Fig., ABCD is a trapezium, with $AB \parallel DC$.

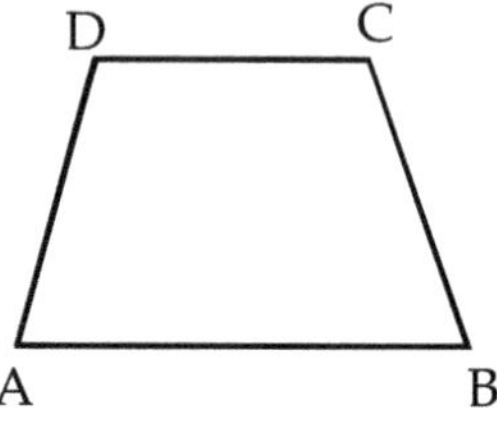

Fig. 2.37

(2) Kite: A quadrilateral, which has two pairs of equal sides next to each other, is called a kite. In following Fig., ABCD is a kite with adjacent sides AB and AD, BC and CD.

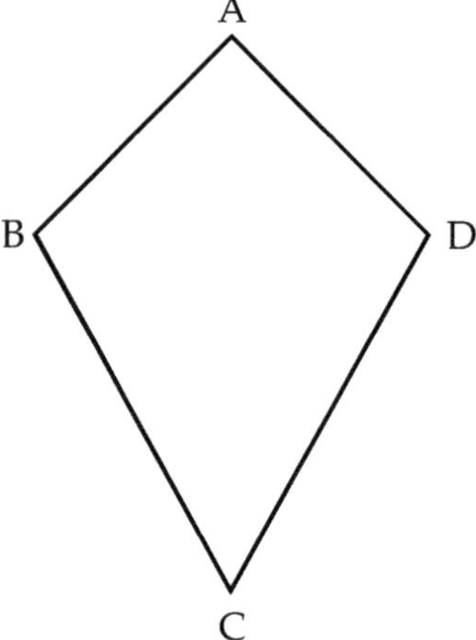

Fig. 2.38

(3) Parallelogram: A quadrilateral which has both pairs of opposite sides parallel, is called a parallelogram. In following Fig., ABCD is a parallelogram with $AB \parallel DC$, $AD \parallel BC$. This is denoted by $||^{gm}$ ABCD (Parallelogram ABCD).

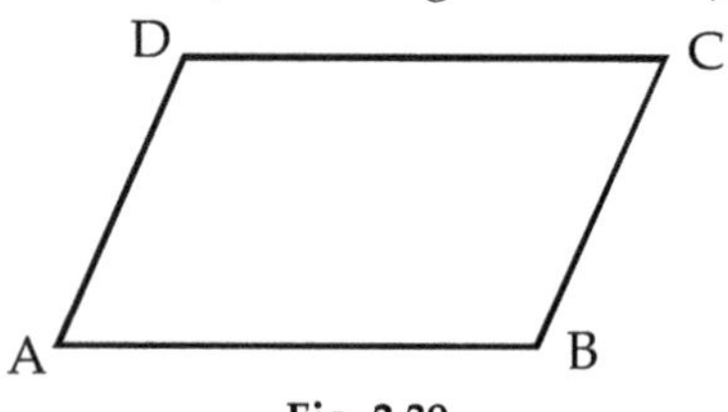

Fig. 2.39

(4) **Rhombus:** A rhombus is a parallelogram in which any pair of adjacent sides is equal. In Fig. 2.40, ABCD is a rhombus.

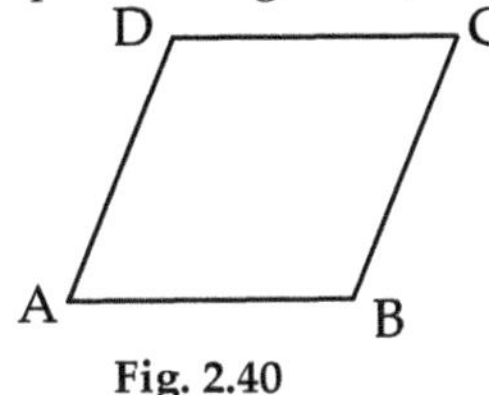

Fig. 2.40

It may be noted that ABCD is a parallelogram with AB = BC = CD = DA i.e., each pair of adjacent sides being equal.

(5) **Rectangle:** A parallelogram one of whose angles is a right angle is called a rectangle. In Fig 2.41. ABCD is a rectangle in which $AB \parallel DC$, $AD \parallel BC$ and $\angle A = \angle B = \angle C = \angle D = 90°$.

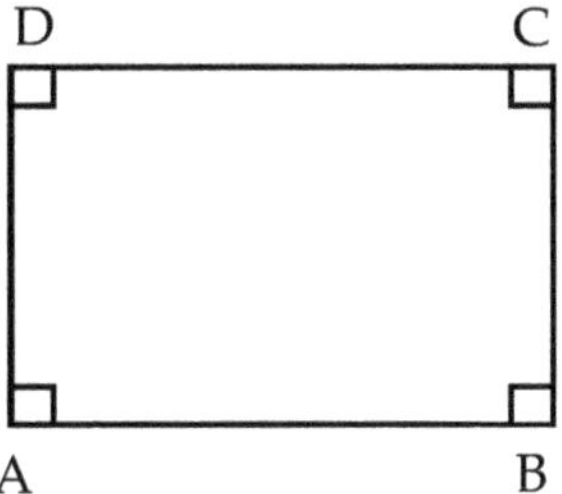

Fig. 2.41

(6) **Square:** A square is a rectangle, with a pair of adjacent sides equal. In other words, a parallelogram having all sides equal and each angle a right angle is called a square.

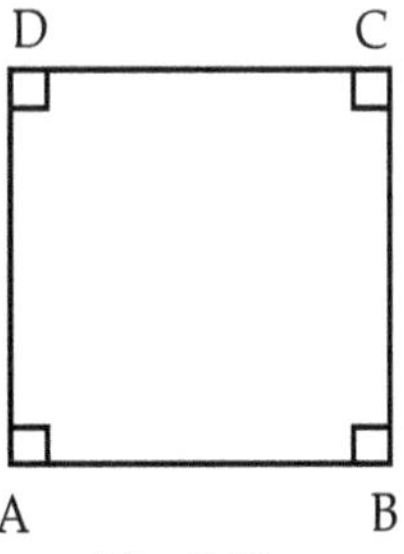

Fig. 2.42

In Fig., ABCD is a square in which $AB \parallel DC$, $AD \parallel BC$, and $AB = BC = CD = DA$ and $\angle A = \angle B = \angle C = \angle D = 90°$.

Q35. Write formulae to calculate the perimeters and areas of different kinds of quadrilaterals.

Ans. Following formulae for perimeters and areas of various figures:

(i) Perimeter of a rectangle = 2 (length + breadth)

Area of a rectangle = length $\times$ breadth

(ii) Perimeter of a square = $4 \times$ side

Area of a square = $(\text{side})^2$

(iii) Perimeter of parallelogram ABCD = 2 (AB+BC)

Area of a parallelogram = base $\times$ corresponding altitude

(iv) Perimeter of a rhombus = $4 \times$ length of a side.

Area of a rhombus = $\frac{1}{2}$ of its diagonals

(v) Perimeter of a trapezium = Sum of the lengths of all 4 sides.

Area of a trapezium = $\frac{1}{2}$ (sum of the parallel sides) $\times$ distance between them.

Q36. Define a Circle with its related terms.

Ans. A circle is a collection of all points in a plane which are at a constant distance from a fixed point in the same plane. The fixed point is known as the centre of the circle.

Radius: A line segment joining the centre of the circle to a point on the circle is called its radius 'r'.

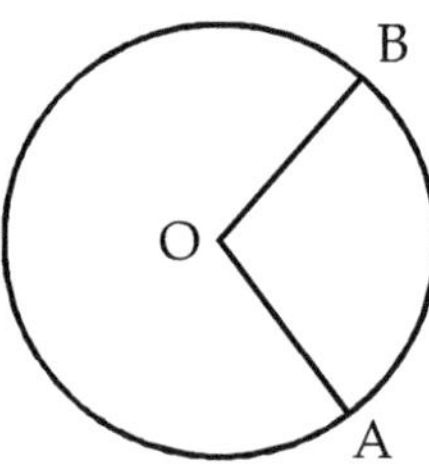

Fig. 2.43

A closed geometric figure in the plane divides the plane into three parts namely, the inner part of the figure, the figure and the outer part.

The inner part of the circle is called the ***interior of the circle.***

The outer part of the circle is called the ***exterior of the circle.***

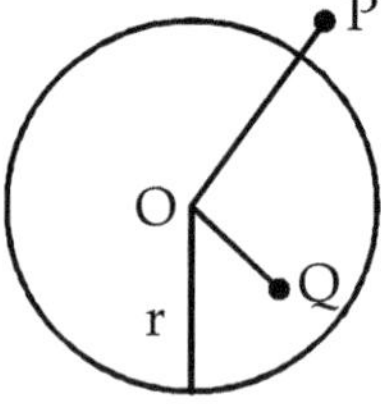

Fig. 2.44

Chord: A line segment joining any two points of a circle is called a chord.

Diameter: A chord passing though the centre of a circle is called its diameter 'd' where d = 2r

Diameter (PQ in the given figure) is the longest chord of a circle.

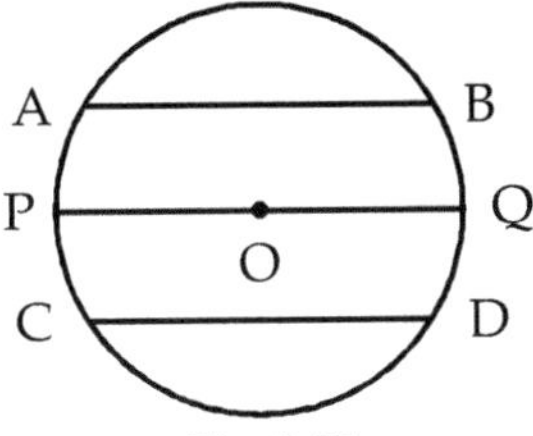

Fig. 2.45

Arc: A part of a circle is called an arc. In Fig. 2.46, ABC is an arc and is denoted by $\overset{\frown}{ABC}$.

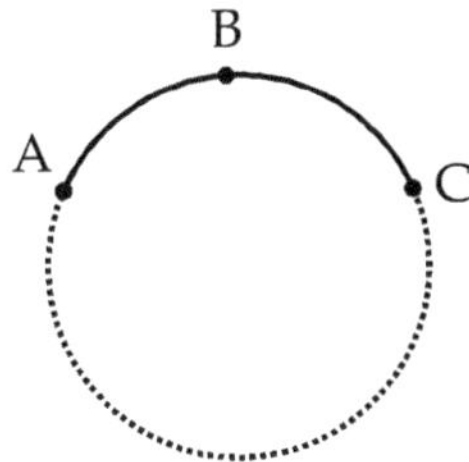

Fig. 2.46

Semicircle: A diameter of a circle divides a circle into two equal arcs, each of which is known as a semicircle.

Sector: The region bounded by an arc of a circle and two radii at its end points is called a sector.

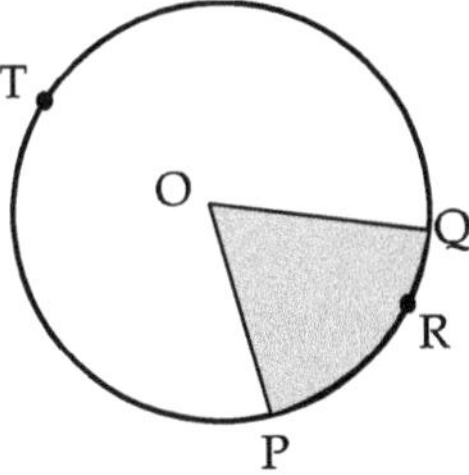

Fig. 2.47

In Fig., the shaded portion is a sector formed by the arc PRQ and the unshaded portion is a sector formed by the arc PTQ.

Segment: A chord divides the interior of a circle into two parts, each of which is called a segment.

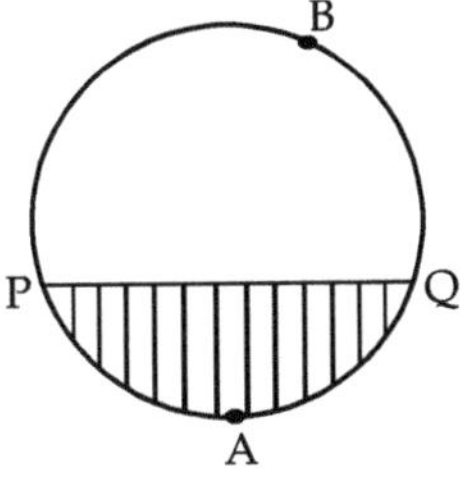

Fig. 2.48

In Fig. 2.48, the shaded region PAQP and the unshaded region PBQP are both segments of the circle. PAQP is called a minor segment and PBQP is called a major segment.

Q37. Write properties of a Circle.

Ans. Some properties of circle:

(1) Angles inscribed in the same arc (i.e., angles in the same segment) are equal.

$m\angle ABD = m\angle ACD, m\angle BAC = m\angle BDC$

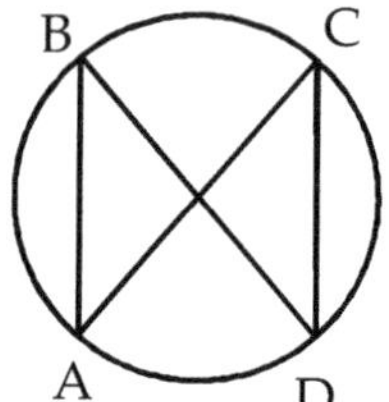

Fig. 2.49

(2) Angle in a semicircle is a right angle. AB is a diameter. Thus, APB is a semicircle. $m\angle APB = 90°$

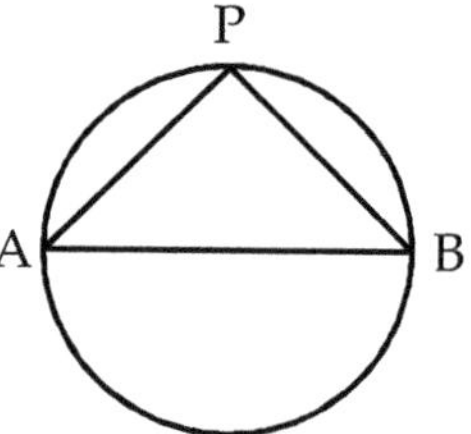

Fig. 2.50

(3) Opposite angles of a cyclic quadrilateral are supplementary. ABCD is a cyclic quadrilateral as its vertices lie on the circle.

$m\angle A + m\angle C = m\angle B + m\angle D = 180°$

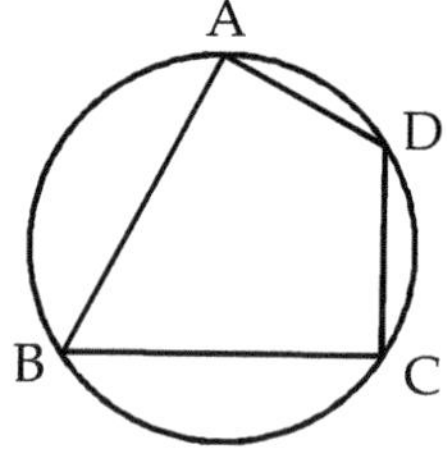

Fig. 2.51

(4) The degree measure of an arc is equal to twice the measure of angle inscribed in the opposite arc.

$m\,\widehat{\text{APB}} = 2\ \text{m}\angle\text{ADB}$

$= 2\ \text{m}\angle\text{ACB}$

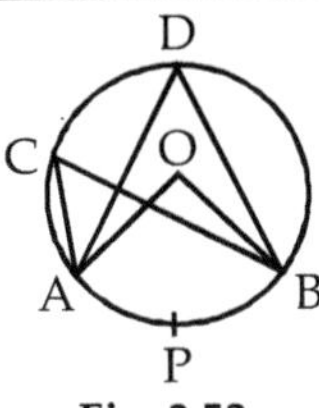

Fig. 2.52

Q38. Discuss the concept of congruency and similarities.

Ans. Congruency: Congruent shapes are the same size with corresponding lengths and angles equal. In other words, they are exactly the same size and shape. They will fit on top of each other perfectly. Therefore, if we know the size and shape of one we know the size and shape of the others. For example:

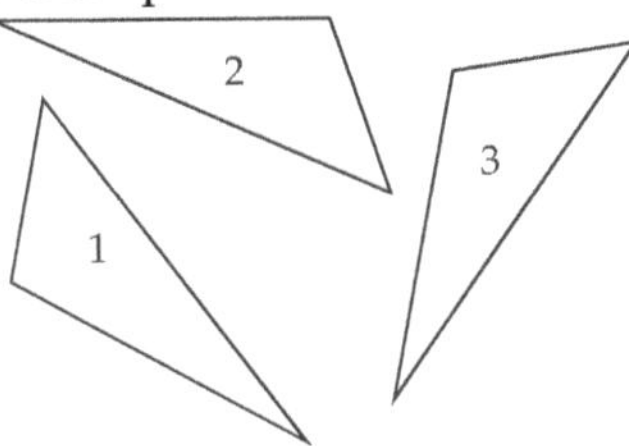

Fig. 2.53

Each of the above shapes is congruent to each other. The only difference is in their orientation, or the way they are rotated. If we traced them onto paper and cut them out, we could see that they fit over each other exactly.

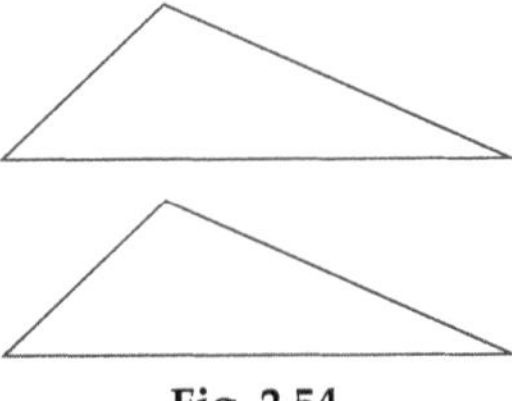

Fig. 2.54

Having done this, right away we can see that, though the angles correspond in size and position, the sides do not. Therefore, it is proved the triangles are not congruent.

Similarity: Similar shapes are like congruent shapes in that they must be the same shape, but they don't have to be the same size. Their corresponding angles are congruent and their corresponding sides are in proportion.

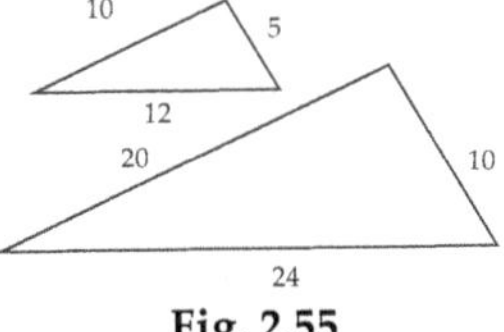

Fig. 2.55

Q39. What are the criterion of congruency of two triangles?

Ans. Criterion of congruency of two triangles are:

Criterion 1: If any two sides and the included angle of one triangle are equal to the corresponding sides and the included angle of the other triangle, the two triangles are congruent.

This criterion is referred to as SAS (Side Angle Side).

In triangles ABC and PQR, if $\overline{AB} \cong \overline{PQ}$,

$\overline{BC} \cong \overline{QR}$ and $\angle ABC \cong \angle PQR$,

$\Delta ABC \cong \Delta PQR$

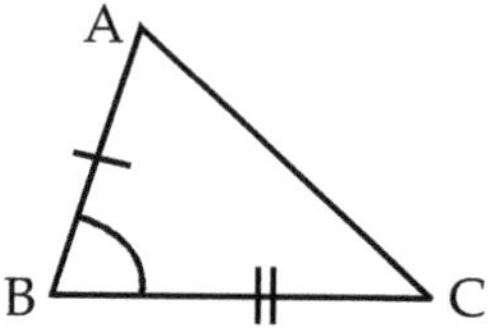

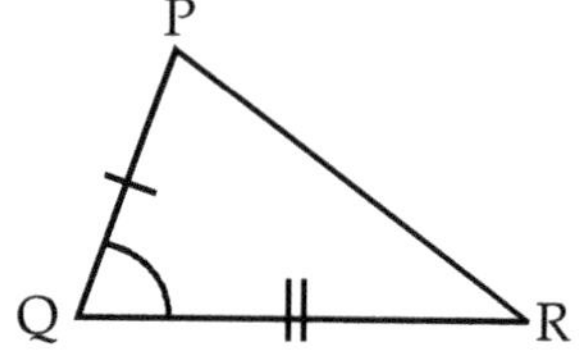

Fig. 2.56

Criterion 2: If any two angles and one side of a triangle are equal to corresponding angles and the side of another triangle, then the two triangles are congruent.

This criterion is referred to as ASA or AAS (Angle Side Angle or Angle Angle Side)

In ΔABC and ΔPQR,

If $\angle B \cong \angle Q$, $\angle C \cong \angle R$, $\overline{BC} \cong \overline{QR}$

Then $\Delta ABC \cong \Delta PQR$

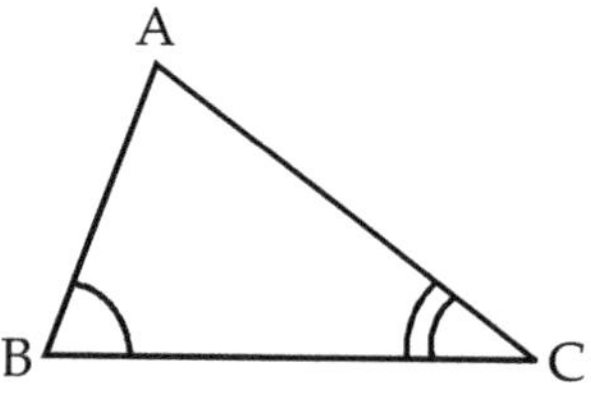

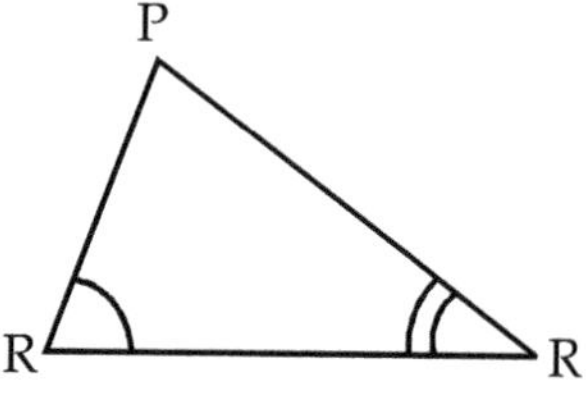

Fig. 2.57

Criterion 3: If the three sides of one triangle are equal to the corresponding sides of another triangle, then the two triangles are congruent.

This is referred to as SSS (Side, Side, Side), criterion.

In ΔABC and ΔPQR, If $\overline{AB} \cong \overline{PQ}$,

$\overline{BC} \cong \overline{QR}$, $\overline{CA} \cong \overline{RP}$, then $\Delta ABC \cong \Delta PQR$

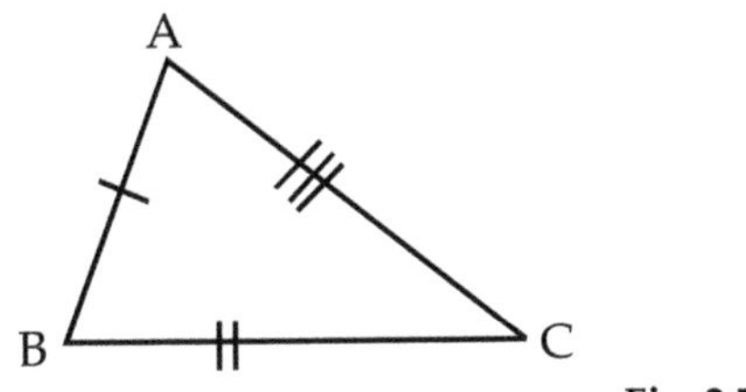

Fig. 2.58

Criterion 4: If the hypotenuse and a side of one right triangle are respectively equal to the hypotenuse and a side of another right triangle, then the two triangles are congruent.

This criterion is referred to as RHS (Right Angle Hypotenuse Side).

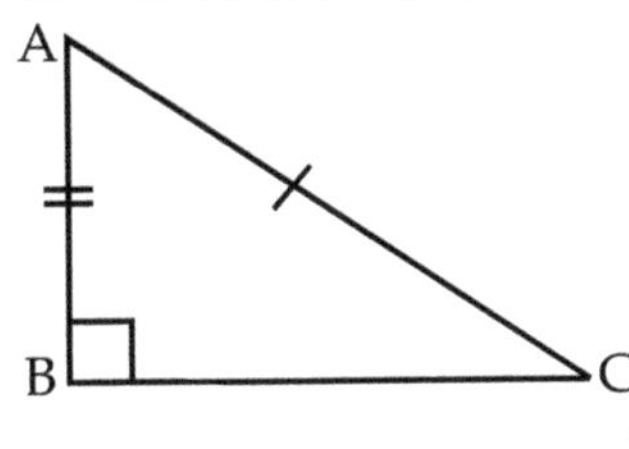

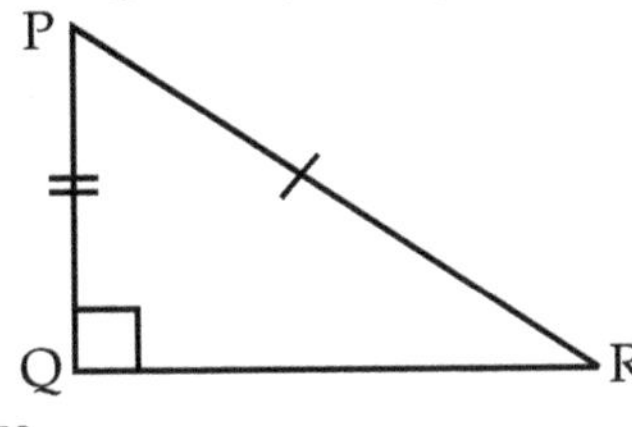

Fig. 2.59

In ΔABC, $\angle B$ is a right-angle and in ΔPQR, $\angle Q$ is a right angle.

If hypotenuses $\overline{AC} \cong \overline{PR}$ and sides $\overline{AB} \cong \overline{PQ}$, then

$\Delta ABC \cong \Delta PQR$.

Areas of two congruent triangles are equal.

Q40. Write brief note on Reflection and Image.

Ans. Nature gives us many examples of the relation between reflection and symmetry; the image of mountains and trees are reflected in the nearby water bodies, dew drops collected on leaves glimmer in the presence of sunlight etc. This concept was also used for decoration of forts and palaces, hundreds of years ago. For example, the roofs and walls of the mirror palace (Jaipur) were decorated with small pieces of mirror, which formed beautiful symmetrical patterns, thus adding to their aesthetic value. This concept is now used for decorating jewelry shops and temples. The concept of reflection in geometry is very much similar to the reflection in plane mirror.

In the process of reflection, the mirror image is nothing but the reflected duplication of the original object. Here, the resultant image is identical to the original object, but reversed in direction. For example, when the alphabet C is viewed in the mirror, the point to point distance of the original object and the reflected image is same with respect to the mirror, but the direction is reversed, as can be seen in the following image.

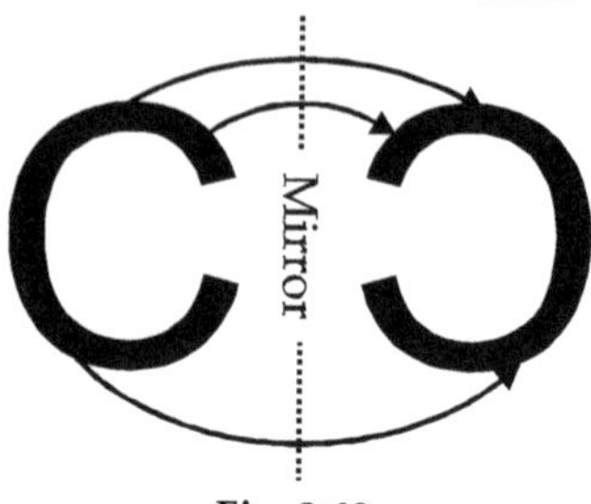

Fig. 2.60

Q41. What is Symmetry? Discuss the types of Symmetry.

Or

Define Linear Symmetry and Rotational Symmetry giving examples.

Ans. Symmetry is an important geometrical concept, commonly exhibited in nature and is used almost in every field of activity. Artists, professionals, designers of clothing or jewellery, car manufacturers, architects and many others make use of the idea of symmetry. The beehives, the flowers, the tree-leaves, religious symbols, rugs and handkerchiefs – everywhere we find symmetrical designs.

A figure has line symmetry, if there is a line about which the figure may be folded so that the two parts of the figure will coincide.

Some figures have more than one line of symmetry.

Rotation Symmetry: If we can rotate (or turn) a star around a center point by fewer than 360° and the star appears unchanged, then the star has rotation symmetry. The point around which we rotate is called the center of rotation, and the smallest angle we need to turn is called the angle of rotation.

The star has rotation symmetry of 72°, and the center of rotation is the center of the star:

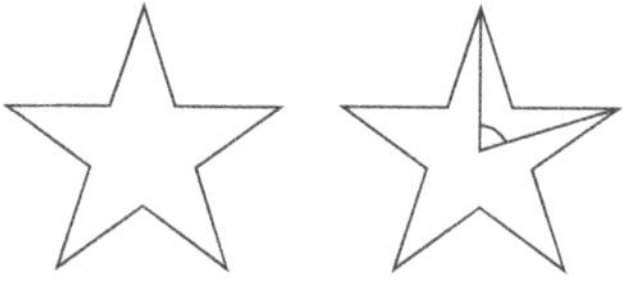

Fig. 2.61

Reflection Symmetry: The simplest symmetry is Reflection Symmetry (sometimes called *Line Symmetry* or *Mirror Symmetry*). It is easy to recognize, because one half is the reflection of the other half.

The central line is called the **Mirror Line** and it doesn't matter what direction

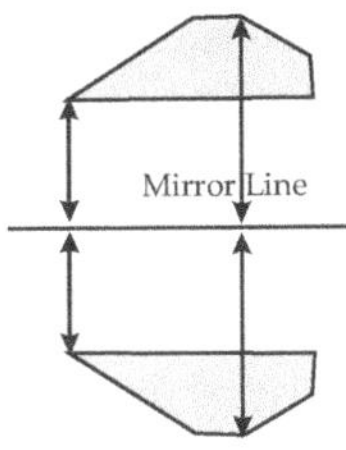

Fig. 2.62

the mirror line goes, the reflected image is always the same size, it just faces the other way.

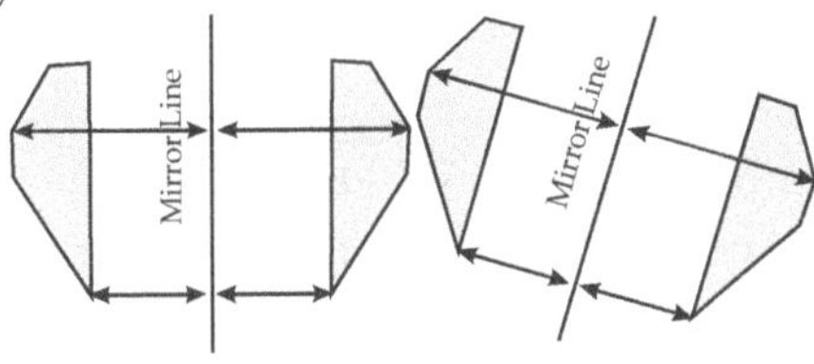

Fig. 2.63

The Line of Symmetry does not have to be up-down or left-right, it can be in any direction.

Q42. What do you mean by Tri-Dimensional Bodies? List its various types.

Ans. Bodies with extensions in three directions mutually at right angles are known as 3D bodies. Different regular 3D shapes are as follows:

(1) Cuboid (2) Cube (3) Cylinder (4) Pyramid

(5) Sphere (6) Prism (7) Cone

Q43. Give the definition of Cuboid and Cube. Write the formulas of calculating their surface area and volume.

Ans. A brick, chalk box, geometry box, match box, a book, etc. are all examples of a cuboid. Fig. 2.64 below represents a cuboid. It can be easily seen from the figure that a cuboid has six rectangular regions as its faces. These are ABCD, ABFE, BCGF, EFGH, ADHE and CDHG. The two adjacent faces meet in a line segment called an edge of the cuboid. For example, faces ABCD and ABFE meet in the edge AB. There are in all 12 edges of a cuboid. Points A, B, C, D, E, F, G and H are called the corners or vertices of the cuboid. So, there are 8 corners or vertices of a cuboid.

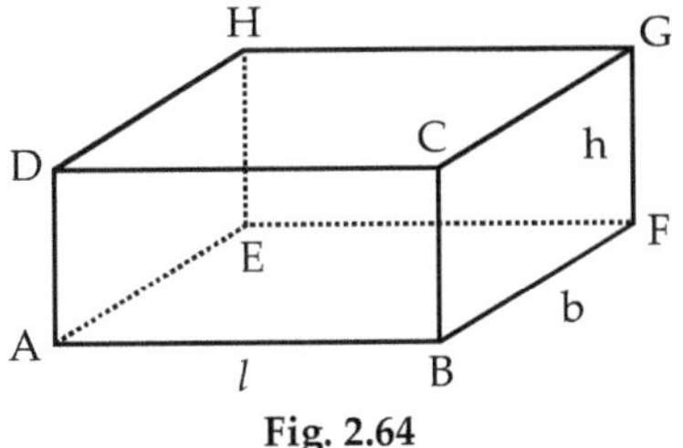

Fig. 2.64

It can also be seen that at each vertex, three edges meet. One of these three edges is taken as the length, the second as the breadth and third is taken as the height (or thickness or depth) of the cuboid. These are usually denoted by l, b and h respectively. Thus, we may say that A B (= EF = CD = GH) is the length, AE (=BF = CG = DH) is the breadth and AD (= EH = BC = FG) is the height of the cuboid.

Surface area of the cuboid is equal to the sum of the areas of all the six rectangles.

Thus, **surface area of the cuboid**

$= l\times b + b\times h + h\times l + l\times b + b\times h + h\times l$

$= 2(lb + bh + hl)$

And, **diagonal of a cuboid** $= \sqrt{l^2 + b^2 + h^2}$

We know that cube is a special type of cuboid in which length = breadth = height, i.e., $l = b = h$.

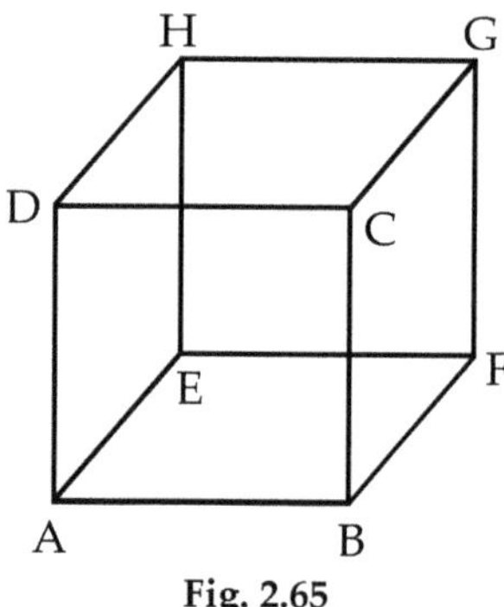

Fig. 2.65

Hence,

Surface Area of a cube of side or edge a

$= 2\ (a\times a + a\times a + a\times a)$

$= 6a^2$

Take some unit cubes of side 1 cm each and join them to form a cuboid as shown in Fig. 2.66 given below:

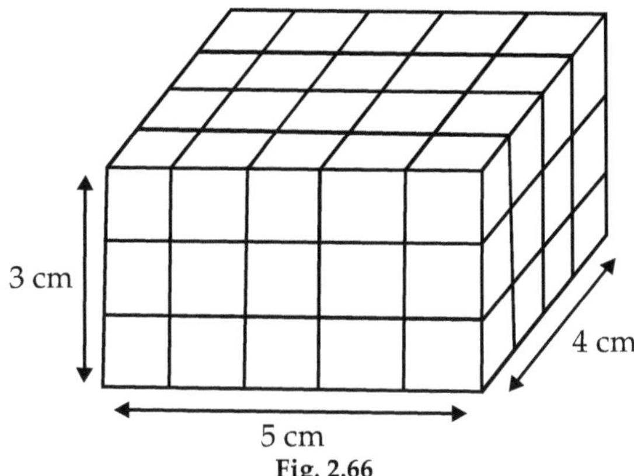

Fig. 2.66

By actually counting the unit cubes, we can see that this cuboid is made up of 60 unit cubes.

So, its volume = 60 cubic cm or 60cm^3 (Because volume of 1 unit cube, in this case, is 1 cm^3)

Also, we can observe that length × breadth × height = 5×4×3 cm^3

= 60 cm^3

We can form some more cuboids by joining different number of unit cubes and find their volumes by counting the unit cubes and then by the product of length, breadth and height.

Everytime, we will find that

Volume of a cuboid = length × breadth × height

or volume of a cuboid = *lbh*

Further, as cube is a special case of cuboid in which $l = b = h$, we have **volume of a cube of side** a = a×a×a× =a^3.

Example: Length, breadth and height of cuboid are 4 cm, 3 cm and 12 cm respectively. Find (i) Surface Area (ii) Volume and (iii) Diagonal of the cuboid.

Solution:

(i) Surface area of the cuboid

$= 2\,(lb + bh + hl)$

$= 2\,(4\times3+3\times12+12\times4)\text{cm}^2$

$= 2\,(12 + 36 + 48)\text{cm}^2 = 192\ \text{cm}^2$

(ii) Volume of cuboid = lbh

$= 4 \times 3 \times 12\ \text{cm}^3 = 144\ \text{cm}^2$

(iii) Diagonal of the cuboid $= \sqrt{l^2 + b^2 + h^2}$

$$= \sqrt{4^2 + 3^2 + 12^2}$$

$$= \sqrt{16 + 9 + 144}$$

$$= \sqrt{169}\,\text{cm} = 13\text{cm}$$

Unit of volume measure: The unit to measure volume of a 3D body is the volume of a unit cube i.e., a cube each side of which is of unit length. If the length of each side of a unit-cube is 1cm, then the volume of the unit-cube is 1cm^3.

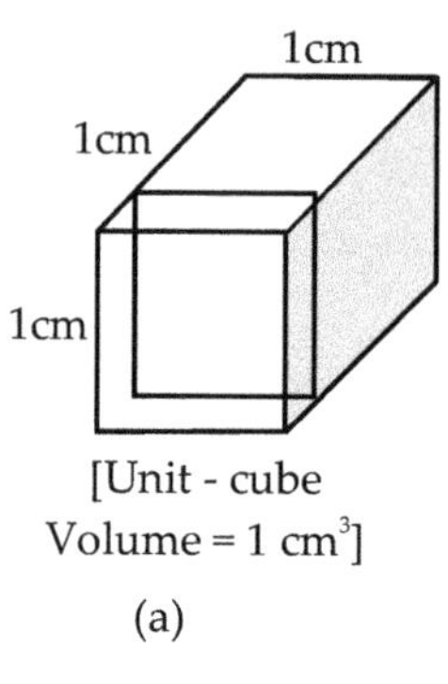

[Unit - cube
Volume = 1 cm^3]
(a)

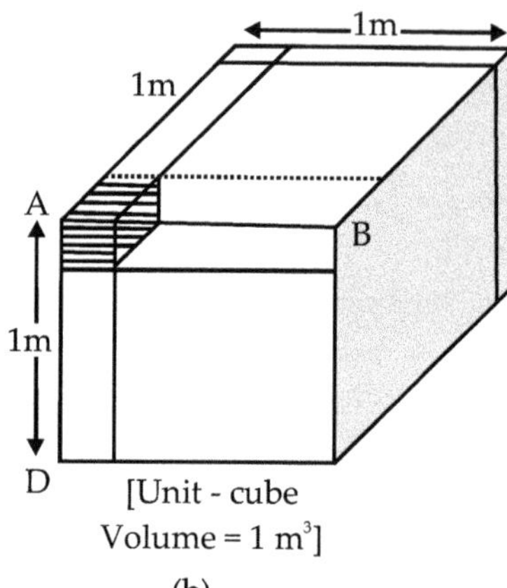

[Unit - cube
Volume = 1 m^3]
(b)

Fig. 2.67

A unit-cube, each side of which is 1cm, is known as a cm-cube.

A unit-cube, each side of which is 1m, is known as a m-cube.

The shaded part of the m-cube (Fig. 2.67 b) is a cm-cube i.e. each edge of it is of length 1cm. Thus if the m-cube is cut into cm-cubes we will get 100 cubes along the edge AB, 100 cubes along the edge AC and 100 cubes along the edge AD.

Hence, the total number of cm-cubes available will be 100 × 100 × 100 = 10,00,000.

Thus 1m^3 = 10, 00,000 cm^3 = 10^6 cm^3

1 cm^3, 1 m^3 etc. are known as cubic units.

Q44. Write the formulae of calculating surface area and volume of a prism.

Ans. Surface area of a prism

Lateral surface area = AB × h × BC + h + CA × h sq-units (where 'h' represents the height)

= h (AB + BC + CA) sq-units ('h' taken common)

= h × perimeter of the base

Area of the ends = 2 × area of each end.

Total surface area of a prism

= lateral surface area + area of the ends

= h × perimeter of the base + 2 × area of each end.

Volume of a prism = base area × height

These rules apply to prisms of bases in the shape of polygons of any no. of sides.

Q45. Write the definition of cylinder with formulas to find its surface area and volume.

Ans. Let us rotate a rectangle ABCD about one of its edges say AB.

The solid generated as a result of this rotation is called a right circular cylinder (Fig. 2.68). In daily life, we come across many solids of this shape such as water pipes, tin cans, drums, powder boxes, etc.

Here, AD (or BC) is called the **base radius** and AB is called the **height** of the cylinder.

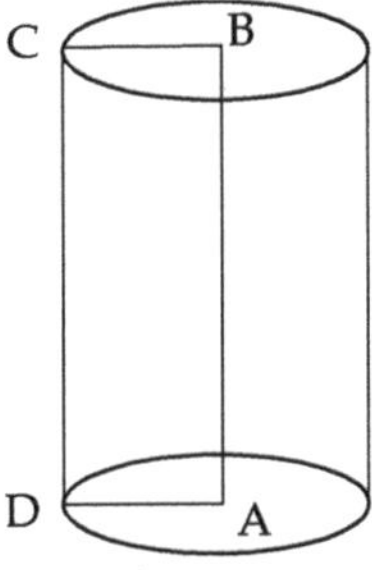

Fig. 2.68

It can also be seen that the surface formed by two circular ends are flat and the remaining surface is **curved.**

Surface Area: Let us take a hollow cylinder of radius r and height h and cut it along any line on its curved surface parallel to the line segment joining the centres of the two circular ends. We obtain a rectangle of length 2π r and breadth h as shown in Fig. 2.69 (ii).

Clearly, area of this rectangle is equal to the area of the curved surface of the cylinder.

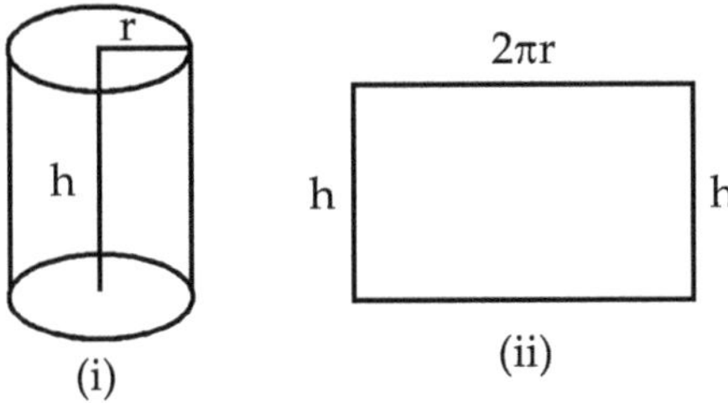

Fig. 2.69

So, curved surface area of the cylinder = area of the rectangle

$= 2\pi\, r \times h = 2\pi rh.$

In case, the cylinder is closed at both the ends, then the total surface area of the cylinder

$= 2\pi rh + 2\pi r^2$

$= 2\pi r (r + h)$

Volume: Volume of a right circular cylinder

= Area of the base × height

$= \pi r^2 \times h$

$= \pi r^2 h$

Q46. What is a Pyramid? Write the formula to find its surface area.

Ans. The base of a pyramid is a triangle or a polygon and it ends in a point at the top. Some such shapes are shown below.

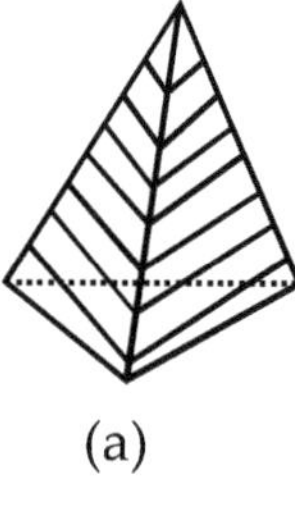

(a)

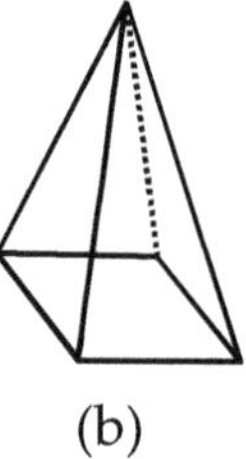

(b)

Fig. 2.70

Pyramid with triangular base has 4 vertices, 6 edges and 4 faces each of which is a triangle.

Pyramid with quadrilateral base has 5 vertices, 8 edges and 5 faces of which slant faces are triangular and the base is a quadrilateral.

The **surface area of a pyramid** = slant surface area + base area

Volume of a pyramid = $\frac{1}{3} \times$ base area × ht.

Q47. What is cone? Write the formula to find the surface area of a cone.

Ans. A funnel without its stem have the a shape which is known as a cone. It has one vertex, one circular edge and 2 faces of which one is curved and the other one is flat and circular in shape.

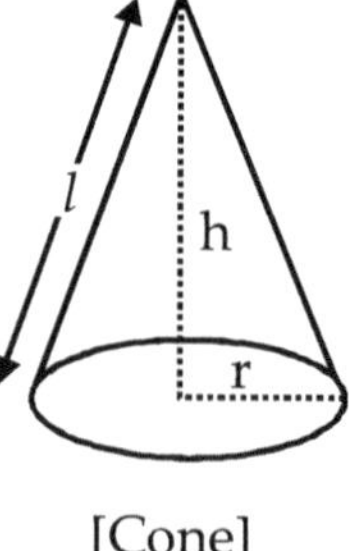

[Cone]

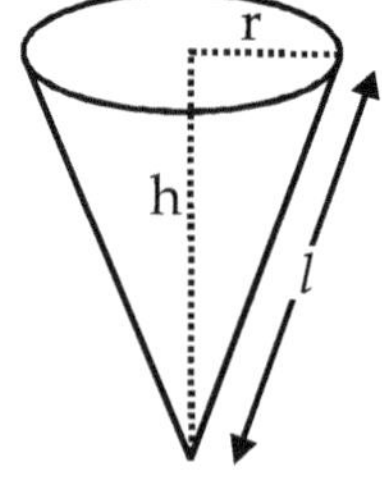

[Inverted Cone]

Fig. 2.71

Total surface area = Curved surface area + area of the base-circle

$$= \pi r\sqrt{h^2 + r^2} + \pi r^2 = \pi r\left(\sqrt{h^2 + r^2} + r\right)$$

[where 'r' is the radius of the circular base and 'h' is the height of the cone as shown in the diagram]

Slant height (l) = $\sqrt{r^2 + h^2}$

Q48. Define a 'Sphere' and write formulae of calculating its Surface Area and Volume.

Ans. A sphere is a perfectly round geometrical object in three-dimensional space that is the surface of a completely round ball. The shape of a football represents a sphere.

It has no vertex and it has no edge too. But it has one curved face.

Fig. 2.72

Surface area of a sphere = $4\pi r^2$

Volume of a sphere = $\frac{4}{3}\pi r^3$ (r is the length of the radius of the sphere and π is to be taken as $\frac{22}{7}$ or 3.14 as suitable).

Q49. Explain the process to construct a line segment of a given length.

Ans. We follow following process to construct a line segment:

(1) We mark a point A on a sheet of paper and draw a line l passing through it.

(2) Then we place the metal end of the compasses at the zero mark on ruler and open the compasses so that the pencil point is on the mark indicating given length on the ruler [Fig. 2.73 (i)].

(3) Now, without changing the opening of compasses, we place the metal end on A and make a small stroke (arc) on the line l so as to cut it at B [Fig. 2.73 (ii)].

(4) Thus, we obtain line segment AB of required length. Similarly, we can construct line segments of other required lengths using compasses.

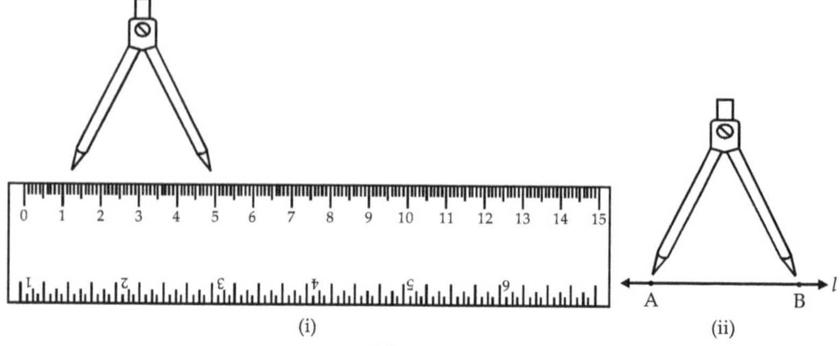

(i) (ii)

Fig. 2.73

Q50. Write the steps of construction of a perpendicular bisector of a Line Segment.

Ans. We follow following steps to construct a perpendicular bisector of MN:

(1) With M as centre and radius more than half of MN, draw an arc.

(2) With N as centre and the same radius a in step 1, draw an arc intersecting the first arc at P an Q.

(3) Join PQ intersecting MN at O

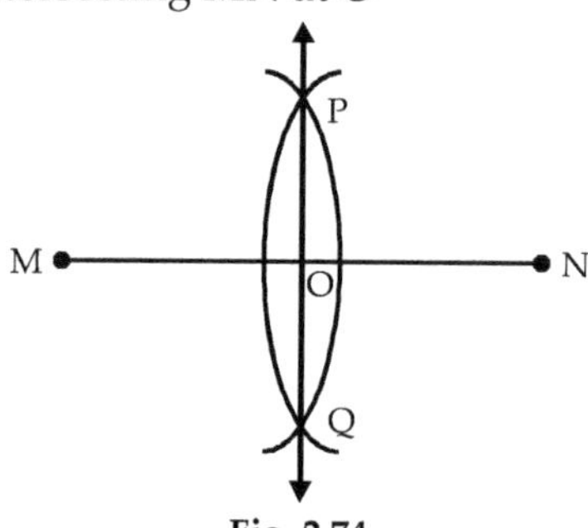

Fig. 2.74

Then PQ is the perpendicular bisector of MN.

Q51. Write steps to construct a perpendicular to a given line at a given point. Also write a steps of constructing perpendicular when point does not lie on the given line.

Ans. To draw a perpendicular to a given line from a point lying on it

Given: A line XY and a point P lying on it.

To construct: A line through P, which is perpendicular to the line XY.

Steps of construction:

(1) With P as centre and any radius, draw an arc to intersect XY at A and B.

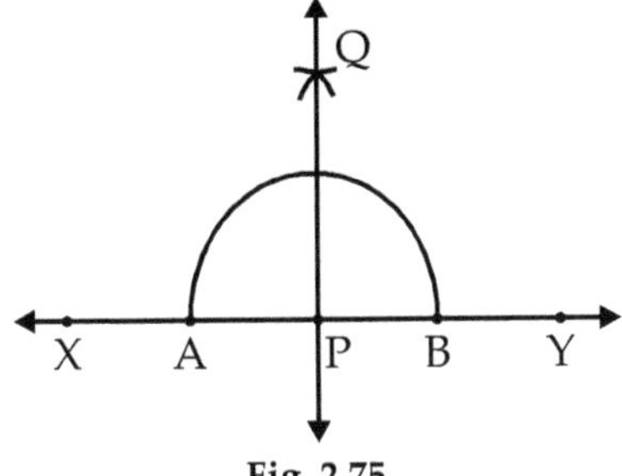

Fig. 2.75

(2) With A as centre and any radius greater than PA, draw an arc.

(3) With B as centre and the same radius, draw another arc to intersect the arc of step 2 at Q.

(4) Join PQ and produce it to form line PQ.
Then PQ is the required perpendicular line.

To draw a perpendicular to a given line from a point not lying on it

Given: A line XY and a point P outside the line XY.

To construct: A line through P which is perpendicular to the line XY.

Steps of construction:

(1) With P as centre and a suitable radius, draw an arc to intersect the line XY at A and B

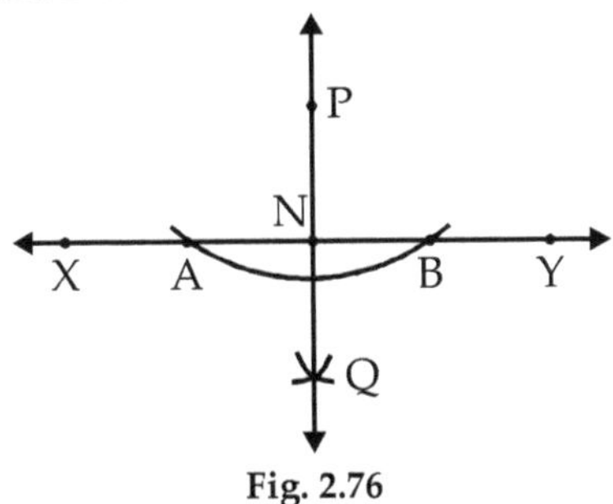

Fig. 2.76

(2) With A as centre and radius greater than $\frac{1}{2}$ AB, draw an arc.

(3) With B as centre and the same radius, draw another arc to intersect the arc of step 2 at Q.

(4) Join PQ, intersecting XY at N, and produce it to form line PQ.
Then PQ is the required line perpendicular to XY and passing through P.

Q52. Write the steps to construct a parallel line to a given line.

Ans. (i) To construct a line parallel to a given line passing through a given point not lying on it

Given: A line l and a point A not lying on it.

To construct: A line parallel to l through A.

Steps of construction:

(1) Take any point B on l and join B to A.

(2) With B as centre and a convenient radius, draw an arc cutting l at C and AB at D.

(3) Now with A as centre and the same radius as in step 2, draw an arc EF cutting AB at G.

(4) Place the steel point of the compasses at C and adjust the opening so that the pencil pint is at D.

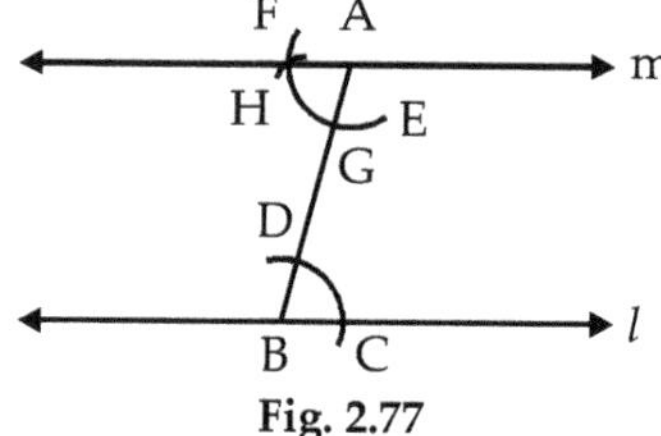

Fig. 2.77

(5) With the same opening as in step 4 and with G as centre, draw an arc cutting the arc EF at H.

(6) Now join AH to draw a line *m*.

Then m is the required line parallel to l and passing through the given point A.

(ii) To draw a line parallel to a given line at a given distance from it.

Given: A line AB is given.

To construct: A parallel line at a given distance (say 5 cm).

Steps of construction:

(1) A point is taken on AB. Name the point as P. At P a line is drawn perpendicular to AB. Name it as PQ.

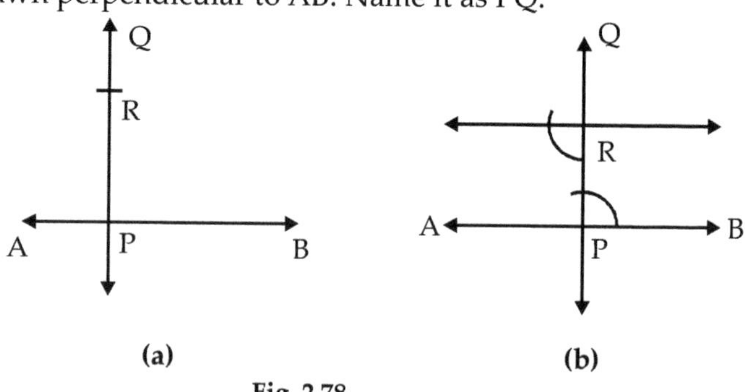

Fig. 2.78

(2) Taking radius of 5 cm, draw an arc with P as centre such that it cuts PQ. Name the point as R.

(3) Draw an angle equal in measure to $\angle RPB$ at R on RP such that it become alternate to $\angle RPB$. Extend the arm of the angle drawn. It gives the required line parallel to AB at a given distance (5 cm) from AB.

Q53. Write the steps to construct an angle equal to a given angle.

Ans. Given: An angle, say $\angle A$ [Fig. 2.79 (i)]

To construct: An angle equal to $\angle A$.

Steps of construction:

(1) Draw a ray PR [Fig. 2.79 (ii)]

(2) With A as centre and any convenient radius, draw an arc meeting the arms of the angle A at D and E.

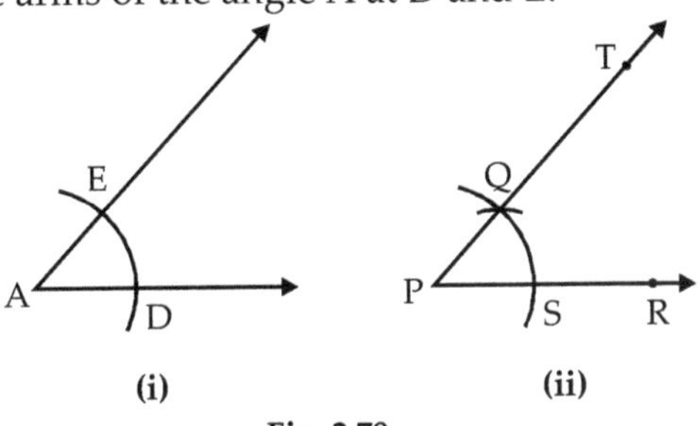

Fig. 2.79

(3) With centre P and the same radius as in step 2, draw an arc intersecting the ray PR at S.

(4) With centre S and radius equal to DE, draw an arc intersecting the arc of step 3 at Q.

(5) Join PQ and produce it to form ray PT.
Then $\angle TPR$ or $\angle P$ is the required angel.

Q54. Draw the bisector of a given angle.

Or

Write the steps to draw an angular bisector of a given angle.

Ans. Given: Any $\angle BAC$.

To construct: The bisector of $\angle BAC$.

Steps of construction:

(1) With vertex A as centre and a convenient radius, draw an arc intersecting side AB at P and the side AC at Q.

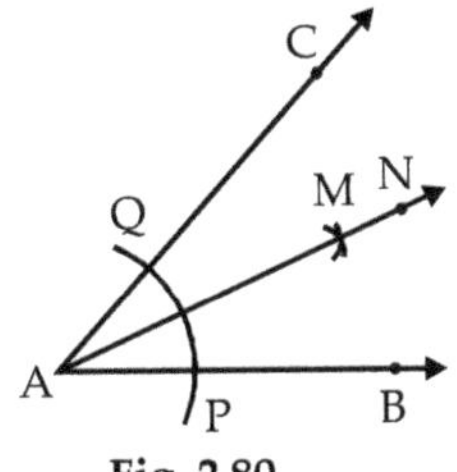

Fig. 2.80

(2) With centre P and radius more than $\frac{1}{2}$PQ, draw an arc.

(3) With centre Q and the same radius as in step 2 above, draw another arc intersecting the arc of step 2 at point M.

(4) Join AM and produce it to form ray AN.

Then ray AN is the required bisector of $\angle$BAC

Q55. Construct an angle of a given degree (say 60°) also construct the angles of its multipliers and sub-multipliers.

Ans. We go through the following steps for this construction:

Steps of construction:

(1) Draw a ray OA

(2) With O as centre and a suitable radius, draw an arc LM that cuts OA at L.

(3) With L as centre and radius OL, draw an arc to cut LM at N.

(4) Join O and N and draw ray OB.

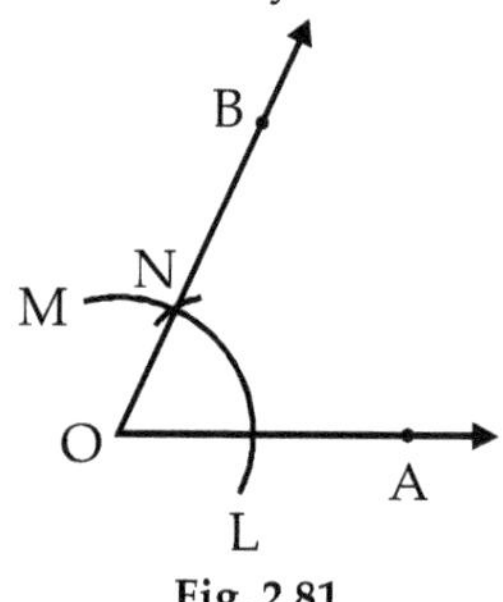

Fig. 2.81

Then $\angle$AOB is the required angle of 60°

Q56. Describe the method of dividing a given line into specified equal parts.

Ans. Let we, start with a line a segment AB that we will divide up into 5 (in this case) equal parts.

Step 1: From point A, draw a line segment at an angle to the given line, and about the same length. The exact length is not important.

Step 2: Set the compasses on A, and set its width to a bit less than one fifth of the length of the new line.

Step 3: Step the compasses along the line, marking off 5 arcs. Label the last one C.

Step 4: With the compasses' width set to CB, draw an arc from A just below it.

Step 5: With the compasses' width set to AC, draw an arc from B crossing the one drawn in step 4. This intersection is point D.

Step 6: Draw a line from D to B.

Step 7: Using the same compasses' width as used to step along AC, step the compasses from D along DB making 4 new arcs across the line.

Step 8: Draw lines between the corresponding points along AC and DB.

Step 9: The lines divide the given line segment AB in to 5 congruent parts.

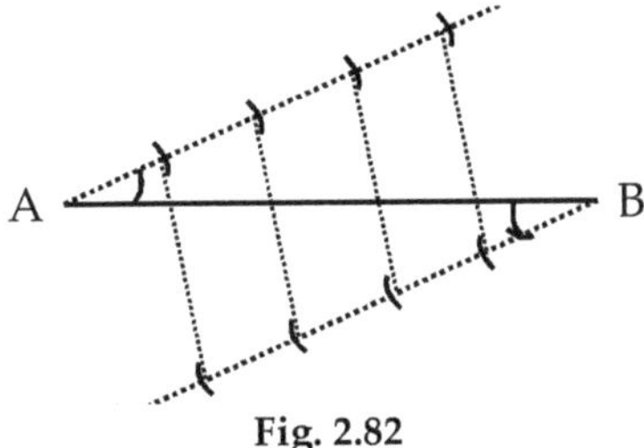

Fig. 2.82

Q57. Describe the method to construct a quadrilateral.

Ans. When we knew the construction of different triangles, it would not be difficult to construct the quadrilaterals. This is because of the fact that every quadrilateral is divided into two triangles by each of its two diagonals.

Therefore, while constructing a quadrilateral first we have to complete constructing its component triangle and then complete the quadrilateral.

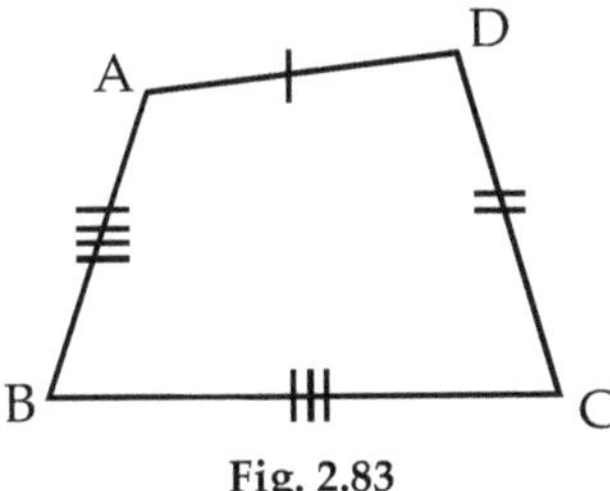

Fig. 2.83

For example, when the lengths of the four sides of the quadrilateral ABCD and the length of AC, one of its diagonals are given, we can draw any of the two triangles, say the triangle ABC and then complete the triangle ADC. Thus the construction of the required quadrilateral can be done.

Similarly, we can undertake the construction of other variations of the quadrilaterals, when:

(i) Two Adjacent Sides and Three Angles are Given

(ii) Three Sides and Two Included Angles are Given

Q58. In the following figure, $AB \parallel CD$ and PQ cuts them. The measures of angles formed are indicated as a, b, c, d, e, f, g and h. If g=35°, find the value of a, b, c, d, e, f and h.

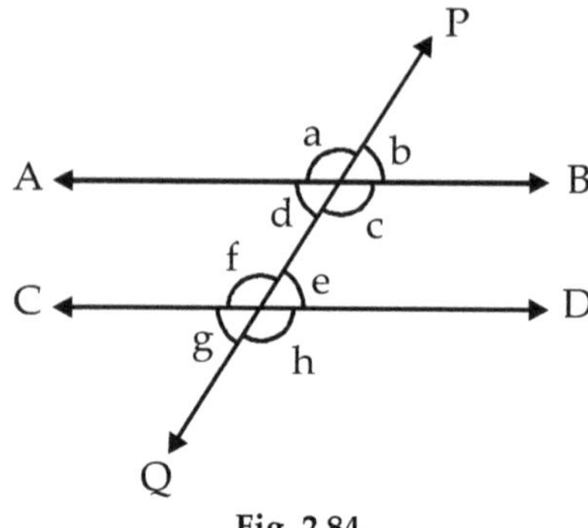

Fig. 2.84

Ans. Given, g = 35°

So,

(i) b = g = 35° (alternate angles)

(ii) e = b = 35° (corresponding angles)

(iii) d = e = 35° (alternate angles)

(iv) e + c = 35° + c =180° (alternate interior angles)

c = 145°

(v) f = c = 145° (alternate interior angles)

(vi) a = f = 145° (corresponding angles)

(vii) h = c = 145° (corresponding angles)

Q59. Form a rectangle of length 16 cm. with the help of 40 cm. long wire. Find the area of rectangle thus formed.

Ans. Perimeter of the rectangle = Length of the wire = 40 cm. (given)

Length of the rectangle formed = 16 cm.

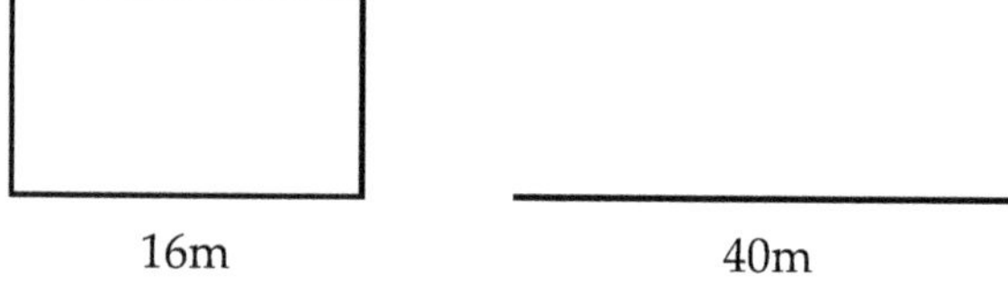

Fig. 2.85

Perimeter of the rectangle = $2(l + b)$

$= 2l + 2b$

Therefore, $40 = 2 \times 16 + 2b$

$\Rightarrow 40 = 32 + 2b$

$\Rightarrow 8 = 2b$

$\Rightarrow b = 4$

Hence, breadth (b) of the rectangle = 4 cm.

Thus, area of the rectangle = $l \times b$

$= 16 \times 4 = 64 \text{ cm}^2$

Q60. Check if the shapes given below have rotation symmetry and if yes, state the order of symmetry in each case.

Ans.

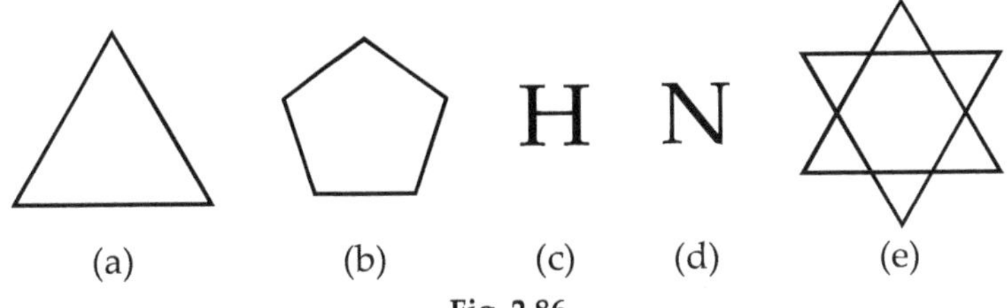

Fig. 2.86

Yes, rotation of the given shapes have symmetry. In each case, the order of rotational symmetry is given below:

Shape (a)	:	Three (3)
Shape (b)	:	Five (5)
Shape (c)	:	Two (2)
Shape (d)	:	Two (2)
Shape (e)	:	Six (6)

Q61. Using ruler and compasses how can the angle of 82.5° measure be achieved in construction?

Or

To construct an angle of measure 82.5° using ruler and compass, what should be the break-up of angle? [April-2016, Q.No.-24]

Ans. Construction of angle of measure 82.5° is as follows:

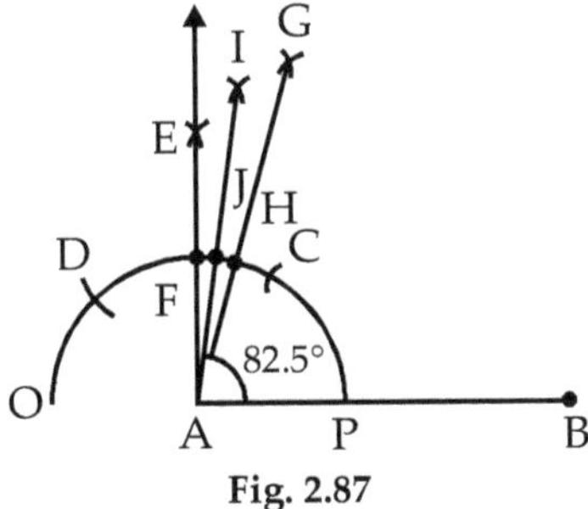

Fig. 2.87

Steps of construction:

(1) First of all, draw a line segment AB.

(2) Taking 'A' as centre, draw an arc 'OP' of any radius intersecting 'AB' at 'P'.

(3) Taking 'P' as centre and radius equal to 'AP', draw another arc intersecting 'OP' at 'C'. Now take 'C' as centre and with same radius, repeat the same process. The new arc will intersect the earlier 'OC' at point 'D'.

(4) Now, taking 'C' and 'D' as centre, draw two arcs with same radius intersecting each other at point 'E'. Join 'E' and 'A'. The line EA intersects arc 'OP' at point 'F' forming a right angle, i.e. $\angle BAE = 90°$.

(5) Taking 'F' and 'C' as centre and with same radius, draw two arcs intersecting each other at point 'G'. Join 'GA' intersecting arc 'OP' at point 'H'.

Now, draw angle bisector of $\angle GAE$, i.e. 'IA'.

Hence, $\angle IAG = \frac{1}{2} \times 15° = 7.5°$

$\because$ GA is the bisector of $\angle CAE = \frac{1}{2} \times 30° = 15°$

$$\therefore \quad \angle IAB = \angle BAE - \angle EAI$$
$$= 90° - 7.5°$$
$$= 82.5°$$

Hence, $\angle IAB = 82.5°$ is the required angle.

Q62. In ΔABC and ΔPQR; If AB = 4 cm, BC = 7 cm; AC = 8 cm, QR = 10.5 cm and PQ = 6 cm, then

(a) Find PR

(b) Find Area of ΔABC : Area of ΔPQR

Ans. (a) To find PR, consider the following figure:

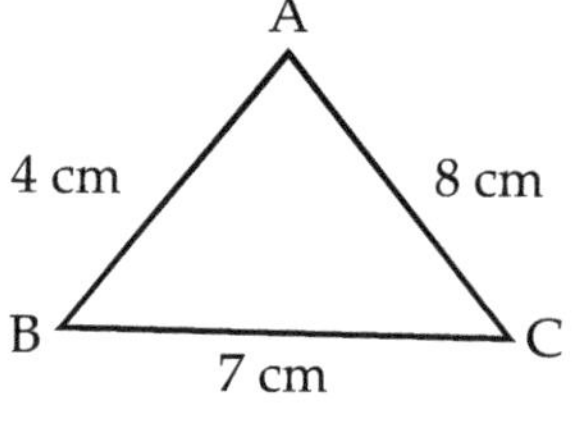

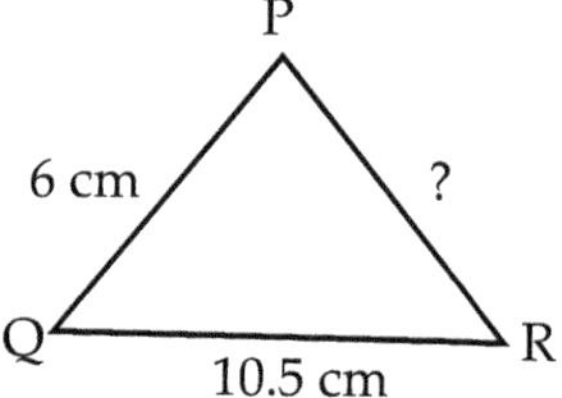

Fig. 2.88

Here, $\frac{AB}{PQ} = \frac{4}{6} = \frac{2}{3}$

and $\frac{BC}{QR} = \frac{7}{10.5} = \frac{2}{3}$

Thus, $\frac{AB}{PQ} = \frac{BC}{QR} = \frac{2}{3}$

Hence, these two triangles are similar triangles.

Therefore,

$\frac{AB}{PQ} = \frac{BC}{QR} = \frac{AC}{PR}$

and,

$$\Rightarrow \frac{AC}{PR} = \frac{8}{PR} = \frac{2}{3}$$

$$\Rightarrow PR = 12 \text{ cm}$$

(b) $Ar\,\Delta ABC : Ar\Delta PQR$

We know that the areas of two similar triangles are proportional to the squares of their corresponding sides.

$$\therefore \; Ar\,\Delta ABC : Ar\Delta PQR = \left(\frac{AB}{PQ}\right)^2 = \left(\frac{BC}{QR}\right)^2 = \left(\frac{AC}{PR}\right)^2$$

$$= \left(\frac{2}{3}\right)^2 = \frac{4}{9} \text{ or } 4 : 9$$

Q63. Using ruler and compasses, draw a shape shown in the figure alongside. The measurements are given below:
PQ = 5 cm and $OP \perp PQ$ and $RQ \perp PQ$. Construct a figure which has line symmetry with PQ as the line of symmetry.

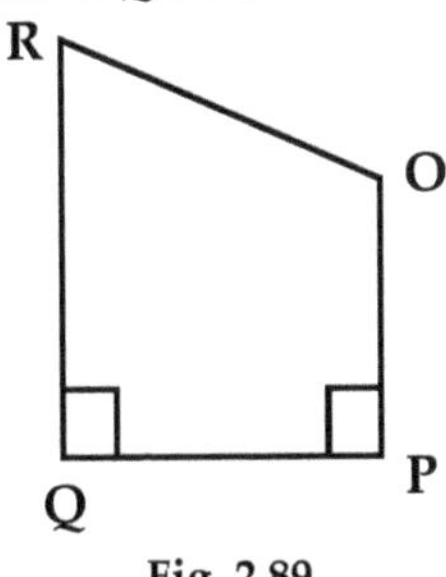

Fig. 2.89

Ans. Steps of construction of the given figure.

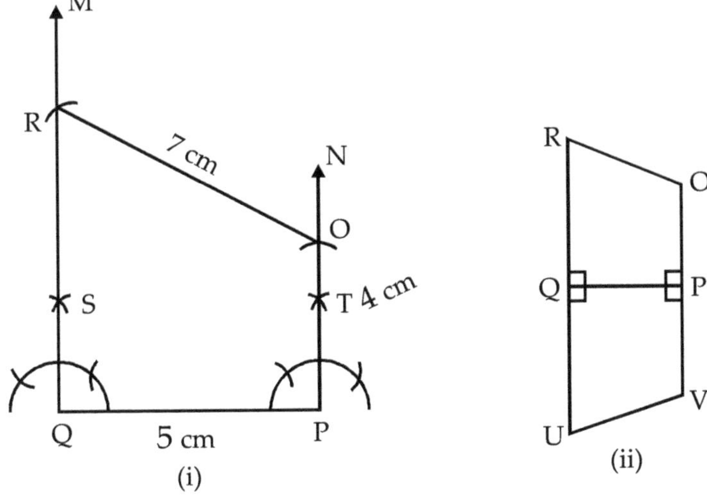

Fig. 2.90

(1) First of all, draw a line segment QP = 5 cm.

(2) Draw $\angle P = \angle Q = 90^\circ$, Hence, we get two points S and T on $\angle PQS$ and $\angle QPT$, respectively. Now, extend QS and PT to QM and PN, respectively.

(3) Taking P as centre draw an arc with radius 4 cm, intersecting PN at O.

(4) Again taking O as centre and radius 7 cm, draw another arc intersecting QM at point R. Join QR. Thus, the obtained ▱OPQR is the required quadrilateral.

(5) Taking PQ as base construct another quadrilateral PQUV following the same method on the opposite side.

Q64. Length, breadth and height of cuboid are 4 cm, 3 cm and 12 cm, respectively. Find:

(i) surface area

(ii) volume

(iii) diagonal of the cuboid

Ans. (i) Surface area of the cuboid = 2 (lb+bh+hl)

$= 2\,(4\times3+3\times12+12\times4)\text{cm}^2$

$= 2\,(12+36+48)\text{cm}^2$

(ii) Volume of cuboid = lbh

$= 4\times3\times12\text{cm}^3 = 144\text{cm}^2$

(iii) Diagonal of the cuboid $= \sqrt{l^2+b^2+h^2}$

$= \sqrt{4^2+3^2+12^2}\text{cm}$

$= \sqrt{16+9+144}\text{cm}$

$= \sqrt{169}\text{cm} = 13\text{cm}$

Q65. Volume of a cube is 2197 cm³. Find its surface area and the diagonal.

Ans. Let the edge of the cube be 'a cm'.

So, its volume = $a^3\text{cm}^3$

Therefore, from the question, we have:

$a^3=2197$

or $a^3=13\times13\times13$

So, a = 13

i.e., edge of the cube = 13 cm

Now, surface area of the cube = $6a^2$

$= 6\times13\times13\text{ cm}^2$

$=1014\text{ cm}^2$

$\therefore$ Its diagonal = $a\sqrt{3}\text{cm} = 13\sqrt{3}\text{cm}$

Thus, surface area of the cube is 1014 cm^2 and its diagonal is $13\sqrt{3}$ cm.

Q66. The radius and height of a right circular cylinder are 7 cm and 10 cm respectively. Find its:

(i) curved surface area

(ii) Total surface area

(iii) Volume

Ans. (i) curved surface area = $2\pi rh$

$$= 2\times\frac{22}{7}\times 7\times 10\text{cm}^2 = 440\text{cm}^2$$

(ii) total surface area $= 2\pi rh + 2\pi r^2$

$$= \left(2\times\frac{22}{7}\times 7\times 10 + 2\times\frac{22}{7}\times 7\times 7\right)\text{cm}^2$$

$$= 440\text{cm}^2 + 308\text{cm}^2 = 748\text{cm}^2$$

(iii) volume $= \pi r^2 h$

$$= \frac{22}{7}\times 7\times 7\times 10\text{cm}^3$$

$$= 1540\text{cm}^3$$

Q67. The base radius and height of a right circular cone are 7 cm and 24 cm. Find its curved surface area, total surface area and volume.

Ans. Here, r = 7 cm and h = 24 cm

So, slant height $l = \sqrt{r^2 + h^2}$

$$= \sqrt{7\times 7 + 24\times 24}\text{cm}$$

$$= \sqrt{49 + 576}\text{cm} = 25\text{ cm}$$

Thus, curved surface area $= \pi rl$

$$= \frac{22}{7}\times 7\times 25\text{cm}^2 = 550\text{cm}^2$$

Total surface area $= \pi rl + \pi r^2$

$$= \left(550 + \frac{22}{7}\times 49\right)\text{cm}^2$$

$$= (550 + 154)\text{cm}^2 = 704\text{cm}^2$$

Volume $= \frac{1}{3}\pi r^2 h = \frac{1}{3}\times\frac{22}{7}\times 49\times 24\text{cm}^3$

$= 1232\text{cm}^3$

Q68. Find the surface area and volume of a sphere of diameter 21 cm.

Ans. Radius of the sphere $= \frac{21}{2}\text{cm}$

so, its surface area $= 4\pi r^2$

$$= 4\times\frac{22}{7}\times\frac{21}{2}\times\frac{21}{2}\text{cm}^2$$

$= 1386 \text{ cm}^2$

Its volume $= \frac{4}{3}\pi r^3$

$= \frac{4}{3} \times \frac{22}{7} \times \frac{21}{2} \times \frac{21}{2} \times \frac{21}{2} \text{cm}^3 = 4851 \text{cm}^3$

Q69. Construct a right triangle, when its hypotenuse and side are given as below:

Hypotenuse = 5 cm and Side = 3 cm

Ans. To construct the triangle, we have gone through the following steps:

Step 1: Draw BC = 3cm

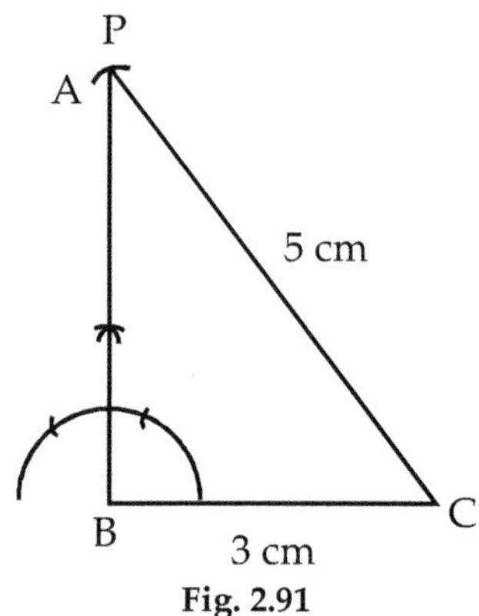

Fig. 2.91

Step 2: At B, construct $\angle CBP = 90°$.

Step 3: With C as centre and radius 5 cm, draw an arc cutting BP in A.

Step 4: Join AC.

ΔABC is the required triangle.

Q70. Define measurement. What are the various methods of measurement?

Ans. Measurement, according to J.P. Guilford, can be defined as a description of data in terms of numbers. Stevents definition is, "Measurement is the process of assigning numbers to objects according to certain assigned rules." Campbell defines it as, "The assignment of numerals to objects or events according to certain rules is called measurement." Still more elaborate and wider definition has been given by Nunnaly, "Measurement consists or rules for assigning numbers to objects in such a way to represent quantities of attributes."

Measurement is required to every individual in his/her life. Each one of us has to measure something or the other. For instance, we may have to spell out the size of the rope required for drawing water from our well, mention the length of the curtain cloth required for our doors and windows, the size of the bedroom of our 'going-to-be-constructed house', etc. In all these contexts, need for measurement arises. In fact, measurement is the quantification of the size of an object. We assign a number to specify the size-length, area or volume of an object, where qualitative description alone may not suffice.

A child's first experience in space are with solid 3-dimensional objects and 2-dimensional figures initially encountered as the surfaces of solid objects such as cubes, cones, cylinders, spheres, rectangular boxes, etc. Matching the 3-dimensional objects and their 2-dimensional representation, (for instance, identifying various parts of a cylinder such as its top, bottom, curved surface, height, etc. both from the 3-dimensional model and 2-dimensional picture) help the children to develop an awareness of different 2-dimensional shapes as well as some basic properties of these objects. Asking children to group objects like: blackboard, duster, book, wire, stick, string, sheet of paper, rectangular box, cylindrical tins, etc. into three groups according to their dimensions, help them understand that with 1-dimensional objects only one number length is associated, with 2-dimensional objects two numbers length and breadth are associated and with 3-dimensional objects length, breadth and height are attached. These kinds of experiences with shapes questions concerning size arise which are essential for developing an understanding of the notions of length, area, volume and their measurement.

The following are the measures that commonly used and the child in the elementary school can experience through different activities and from the real life experiences.

(1) Distance-measure: Length, breadth, height and radius are all distance measures. Following figure represents the distance between two specific points:

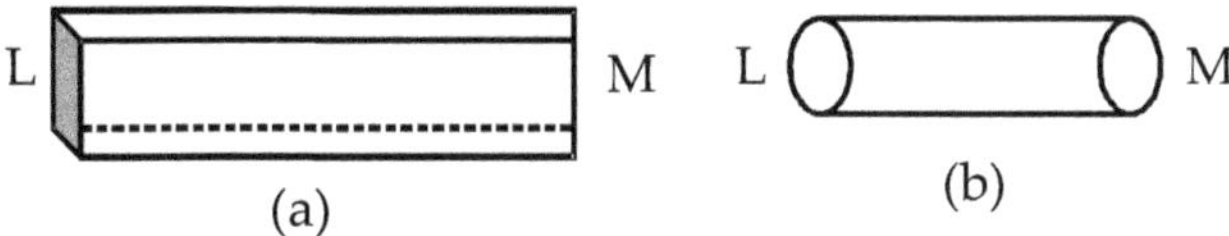

Fig. 2.92

In above fig. 2.92, there are three blocks of wood. Each of them has 2 ends (L, M). There is some distance between the two ends. It can be seen that the distance between the two ends of the block in (a) is more than the distance between the two ends of (b).

Thus, the distance between the two ends of the block is a common characteristic of the block. This is known as the **length-measure.**

(2) **Area-measure:** Each 2-D shape encloses some region on a plane. The measure of enclosed region is known as the area-measure.

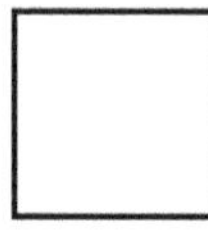

Fig. 2.93

The figure above encloses a part of the page of paper. Thus, each 2-D shape has an **area-measure**.

(3) **Volume-measure:** A portion of the space is occupied by 3-D bodies. The extent of space occupied by a 3-D body is its volume-measure. A 3-D body (not soluble in water) displaces a certain quantity of water when submersed in it. The quantity of water it displaces is known as the **volume-measure.**

(4) **Weight-measure:** When we carry a body or lift it above the ground, in case of some, we do not have to strain too much, whereas in case of some others, we have to strain too much. 3-D bodies also show a force with which those are pulled towards the earth. The bigness or the smallness of the pull of the earth on 3-D bodies represents their weight-measure. The characteristic of the body that gives the feeling of heaviness speaks of the **weight-measure**.

(5) **Time-measure:** When did an event happen during the day? How long do we take to complete a work? To answer such questions we need to be acquainted with the **time-measure.**

Q71. If 1 kg of rice costs `25, Find the cost of 5 Quintals of rice. If this quantity of rice is packed in small packets of 20 kg each, how many packets can be made with this quantity of rice?

Ans. 1 Quintal = 100 kg

5 Quintals = 100 × 5 = 500 kg

The cost of 5 Quintals of rice = 500 × 25 = `12500

20 kg = 1 packet

$$1 \text{ kg} = \frac{1}{20}$$

$$500 \text{ kg} = \frac{1 \times 500}{20} = 25 \text{ packets}$$

Thus, the cost of 5 Quintals of rice is `12500 and 25 packets can be made with the given quantity of rice.

Q72. How are similar objects measured with a degree of comparison?

Ans. Comparing the size of two objects is the first step in measurement: Comparison of size can be done by:

(1) observation;

(2) superimposition;

(3) indirect methods;

(4) using non-standard units; and

(5) using standard units.

Initially, we are not required to go for the 4th and the 5th method. We can use the first three methods and perform various activities to teach the children the concept of 'size' of an object.

Example 1: A teacher of class-IV came to the class with a bag full of many objects. She first divided the class into two groups. To one group, she gave about 10 pencils of different sizes and to other group, she gave a pen, a pencil, a scale, a rod, a sketch pen, a rubber, etc. She asked both the groups to arrange their things in the order of their length. Children were able to do this task easily. She performed many activities of this kind to teach the concepts of big, small, tall, short, fat, thin, wide and narrow.

The teacher continued with her discussion about comparison of size. First, she wanted to take up comparison of size by superimposition.

Example 2: A teacher of class-IV showed two ribbons to everyone in her classroom, the colour of ribbons was red and black. She asked the students that which one of the two is longer?

Then she superimposed one over the other and showed it to the entire class. The children took no time in saying that black was longer. Then children superimposed chalk pieces, pencils and other things whatever was available to them and found out the longer of the two.

The teacher then turned to 3-D objects. She made a pillar with some matchboxes. She asked children also to make similar pillars with matchboxes. Children then found out the biggest pillar and checked it by counting the number of matchboxes. Then she took out two balls from her bag and made children say which ball was bigger. Similarly, children took no time in saying that Lakshay's pencil box was bigger than Mayank's when their teacher showed both these boxes to them. The children seemed to enjoy doing all these activities.

In the same way, the idea of volume can be informally introduced with the help of the following activity:

Example 3: We can take two glass vessels of different shapes and ask the children, which one is bigger. If they are not able to answer, we can ask them to fill one vessel with water upto the brim and then pour this into the second vessel. Now we may ask questions to them, such as which one is bigger? Which one hold more? Which one has more capacity, etc.?

Now they will be able to answer these questions. It is the indirect method of comparing size. Indirect methods are useful as students are able to learn the use of standard units with the help of these methods.

Q73. Distinguish between non-standard and standard units of measurement.

Or

Why are standard units of measurement required?

Or

Name any two non-standard units of length using body parts.

[April-2016, Q.No.-23]

Ans. Measuring each single object can be done either by using non-standard units or standard units. Usually, individuals do not use standard units of measurement always rather most of us use non-standard units of measurement.

The non-standard units refer to the measurement through different objects like a stick, human body parts, etc. These are physical units because these can be seen, touched and counted. Children need to be given the experience of measuring lengths of objects using a variety of physical units, for example, matchboxes, pencils of uniform length, sticks, crayons, etc.

However, following are also various *non-standard units of length based on the human's body parts,* which were used in olden days:

(i) **Finger:** Breadth of first finger.

(ii) **Palm:** Length of hand from tip of a finger till end of the hand.

(iii) **Cubit:** Length of one arm till the tip of middle finger.

(iv) **Pace:** Length of one footstep.

(v) **Inch:** Length from tip of thumb till its joints with the palm.

Such units cannot give us correct lengths.

Measuring the length of many objects using span, foot/pace by all the children, may help the children in forming the conclusion that these units give different length for the same object if measured by different persons. This necessitates the use of a standard unit for measurement.

Students learn the use of standard units only with the help of non-standard units.

Similar to non-standard units of length, unit area, unit volume/capacity and unit weight are also used to measure area, volume/capacity and weight, respectively. Each of these is taken as a unit of measurement of the specific attribute. These units can be of different forms as per the situation and requirement.

In contrast to non-standard units, standard units are same all over the world. For instance, a meter scale is a standard measure used in almost all countries throughout the world. Anywhere, the length of a meter is fixed and does not depend on the person or situation or time.

The standard units are easier to use as it is simple and is understood easily by everybody throughout the world. Thus, these units have been nearly perfected for accurate measurements. Sub-units (e.g., centimeter and millimeter are sub-units of meter) and compound units (e.g., kilometer is a compound unit of meter) are well-defined in most of the standard units, which are usually not available with non-standard units.

Non-standard units of measurements have been evolved to meet some immediate or some local needs. If we are preparing a sweet dish, we do not always go for the measures of rice, sugar and milk by the cooking manuals. By experience, we can have handful of rice, five spoonful sugar and two glasses of milk and yet the dish would be as tasteful as the dish prepared by following the accurate measures of those ingredients. These non-standard measures may work well for us, but may not be as useful for another person who might have different measures fulfilling his/her requirements.

Some commonly agreed units in a locality/community are used to measure length, weight, area and volume since a long time. These are standardised units within that locality/community or culture. We find such units in every culture. However, such units are limited to one culture and may not be intelligible in another culture.

Q74. What is the importance of non-standard units to children?

Or

How are the non-standard units helpful to children?

Or

Why is the use of non-standard units at the early stage of schooling important? Give reasons.

Ans. The importance of non-standard units to children can be understood by providing them experience to measure with the non-standard units, as it is helpful to them in a number of ways:

(i) Children are introduced to the concept of measuring in units through familiar objects rather than going straight into these mysterious things called centimetres. In this way, they are not required to handle a new vocabulary for the unit at the same time as meeting a new measuring experience.

(ii) The non-standard units are more appropriate size of a unit for the first practical measuring tasks that young children undertake. Centimetres may be too small, and therefore, too numerous for their first experience of measuring the length of the desktop, or the height of a friend and metres are clearly too large a unit for this purpose.

(iii) The experience of measuring with non-standard units can open children to the idea that scales can be invented for a particular measuring task when a standard scale is not available, or when the standard scale is inappropriate.

(iv) Through using non-standard units, children will become aware of the need for a standard unit when, for example, they discover that the classroom is twenty pace wide when they measure it, but only eleven paces wide when the teacher measures it.

Q75. How can a teacher introduce standard units of measurement in her classroom?

Ans. In a classroom, standard unit should be introduced only when the need for such a unit is felt by the children. If the teacher immediately draws a segment on the blackboard and measures its length with a ruler, children fail to understand, why 'centimetre' is called a standard unit. In this regard, a primary school teacher can adopt the following method in her classroom:

- The teacher may call a few children to her table one by one and may ask them to measure the length of her table in span and record their findings.
- Then she may ask each one of them about their findings. The result may vary from 6 to 7 span. But the teacher may get different measure (5 span). This could be because her hand is bigger. Each one of us has different span length so we get different answers.

- The teacher then may call another set of children and may ask them to measure the table with the stick. Let each one of them measure it to be 4 sticks. In this case, she can consider this stick to be a standard object to measure. This is the stage, when children realises the need for a standard unit of measurement.

If she introduces the standard unit in this manner, it would be quite meaningful for the children. Then she should draw their attention towards salespersons at a textile shop measuring out cloth pieces. She should tell them that they might have seen a stick used by them, which is a metre scale. This stick is used everywhere to measure length and so is accepted by everybody all over the world. Hence, it is a standard unit for measuring length. When the children are well conversant with the above process, they are now ready to use the standard metre scale.

Q76. Write the key points which a teacher should take care while introducing her students to use scale accurately?

Ans. A teacher should take care of the following points while introducing her students to use scale accurately:

(1) Familiarising children with the marking of sub-units on the scale.

(2) Appropriately placing the scale with the object of measurement.

  (a) Demonstrate to children to place the scale alongside the object so that the '0' mark of the scale coincide with one end/edge of the object. This is very important for the beginners.

  (b) Allow the children to place the scale such that one end point of the object coincides with any point on the scale other than the '0' point (say 1, 2, or 3) and mark the difference in the reading of the scale, coinciding with the other end point of the object.

(3) Estimating the length before exactly determining it.

(4) Correctly calculating the length.

  (a) At first, when the child aligns the '0' point of the scale with one end point of the object being measured, then the figure on the scale coinciding with the other end point of the object determines its length.

  (b) When the child aligns any point other than the '0' point (say 1, 2, or 3, etc.), then difference in readings on the scale at the two end points determines the length of the scale.

(c) While using a particular unit of length for the first time, for example, the centimeter, the children should be provided with materials like wires, rods, etc. whose length could be measured by complete units (i.e. 3 cm, 5 cm, 10 cm, etc.) without using any part of the unit. When they become competent in such measurements, they can be given objects where they can use the sub-units or parts of the unit (for example millimeters).

(5) Developing the measuring skills.

(6) Choosing appropriate ruler or scale.

At the early stage of measuring length with standard units in the classroom, scales or rulers of 30 cm length would be handy for use by children as this scale would be appropriate for measuring most of the familiar objects around them. Scales or tapes of larger lengths may be required, depending on the length of the objects to be measured. If the length of the classroom or verandah of the school is going to be measured meter scales of larger length need to be selected for use and when small lines drawn on the notebooks or small objects are required to be measured, then scale of 15 cm length would be more appropriate.

Q77. What in and out of the classroom activities, a teacher could organise to encourage her children to learn measurement?

Ans. To encourage her children to learn measurement, a teacher can carry out the following activities:

- Preparing non-standard scales using coloured sticks with equal parts marked with contrast colours.
- Preparing centimeter scales of different measures like 5 cm, 10 cm, etc. with each centimeter portion of the strip coloured differently from the other.
- Demarcating play field for playing games like kabaddi, kho-kho, badminton, etc.
- Participating in long jump, high jump and measure distances or heights jumped for each jump.
- Drawing designs using straight lines of different lengths.

Q78. What is area? Discuss how can a teacher introduce the concept of area to her students.

Or

Construct an activity for the students to help them to understand the concept of area.

Ans. Area is the quantity that expresses the extent of a two-dimensional figure or shape, or planar lamina, in the plane. Area describes how much surface is occupied by something. The measurement for area uses the same units of measurement for length. The only difference is that the units are "Squared" since area is a product of two dimensions (usually length and width, which uses the same unit).

A teacher can introduce the concept of area to her students through the following:

The teacher first make children understand that the size of a plane figure is its spread. Once children understand this, then they are able to compare two regular figures by spreading some known objects on them, they soon start to realise that different smaller units used to fill up the plane figures would give different area. So now, they should be introduced to the unit of measurement of area.

Now, the teacher gave a rectangular piece of paper of the same size to each student and told them to measure the size of the paper using only one square. Each student marked off the size of the square on the paper along the edges of the square with a pencil, as shown in Fig. given below:

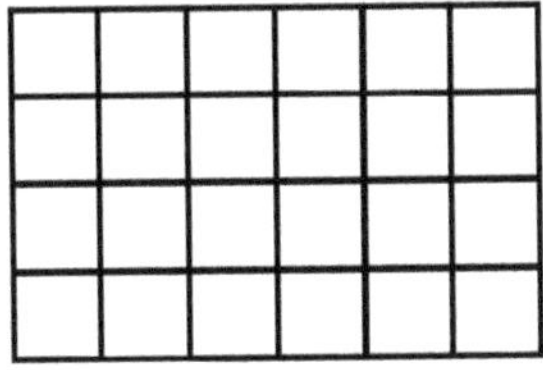

Fig. 2.94

After obtaining correct and same answer from the children of entire class, the teacher then made them find the area of the small square cardboard given to them by measuring its sides. They all found that it was 1 cm along all its edges. The teacher then conveyed to them that "the small square is of a particular size. Since it is one centimetre along all edges, we can call it a 'centimetre square'. So instead of saying the area is '24 squares', we say the area is 24 centimetre square. Area is expressed in centimetre squares. Centimetre square is a unit for measuring area".

She told the children that the area of bigger plane figures like fields, playgrounds, etc. is marked in metre square in the same way.

The above activity may also help children derive the formula for calculating the area of a square or a rectangle by themselves. They may be asked questions like:

- How many squares are there in one row?
- How many rows are there?
- 4 rows with 6 squares in a row, how many in total?
- How would you find the total number, without counting all squares?
- If there are 5 squares in one row and 4 such rows, what is the area, etc.?

This may help children understand why
area of a rectangle = length × breadth, and in particular,
area of a square = (length)^2.

This kind of pictorial representation would help them have a lasting impression on their mind and they would know when and how to use the formula.

Q79. Describe standard units of area. Show relation between the units of high and low area.

Ans. For any standard unit of measuring area, the area of a square is considered suitable. For example, a square of side of one metre; its area will be $1\,\text{m} \times 1\,\text{m} = 1\,\text{m}^2$. This area is called square metre, which is world's SI unit of area. Hence, the area of squares having sides 1mm or 1 cm or 1 m, etc. are considered units of area.

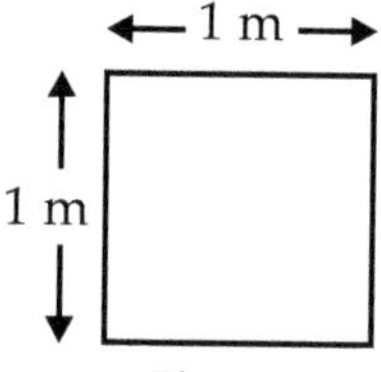

Fig. 2.95

Multiple and Sub-multiple Units of Area (Units of high and low area)

$$1\,\text{Square kilometre}\,(\text{km}^2) = 1\,\text{km} \times 1\,\text{km}$$
$$= 1000\,\text{m} \times 1000\,\text{m}$$
$$= 1000000\,\text{m}^2$$
$$= (10)^6\,\text{m}^2$$

$$1\,\text{Square metre}\,(\text{m}^2) = 1\,\text{m} \times 1\,\text{m}$$
$$= 100\,\text{cm} \times 100\,\text{cm}$$
$$= 10000\,\text{cm}^2$$
$$= (10)^4\,\text{cm}^2$$

$$1\,\text{Square centimetre}\,(\text{cm}^2) = 1\,\text{cm} \times 1\,\text{cm}$$
$$= 10\,\text{mm} \times 10\,\text{mm}$$
$$= 100\text{mm}^2$$
$$= (10)^2\,\text{mm}^2$$

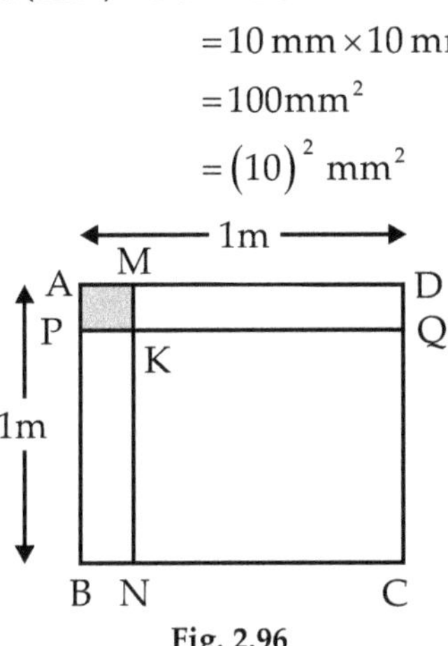

Fig. 2.96

Usually, the standard unit of measuring area of land in the traditional system of measurement is 'Acre'.

In metric system, 'Hectare' is the unit of measuring area of land along with 'Are'.

1 hectare = 10,000 m^2

And, 1 are = 100m^2.

From these, we can calculate to find that:

1 hectare = 100 are

And, 100 hectares = 1 km^2.

Incidentally, 1 hectare = 2.471 acres.

Q80. How can be the area of unequal and irregular figures calculated?

Ans. For finding the area of irregular figures, centimetre graph or a device named 'THREAD GRAPH' is used. It's a graph made up of thread. It consists of a wooden/plastic/cardboard frame joined together to form a square.

Each cell is a square of side 1 centimetre. Therefore, the area enclosed by each cell is a 'centimetre square'. To find the area of any figure say a leaf, we place the graph over it, look from direction above and count the squares covering the leaf. If the leaf covers half of a cell or more (as in Fig. given below), it should be taken as one square. If it covers less than half of a square, that can be omitted. The total number of squares counted gives an approximate area of the figure in centimeter squares.

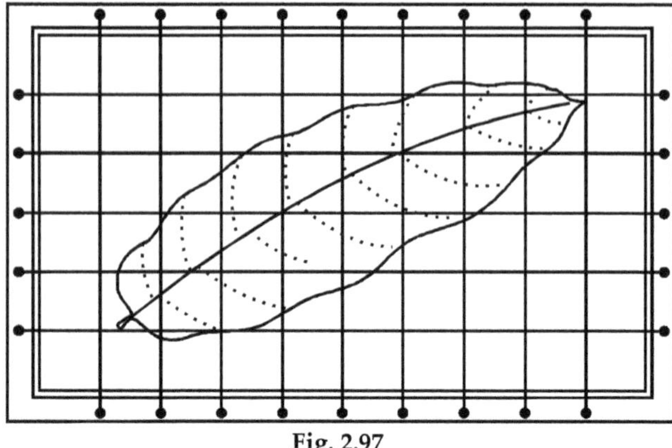

Fig. 2.97

The thread-graph is a useful device for classroom demonstration by the teacher. Graph paper with markings in cm (not in mm) may also be used instead. Using the graph paper also, area can be obtained easily by outlining the boundary of the leaf on a graph paper and then counting the number of squares as above.

Q81. Define volume. Discuss an activity through which a teacher is able to teach children about the concept of volume.

Or

How can the volume of a solid object be measured whose shape is uneven?

Or

How can you find the method to find the volume of an uneven object?

Ans. The total amount of space occupied by an object is known as the volume of that object. Thus, any object around us occupies space, be it a table, chair, desk, book, ball, bat, pencil, chalk, each occupies some definite portion of the space. The volume of an object has three dimensions, i.e. length, breath and height (thickness).

An activity through which a teacher is able to teach children about the concept of volume is:

A teacher can show children some wooden blocks of cubes and cuboids as shown in the figure below and ask them to compare the volumes of these blocks.

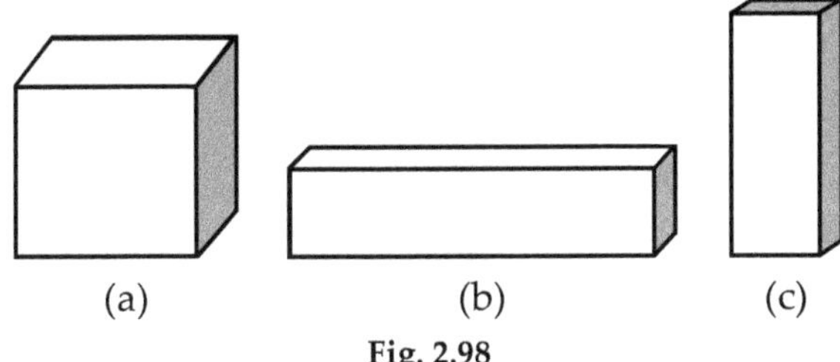

Fig. 2.98

Here, the children face the difficulty to estimate the volumes of the blocks. For this, they need to know the ways of determining the volume of an object.

For volume measurement, small unit of cube of 1cm× 1cm ×1cm is usually used as a standard unit.

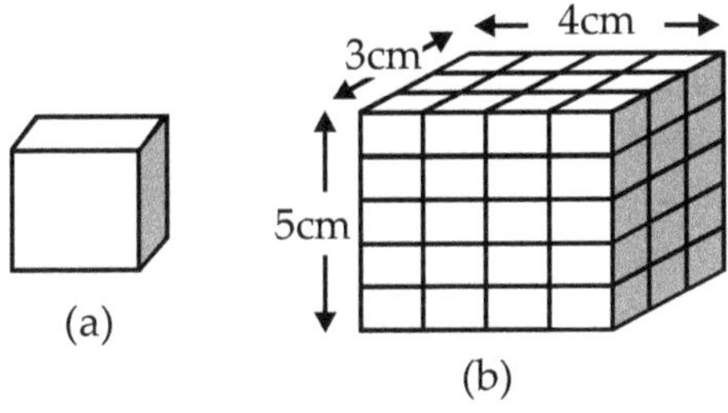

Fig. 2.99

This unit cube with each edge measuring 1cm is called a centimeter cube. Its volume is taken as **one cubic centimeter** and is denoted by **1cm^3**.

For measuring large objects, larger unit of volume like **one cubic meter** or **1m^3** may also be used.

We see how we can measure the volume of a regular solid like a cuboid. The cuboid is of size 3cm × 4cm × 5 cm. A teacher can observe that there are the cuboid consists of 5 slabs of 1cm thickness and in each slab, there are 3 rows with each row having 4 centimeter cubes. That means each slab has (4×3) 12 cm cubes and in 5 slabs there are altogether 60 cm cubes. Hence, the volume of a (3cm × 4cm × 5cm) cuboid is 60 cubic cm or 60cm^3.

From this example, teacher may deduce that **the volume of a cuboid = (l × b × h) cubic units,** where l = the length, b = the breadth and h = the height of the cuboid.

In a cube, we know that $l = b = h$, hence the **volume of a cube = l^3 cubic units**.

Q82. The length, breadth and height of a tank is 3 m, 2 m and 1 m, respectively. How much water can be filled in it? Give your answer in litre.

Ans. Volume of a tank = l × b × h

Since, 1m = 100 cm

Hence, V= 300 ×200×100

= 6000000 cm^3

Now, 1000 cm^3=1 litres

$\Rightarrow 1 \text{ cm}^3 = \frac{1}{1000}\text{litre}$

$\therefore$ V= 6000000 cm^3 = $\frac{6000\cancel{000} \times 1}{1\cancel{000}}$ = 6000 litres

Thus, 6000 litres of water can be filled in the tank.

Q83. What is the method to find out the volume of a solid by measuring that of the displaced water by it? Discuss.

Ans. The volumes of solid objects are measured using cylindrical glass jars with calibration of volume expressed in cubic centimeter (cc). In this method, the calibrated glass jar is filled with liquid to some extent and the initial level of the liquid is noted. Then the object whose volume is to be determined is totally submerged in the liquid and the level of the liquid in the jar is noted. The difference between the two levels gives the volume of the object.

The other way is to fill any vessel completely with liquid in such a way that any additional drop of the liquid will overflow out of the vessel. Then submerge the object into the liquid in the vessel and take care to collect every drop of the liquid displaced out of the vessel due to the submergence of the object. The volume of the displaced liquid is equal to the volume of the object. This is how we can find out the volume of liquids.

Q84. How can we measure the volume of liquids? Discuss.

Or

How can a teacher is able to make her students understand about the method to measure volume of the liquids?

Or

Discuss some activities that can be conducted by children in and out of school so that they are able to understand about the measurement of volume of the liquids.

Ans. Liquid substances have no definite shape. They take the shape of the vessel in which they are kept.

The capacity of a vessel or a container means the volume of liquid, or sand, or salt or any such substance that the vessel can hold. If a bucket can be filled completely with 20 bottles (of equal size) of water, then the capacity of the bucket is 20 such bottles of water. And if one bottle holds 1 liter of water, then the capacity of the bucket is 20 liters.

At the initial stage of learning, the children should be given a lot of opportunities to use non-standard units of measuring capacities of different vessels. Some such activities that can be conducted by children in and out of school are:

- Filling sugar in the can using a small cup.
- Filling pots with water using a fixed bottle.
- Filling tea pots/kettles, or any other pots with water using cups.
- Filling drinking water storage in the school with water using a bucket.
- Measuring volume of rice/paddy/wheat/any seeds with a small tin/plastic can.
- Measuring sand with a tin can.

Always there is an emphasisation on the use of one measure in measuring a particular item while practicing with the non-standard units like spoon, cup, jug, tin can, plastic mug, etc. Different cups can be tried to measure an amount of rice, and also measure the same amount of rice with only one cup. There will be a difference in the two measures.

When the children become efficient in using non-standard units of measuring volumes, then the standard units of cubic centimeter (cc) and liter can be meaningfully introduced. The devices used to measure oil in the retail shops can be seen by the children as the devices of measurement.

The standard unit of measuring the liquid is a litre or liter. 1 litre is equal to 1000 cubic centimeters or 1000 cm^3. It means if a vessel contains 1000 litres of water, then its volume is 1000 cm^3.

Q85. Discuss the concept of measuring weight.

Or

How can a teacher encourage her children to perform some activities based on measuring weight?

Ans. Weight is the force by which the earth attracts the objects towards its centre. In mathematical sense, it is measured in kilogram. Children might have experienced the weighing of rice, vegetables, groceries and other food items using standard weights and common balance. But, at the beginning stage, children should be familiarised with the process of weighing with a balance using non-standard weights like small stones, pieces of brick, wood, iron or any metal.

Thus, here a teacher may encourage her children to perform the following activities:

- **To prepare a model of common balance with a beam and two pans hanging from the two extremes of the beam:** They can attach a thread at the exact middle point of the beam. When equal weights are placed on the two pans, the beam remains horizontal to the ground when it is raised with the thread at the middle of the beam.
- **Weighing with non-standard units:** Children should be encouraged to use the improvised balance they have made in weighing different materials like sand, leaves, seeds, etc. with non-standard units. Through such activities, they would develop the skills of using the balance properly.

  When they become well versed with using the improvised scales and non-standard weights, they will feel the need of a proper balance and the standard weights.

  Gram and kilogram are commonly used units to measure weights of familiar objects. Children are more exposed to weighing vegetables and groceries in kilograms and grams.

Q86. Describe the metric system of measurement.

Or

Write basic unit for measure of mass. Relate it to three higher units. [April-2016, Q.No.-32]

Ans. The metric system is an international system of measurement that is based on powers of 10. To express a certain metric unit as a larger or smaller metric unit all that is required is to move the decimal point a proper number of places to the left or right.

Earlier, the scientists of different nations were using different systems of units for measurement. Three such systems, the CGS, the FPS (or British) system and the MKS system were in use extensively till recently.

The base units for length, mass and time in these systems were as follows:

- In CGS system, they were centimeter, gram and second, respectively.
- In FPS system, they were foot, pound and second, respectively.
- In MKS system, they were meter, kilogram and second, respectively.

The system of units which is at present internationally accepted for measurement is the *Systeme Internationale d' Unites* [French for

International System of Units] the units and abbreviations were developed and recommended by General Conference on Weights and Measures in 1971 for international usage in scientific, technical, industrial and commercial work. Because SI units used decimal system, conversions within the system are quite simple and convenient. SI is the broadest of these 4 systems by having 7 base units covering length (meter), mass (kilogram), time (second), electric current (ampere), temperature (kelvin), amount of substance (mole) and luminous intensity (candela). With units that can be derived from these 7 base units, SI addresses mechanics, electromagnetism, chemistry, radioactivity, medical sciences, illumination, commerce and numerous other fields.

The metric system uses units such as meter, liter and gram to measure length, liquid volume and mass.

In addition to the difference in the basic units, the metric system has different measures for length include kilometer, meter, decimeter, centimeter, and millimeter. Notice that the word "meter" is part of all of these units.

The metric system also applies the idea that units within the system get larger or smaller by a power of 10. This means that a meter is 100 times larger than a centimeter, and a kilogram is 1,000 times heavier than a gram.

(1) **Unit for length Measure:** Unit of length measure in the metric system is metre or meter.

	Unit : Metre (m)
Higher Units	Kilo meter (km)= 1000m
	Hecto meter (hm)= 100m
	Deca meter (dam)= 10m
Sub-Units	Deci meter (dm) = $\frac{1}{10}$ m
	Centi meter = $\frac{1}{100}$ m
	Milli meter = $\frac{1}{1000}$ m

From among these, kilometer, meter and centimeter are frequently used in measurement of lengths of varying distances and commonly understood.

Although metric system has been adopted in our country since 1958, yet the unit of length like inch (=2.54 cm), foot (=12 inch) and yard (=3 feet) are still used in several events of measurement like in land measurement and also by tailor for measuring cloth for making dresses.

(2) **Units for Capacity Measure:** It is a common experience that liquid has no shape. It takes the shape of the container in which it is kept. Thus, for deciding the unit for measuring the quantity of liquid, we either use weight measure unit or we use volume measure unit.

Litre is the unit of capacity measure (i.e., volume-measure). The volume-unit is known as 1 litre (equal to 1000 cm^3). Different containers are made of different capacity measures.

	Unit : Litre (l)
Higher Units	Kilo litre $(kl) = 1000\ l$
	Hecto litre $(hl) = 100\ l$
	Deca litre $(dal) = 10\ l$
Sub-Units	Deci litre $(dl) = \frac{1}{10} l$
	Centi litre (cl) = $\frac{1}{100} l$
	Milli litre (ml) = $\frac{1}{1000} l$

Litre is the most frequently used unit to measure the liquid substances like milk, water and oils.

(3) **Unit of Mass or Weight:** We know the main standard unit of mass or weight is **kilogram**, which we write in short as **'kg'**. 1000th part of this kilogram is **gram,** which is written in short as **'g'**.

Thus, 1000 gram = 1 kilogram and 1 kilogram = 1000 gram.

This gram (g) is a very small unit of mass.

100 kg wt. is called one quintal wt.

10 quintal wt. is known as one metric ton.

Thus, 1 Quintal = 100 kg and 100 kg = 1 quintal.

1 metric ton = 10 quintal = 10 x 100 kg = 1000 kg

Q87. What is time measure? Discuss various units of time.

Ans. Time-measure is related to the revolution of the earth about its axis and rotation of the earth around the sun.

There are different units of time. Second, minute, hour, day, week, month and year are the units of time, which have the following relations between each:

60 seconds = 1 minute or 1 minute = 60 seconds

60 minutes = 1 hour or 1 hour = 60 minutes
24 hours = 1 solar day (day + night)
7 days = 1 week
12 months = 1 year
52 weeks = 1 year
365 days or 366 days make a year
10 years make a decade
50 years make half century
100 years make a century

Q88. Define solar day.

Ans. A solar day is the time, which the earth takes to rotate once about its axis. It is the fundamental unit of time, which begins at midnight and runs through 24 hours, until the next midnight. A day is commonly divided into two sets of 12 hours for ordinary timekeeping purposes; those hours from midnight to noon are designated as AM (ante meridiem, "before noon"), and those from noon to midnight are designated as PM (post meridiem, "after noon").

Q89. What is a solar year? Discuss the relation between a solar year and a solar day.

Or

What is a solar year? How can it leads to the formation of a leap year?

Or

Define 'solar year'. [April-2016, Q.No.-26]

Or

What is a 'solar year'? How will you relate 'solar year' to 'solar day'? [October-2016, Q.No.-33]

Ans. The duration in which the Earth completes one rotation about the Sun is known as a *solar year*. The Earth's revolution around the Sun determines the length of the year. Earth makes a full orbit and it travels 360° around the Sun to end up back where it started, in 365.256363004 days.

Thus,

1 solar year = 365 days 5 hours 48 minutes 47 seconds

Roughly, 1 solar year = 365 ¼ days

A calendar year is taken to have 365 days.

Hence, in 4 years, we lose 1 day. To make it up, in every 4 years, one year is taken to have 366 days and this year is known as a leap year.

Leap years are added to the calendar to keep it working properly. The 365 days of the annual calendar are meant to match up with the solar year. A solar year is the time it takes the Earth to complete its orbit around the Sun — about one year. But the actual time it takes for the Earth to travel around the Sun is in fact a little longer than that—about 365 ¼ days (365 days, 5 hours, 48 minutes, and 47 seconds, to be precise).

So the calendar and the solar year don't completely match—the calendar year is shorter than the solar year.

As exceptions are always existing, in a leap year too it does. The year numbers that have zeroes at the ten's place and unit's place and are merely divisible by 4 only are not leap years. But from among them, which are multiples of 400 are leap years.

Therefore, 2000 was a leap year, whereas 1900, 1800, 2100, 2200, 2300, etc. are not leap years.

Q90. Discuss the concept of clock.

Ans. Measurement of time is related to the revolution and rotation of earth. However, to measure time, we use clocks and watches. Following figure shows a clock:

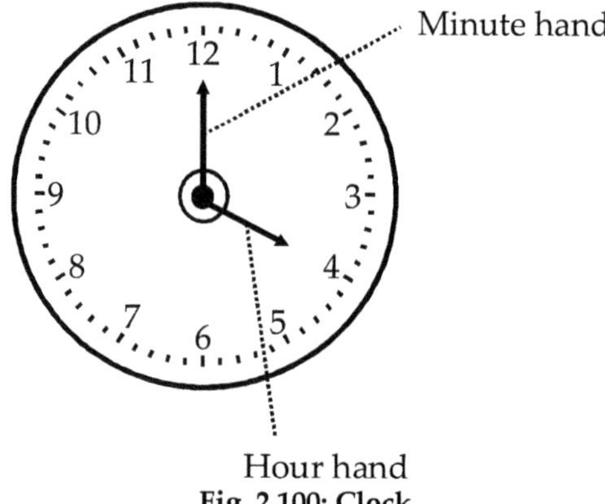

Fig. 2.100: Clock

A clock has 12 equal divisions marked from 1 to 12. There are 5 equal divisions in between two successive numbers. Thus, there are 60 small divisions in all. Each big division represents an hour and each small division a minute. A clock has two hands, one shorter (hour hand) and the other longer (minute hand).

The shorter hand of a clock reaches from one number to the next in one hour. The minute hand or longer hand of clock reaches from one number to another in 5 minutes.

There are two types of clock. The first one is the 12 hour-clock and the other is the 24-hour clock. Usually, we use 12 hour-clock. In such a clock, the numbering of hours on the dial of the clock are limited within 1 to 24. The hour hand rotates once over the clock-face in 12 hours and the minute hand rotates once in 1 hour. Mid night and noon are indicated by 12. We can say 12 midnight and 12 noon.

The time between 12 o' clock night and the next 12 o' clock night is called a day. A day is of 24 hours. That's why, the hour hand makes two rounds of a 12-hour clock in a day. The time between 12 o' clock night and 12 o' clock day is called AM (Ante-Meridiem). The time between 12 o' clock day and 12 o' clock night is called PM (Post-Meridiem).

The bigger hand of a clock makes an angle of 360° in 60 minutes. Hence, the clock's bigger hand makes an angle of 6° in 1 minute.

In the same way, the clock's smaller hand makes an angle of 360° in 12 hours or 720 minutes. So, it makes an angle of 30° in an hour or 60 minutes.

Generally, a 24-hour clock is used in railways and airways. Midnight is indicated as 24 hr and the subsequent hours are counted as 1hr, 2hr, 3hr, and so on till the following midnight. There is no use of am and pm in this system. Here, the clock-face shows the numbers from 1 to 24 and the hour hand rotates once over the clock face in 24 hours.

Q91. Which is the SI unit of time? Also enumerate some other units of time.

Ans. The Standard Unit (SI Unit) of time is seconds. We also use many other different units of time as:

60 seconds (s)	=	1 minute (m)
60 minutes (m)	=	1 hour (h)
24 hours (h)	=	1 day
365 days	=	1 year (simple)
366 days	=	1 year (leap)

Q92. How can children develop a sense of time?

Ans. In order to relate to the concept of time and its measurement, children are required to develop certain specific skills. They need to understand how calendar and clock functions but also how they enable us to calculate the duration of time between two events.

They have to know some time-related concepts and the abilities such as the ability to order events, that is which event happened earlier/later than the other and by how much of a duration which is essential learning for a child for carrying out daily routine. It is also important that children learn the associated vocabulary like now, later, before, sometime, yesterday, today, tomorrow, etc.

It is important for children to realise the passage of time in terms of happenings, i.e. past, present and future. Children should be able to differentiate that something has happened, something is happening and something will happen and are able to communicate it using appropriate language. It is important for children to realise that we are talking of a specific point of time or we are referring to a period of time over which an event has happened. They should be able to differentiate between 3 o'clock and 3 hours. It is important that they do not confuse between the happening of an event three years ago and an event, which happened for three years.

Thus, children can learn and relate to the usage of watch and calendar in their activities in a meaningful way.

For example, if we ask a 7-year-old child who is older than her father, it may not be difficult for her to answer. Of course, if we ask her 'who was born first', she may need to think a while before answering. But if we ask her 'Who was born earlier" her father or grandfather, it may be a real problem for her to answer. This shows that the immediate past is not difficult for her to conceive but she has no idea of the remote past, this means that the terms '400 BC' or 'Vedic age' have no meaning for her. So we have to teach children these aspects.

Q93. What are instant and duration of time?

Ans. The **instant of time** means the time at which an event occurs. We use time in this sense when we look at our watch or a clock to find the time of the day, or make an appointment for a particular day of the month or recall the year in which some event took place.

The **duration of time** is the time that passes between two events. For example, the time between the first bell in the school and the last bell is the duration of school day. So, there are two events associated with a duration (or time-interval), one the beginning and the other the ending. This shows that to find the time-interval, one should be aware of the order in which the events occur.

A watch or clock and a calendar are wonderful tools for teaching children that there is an orderly way to mark the passage of time. They can count the time or days between different events, and thus, will have the idea of duration.

Q94. Identify leap years from the following:

1536, 1600, 1682, 1700, 1820, 1980, 2000, 2006, 2012

After that, solve the following problem:

Rama left out from home to the college hostel in the morning on 11.11.2011 and came home back in the night on 12.12.2012. For how many days she stayed out of the house?

Ans. Leap Years: 1536, 1600, 1820, 1980, 2000, 2012

Now,

Years	Months	Days
2012	12	12
2011	11	11
01	01	01

Year = 1 year (leap) = 366 day (∵ 2012 is a leap year)

Month = 1 month = 30 days (Nov. to Dec.)

Days = 1 day

Total No. of days = 397 days

But,

∵ She left her house in the morning on 11.11.2011

∴ 1 more day she spent out of her house.

Thus, the total no. of days she spent out of house = 397 + 1 days = 398 days.

Q95. On the 10th January 2008, the repair work of a school building started and continued for a period of 65 days. On which day was the work completed?

Ans. The work of school building started on 10th January 2008, in the morning.

The work was completed in 65 days.

65 days = 22 days (in January) + 29 days (in February)
= 51 days

The work done in the month of March = 65 – 51 days
= 14 days

Thus, the work was completed on 14th of March in 2008.

Q96. What do you mean by data and the process of data collection?

Ans. Data is a collection of information gathered in a systematic manner with the aim of deriving certain related and useful conclusion. Data are a number of facts. "Data" is the plural of the Latin word "datum" which means "fact". Measuring and noting down some information is called the process of **data collection**.

Q97. What are the various sources for collection of data? Explain with the help of examples.

Ans. Following are the various sources for collection of data:

(1) Primary Data: Data are said to be **primary** if the investigator himself is responsible for the collection of data. Some examples of primary data are voters' lists, data collected in census-questionnaire, etc.

Here, the data are collected directly from the source. This is an instance of the data being collected from the *primary source.*

(2) **Secondary Data:** It is not always possible for an investigator to collect data due to lack of time and resources. In that case, s/he may use data collected by other governmental or private agency in the form of published reports. They are called **secondary data**. Data may be primary for one individual or agency but it becomes secondary for other using the same data.

If someone wants to know the number of persons in various income groups in a town/village, then the sources of information about the income groups are the records (census report) available in the Municipality/Panchayat office. This is not a direct source of information. These data are collected indirectly, i.e. from the documents containing the information collected for some other purpose. Such indirect sources are called *secondary source*.

Q98. What do you understand by presentation of data? How can we arrange data in tabular form? Write procedure.

Or

Explain ungrouped frequency distribution with the help of an example.

Or

Explain grouped frequency distribution with the help of an example.

Ans. When the work of collection of data is over, the next step to the investigator is to find ways to condense and organise them in order to study their salient features. Such an arrangement of data is called **presentation of data**. However, we can also present our data in tabular form, which is known as the tabular representation of data.

The tabular representation of data is in two forms, i.e. raw data and arrayed data.

The **Raw data** is collected from different sources, which are not arranged or organised in any manner. And, if the raw data is arranged in ascending (increasing) or descending (decreasing) order, then it is called *arrayed data*.

Example: Suppose there are 20 students in a class. The marks obtained by the students in a mathematics test (out of 100) are as follows:

45, 56, 61, 56, 31, 33, 70, 61, 76, 56,
36, 59, 64, 56, 88, 28, 56, 70, 64, 74

Solution: We can prepare a table for given data in the following manner:

Table 2.5

Marks	Number of Students
28	1
31	1
33	1
36	1
45	1
56	5
59	1
61	2
64	2
70	2
74	1
76	1
88	1
Total	**20**

This presentation of data in the form of a table is an improvement over the arrangement of numbers (marks) in an array, as it presents a clear idea of the data. From the table, we can easily see that 1 student has secured 28 marks, 5 students have secured 56 marks, 2 students have secured 70 marks and so on. Number 1, 1, 1, 1, 1, 5, 2, ... are called respective **frequencies** of the observations (also called variate or variable) 28, 31, 33, 36, 45, 56, 70, ...

Such a table is called a frequency distribution table for ungrouped data or simply ungrouped frequency table.

When the number of observations is large, it may not be convenient to find the frequencies by simple counting. In such cases, we make use of bars (|), called **tally marks** which are quite helpful in finding the frequencies.

In order to get a further condensed form of the data (when the number of observation is large); we classify the data into **classes** or **groups** or class intervals as below:

Step 1: We determine the **range** of the raw data, i.e. the difference between the maximum and minimum observations (values) occurring in the data. In the above example, range is 88 – 28 = 60.

Step 2: We decide upon the number of classes or groups into which the raw data are to be grouped. There is no hard and fast rule for determining the number of classes, but generally, there should not be less than 5 and not more than 15.

Step 3: We divide the range (it is 60 here) by the desired number of classes to determine the approximate **size** (or width) of a **class-interval**. In the above example, suppose we decide to have 9 classes. Than the size of each class is $\frac{60}{9} \approx 7$.

Step 4: Next, we set up the **class limits** using the size of the interval determined in Step 3. We make sure that we have a class to include the minimum as well as a class to include the maximum value occurring in the data. The classes should be non-overlapping, no gaps between the classes, and classes should be of the same size.

Step 5: We take each item (observation) from the data, one at a time, and put a tally mark (|) against the class to which it belongs. For the sake of convenience, we record the tally marks in bunches of five, the fifth one crossing the other four diagonally as ~~||||~~.

Step 6: By counting tally marks in each class, we get the frequency of that class. (Obviously, the total of all frequencies should be equal to the total number of observations in the data)

Step 7: The frequency table should be given a proper title so as to convey exactly what the table is about.

Using the above steps, we obtain the following table for the marks obtained by 20 students.

Table 2.6: Frequency Table of the marks obtained by 20 students in a mathematics test

Class Interval (Marks out of 100)	Tally Marks	Frequency
28-34	|||	3
35-41	|	1
42-48	|	1
49-55	—	0
56-62	~~||||~~ |||	8
63-69	||	2
70-76	||||	4
77-83	—	0
84-90	|	1
Total		**20**

The above table is called a **frequency distribution table** for grouped data or briefly, a **grouped frequency table**. The data in the above form are called **grouped data**.

In the above table, the class 28-34 includes the observations 28, 29, 30, 31, 32, 33 and 34; class 35-41 includes 35, 36, 37, 38, 39, 40, 41 and so on. So, there is no overlapping.

For the class 28-34, 28 is called the **lower class limit** and 34, the **upper class limit**, and so on.

Range = upper class limit – lower class limit = 34 – 28 = 6

Range helps in determining the length of class intervals.

Here, Class Interval = (34 – 28) + 1 = 7

From this type of presentation, we can draw better conclusions about the data. Some of these are:

(i) The number of students getting marks from 28 to 34 is 3.

(ii) No student has obtained marks in the class 49-55, i.e. no student has obtained marks 49, 50, 51, 52, 53, 54 and 55.

(iii) Maximum number of students has got marks from 56 to 62, etc.

We can also group the same 20 observations into 9 groups 28-35, 35-42, 42-49, 49-56, 56-63, 63-70, 70-77, 77-84 and 84-91. Here, the class interval is: 35 – 28 = 7.

It appears from classes 28-35 and 35-42, etc. that the observation 35 may belong to both those classes. But no observation could belong simultaneously to two classes. To avoid this, we adopt the convention that the common observation 35 belongs to the higher class, i.e. 35-42 (and **not** to 28-35). Similarly, 42 belongs to 42-49 and so on. Thus, class 28-35 contains all observations, which are greater than or equal to 28 but less than 35, etc.

Table 2.7: New Frequency Table of the marks obtained by 20 students in a mathematics test

Class Interval (Marks out of 100)	Tally Marks	Frequency
28-35	|||	3
35-42	|	1
42-49	|	1
49-56	—	0
56-63	~~||||~~ |||	8
63-70	||	2
70-77	||||	4
77-84	—	0
84-91	|	1
Total		**20**

Q99. What are the various pictorial representations for the depiction of data? Discuss with the help of suitable examples.

Or

Write the method for presenting numeric data in a pictograph.

Or

How can we represent numerical data with the help of bar graph? Give an example.

Or

What do you know about histogram? Explain with the help of an example.

Or

Explain pie-chart with the help of an example.

Or

Give two characteristics of a bar diagram. [April-2016, Q.No.-27]

Ans. There are variety of ways to present the data called **graphical (pictorial) representation** which is more convenient for the purpose of comparison among the individual items. Also pictures are generally eye-catching, easier to understand and leave a more lasting impression on the mind of the observer.

Various pictorial representations for the depiction of data are given as follows:

(1) Bar Graph: A bar chart or a bar diagram is a chart that present qualitative (grouped) data with rectangular bars with lengths proportional to the values that they represent. For example, suppose a group of students undertake a project to find out how the students of their class travel to school. Their findings are:

Table 2.8: Tabular Data

No. of students using the schools bus	...	...	...	20
No. of students using public transport	...	...	...	10
No. of students cycling to their school	...	...	...	4
No. of students taken by their parents in a car	...	...	...	2
No. of students taken by their parents on a two-wheeler	...	...	...	7
No. of students walking to school	...	...	...	2
	Total No. of students			45

The bar chart consists of bars of equal thickness, with the length/height being proportional to the quantity the bars represent.

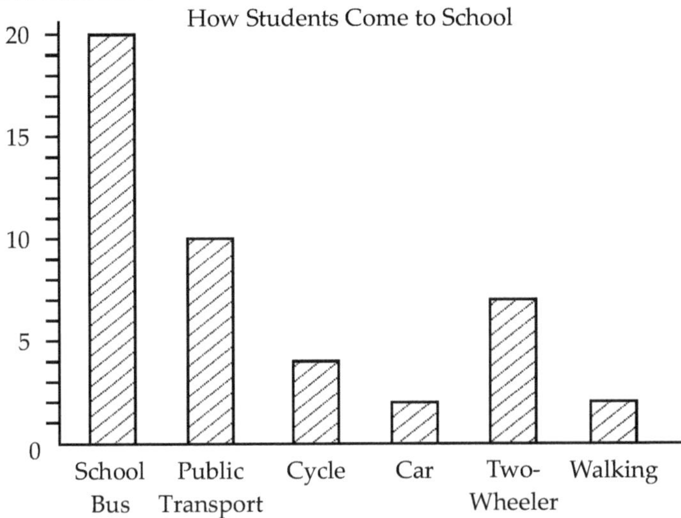

Fig. 2.101: Bar Graph

Points to be remember:

(1) The bar-chart has a heading.

(2) Sub-divisions are made on the vertical axis, using a suitable scale. (Suitable means that the scale is so chosen that the space on the graph paper be optimally used by the given data).

(3) Bars are of equal thickness and do not touch each other.

(4) Each bar is assigned a heading to denote what it represents.

(5) The height of each bar represents the number it is supposed to represent.

Bars could be drawn horizontally also. Then the numbering would be on the horizontal axis.

Steps for solution: We draw the bar graph of this data in the following steps:

(1) We represent the Heads (variable) on the horizontal axis choosing any scale, since the width of the bar is not important. But for clarity, we take equal widths for all bars and maintain equal gaps in between. Let one vehicle be represented by one unit.

(2) We represent the number of students on the vertical axis. We can choose the scale as 1 unit = 5 students.

(3) To represent one first Head, we draw a rectangular bar with width 1 unit.

(4) Similarly, other Heads are represented leaving a gap of 1 unit in between two consecutive bars.

Therefore, in some ways, it serves as a better representation of data than the tabular form.

Multiple Bar Diagram: A multiple bar diagram is used when a number of items are to be compared in respect of two, three or more values. These can be prepared either by changing the width of the bar or by using different colours for each character. In these types of graph, we can express more than one sub-attribute of variable. Following is an example of multiple bar diagram:

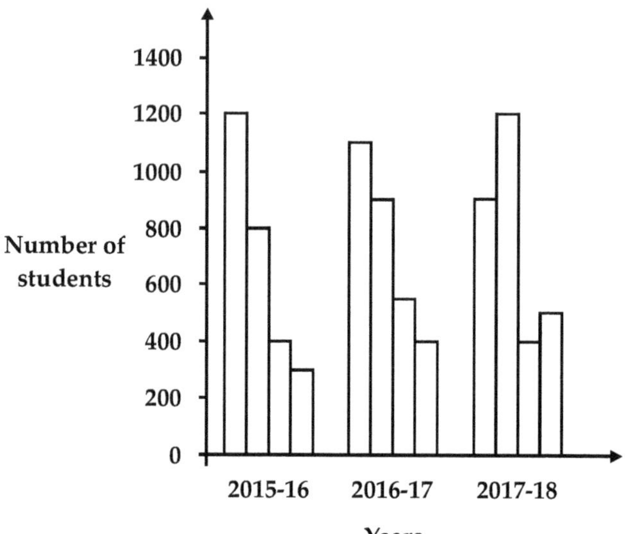

Fig. 2.102: Multiple-Bar Diagram

(2) Histogram: This is a form of representation like the bar graph, but it is used for continuous class intervals. For instance, consider the following frequency distribution table, representing the weights of 36 students of a class:

Table 2.9: Tabular Data

Weights (in kg)	Number of students
30.5-35.5	9
35.5-40.5	6
40.5-45.5	15
45.5-50.5	3
50.5-55.5	1
55.5-60.5	2
Total	**36**

We can represent the data given in table 2.10 graphically by adopting the following steps:

(i) We represent the weights on the horizontal axis on a suitable scale. We can choose the scale as 1 cm = 5 kg. Also, since the first class interval is starting from 30.5 instead of zero, therefore, we show it on the graph by marking a *kink* or a break on the x-axis.

(ii) We represent the number of students (frequency) on the vertical axis on a suitable scale. Since the maximum frequency is 15, we need to choose the scale to accommodate this maximum frequency.

(iii) We now draw rectangles (or rectangular bars) of width equal to the class-size and lengths according to the frequencies of the corresponding class intervals. For example, the rectangle for the class interval 30.5 – 35.5 will be of width 1 cm and length 4.5 cm.

(iv) In this way, we obtain the graph as shown in Fig. below:

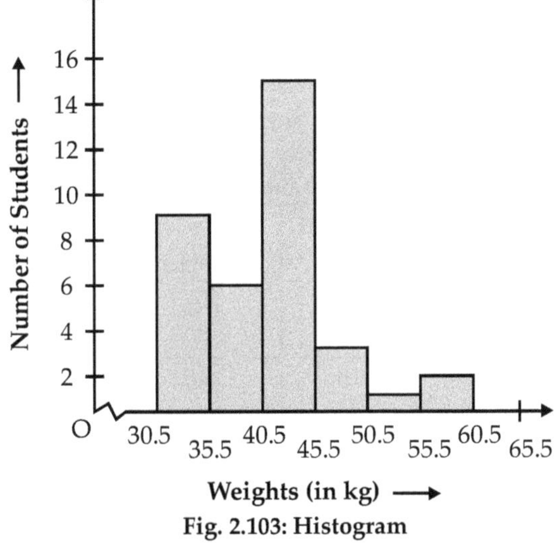

Fig. 2.103: Histogram

Since there are no gaps in between consecutive rectangles, the resultant graph appears like a solid figure. This is called a *histogram*, which is a graphical representation of a grouped frequency distribution with continuous classes. Also, unlike a bar graph, the width of the bar plays a significant role in its construction. Here, in fact, areas of the rectangle erected are proportional to the corresponding frequencies.

(3) **Pie Chart:** Another mode of representing data is through the use of a pie chart (also called circle graph). The entire circle is taken to represent one whole and all the constituents of the entire data are represented proportionally in the pie chart.

Following is the method to determine the proportion: The angle around the centre of a circle is 360°. If we divide a circle into four equal parts by drawing two mutually perpendicular diameters, we get four quadrants. Each quadrant is 1/4 of the circle and the angle made by the two arms of a quadrant is also 1/4 of the entire angle, i.e. it is 90°. Similarly, a semi-circle divides the circle into two equal parts and the angle of 360° is also divided into two halves. Thus, we can make proportional parts of a circle.

Each proportion (division) of the data is shown by a sector. We can find the central angle for each sector, which is given by:

$$\theta = \frac{f}{N} \times 360^{\circ}$$

Where, f = frequency of the division, and N = Sum of the frequencies (total).

The following table depicts to the "mode of transport to school" problem.

Table 2.10: Tabular Data

Mode of transport used	Number	Angle in the sector	Approximate percentage of the whole
Those using school bus	20	160°	44.5%
Those using public transport	10	80°	22.2%
Those using cycle transport	4	32°	8.9%
Those using parent's car	2	16°	4.4%
Those using parent's two-wheeler	7	56°	15.6%
Those walking to the school	2	16°	4.4%
Total no. of students	45	360°	100%

A pie chart depicting the above information will look like the figure given below:

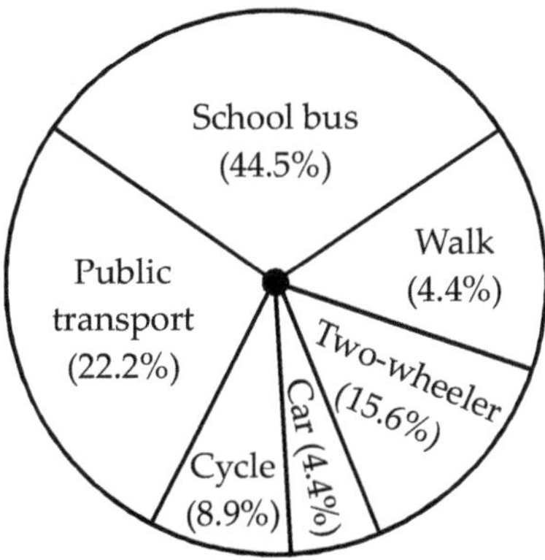

Fig. 2.104: Pie-Chart

Constructing a pie chart involves the following steps:

(i) Firstly, calculate the angle of the given sectors by using formula $\theta = \frac{f}{N} \times 360^{\circ}$ and approximate per cent of each item in the data.

(ii) Draw a circle and construct sectors using the sectoral angle.

(iii) Label each sector and write the per cent of the whole.

(iv) Now, construct pie chart for given data.

(4) **Pictogram:** Sometimes the picture of an object is used to display information. For example, if we want to depict pictorially the production of cycles in the country over a number of years, we choose a suitable scale such as one cycle representing 1 lakh cycles and draw the required number of cycles. The last cycle representing some fraction of a lakh will be drawn only partly in the same proportion. Sometimes a dotted outline may be given to complete the picture. A pictorial representation of this type is called a pictogram.

Example: The production of motor cars in a certain country over a period of five years is shown by the following table:

Table 2.11

Years	No. of Cars (in Ten Thousands)
1990	3
1991	5.5

1992	6
1993	7.5
1994	8

Taking one car to represent ten thousand, we can depict the above information in a pictogram as shown:

Production of Cars in the Country

(= ten thousand)

Fig. 2.105: Pictogram

Q100. Discuss two major features of the distribution.

Ans. The two major features of the distribution are as follows:

(1) Central Tendency: The scores of observations tend to cluster around a specific value, which is nearer to the middle of the distribution. This characteristic of the distribution of data is called its **central tendency**. A measure of central tendency refers to a central value, which is representative of the entire set of data to which it belongs. It aims to provide an accurate description of the entire data.

(2) Variability or Dispersion: Only knowing the measure of central tendency is not sufficient to study the nature of the distribution of data. Besides the central value, we have to know the nature of spread of individual observations around the central value. Here, two distributions are given below:

(i) 10, 11, 12, 13, 14, 15, 16

(ii) 5, 9, 10, 13, 19, 17, 18

In these distributions, the central value is 13. But, in the distribution (i), the scores are clustered nearer to the central value 13 than the score in the distribution (ii). This is a very simple example to show that we need to know the spread of scores or variation of scores around the central value for a complete analysis of the distribution. The spread or variability nature of data is otherwise called *variation* or *dispersion*.

Q101. Discuss "measures of Central Tendency." Name these measures.

Ans. A representative value for the given data is called the measure of central tendency. Mean (arithmetic mean), median and mode are three measures of central tendency. A *measure of central tendency* gives us a rough idea where data points are centred.

Q102. Discuss the mean in detail.

Or

Discuss the method of determining Arithmetic Mean for ungrouped data and grouped data with the help of suitable examples.

Ans. The **arithmetic mean** (or simply the **mean**) of a list of numbers is the sum of all of the list divided by the number of items in the list. If the list is a statistical population, then the mean of that population is called a **population mean**. If the list is a statistical sample, we call the resulting statistic a **sample mean**.

The mean is the most commonly-used type of average and is often referred to simply as the *average*.

(1) Mean (Arithmetic average) of Ungrouped Raw Data: To calculate the mean of raw data, all the observations of the data are added and their sum is divided by the number of observations. Thus, the mean of n observations $x_1, x_2, \ldots x_n$ is

$$\frac{x_1 + x_2 + \ldots + x_n}{n}$$

It is generally denoted by $\overline{x}$. So

$$\overline{x} = \frac{x_1 + x_2 + \ldots + x_n}{n}$$

$$= \frac{\sum_{i=1}^{n} x_i}{n} \qquad \ldots \text{(i)}$$

where the symbol "Σ" is the capital letter 'SIGMA' of the Greek alphabet and is used to denote summation.

To economise the space required in writing such lengthy expression, we use the symbol Σ, read as **sigma**.

In $\sum_{i=1}^{n} x_i, i$ is called the index of summation.

Therefore, the mean $\overline{x} = \dfrac{\text{Sum of all the observations}}{\text{Total number of observations}}$

Example: The weight of four bags of wheat (in kg) are 103, 105, 102, 104. Find the mean weight.

Solution: Mean weight

$$(\bar{x}) = \frac{\text{Total weight of four bags}}{\text{Total number of bags}} = \frac{103+105+102+104}{4}\text{kg}$$

$$= \frac{414}{4}\text{kg} = 103.5 \text{ kg}$$

(2) Mean of Ungrouped Frequency distribution: We will explain to find mean of ungrouped data through an example.

Find the mean of the marks (out of 15) obtained by 20 students.

2 10 5 8 15 5 2 8 10 5

10 12 12 2 5 2 8 10 5 10

This data is in the form of raw data. We can find mean of the data by using the formula (I), i.e., $\frac{\sum x_i}{n}$. But this process will be time consuming.

We can also find the mean of this data by first making a frequency table of the data and then applying the formula:

$$\text{mean} = \bar{x} = \frac{\sum_{i=1}^{n} f_i x_i}{\sum_{i=1}^{n} f_i} \qquad \text{...(ii)}$$

where f_i is the frequency of the ith observation x_i.

To find mean of this distribution, we first find $f_i x_i$, by multiplying each x_i with its corresponding frequency f_i and append a column of $f_i x_i$ in the frequency table as given below:

Table 2.12

Marks (x_i)	Number of students (f_i)	$f_i x_i$
2	4	$2 \times 4 = 8$
5	5	$5 \times 5 = 25$
8	3	$3 \times 8 = 24$
10	5	$5 \times 10 = 50$
12	2	$2 \times 12 = 24$
15	1	$1 \times 15 = 15$
	$\Sigma f_i = 20$	$\Sigma f_i x_i = 146$

$$\text{Mean} = \frac{\sum f_i x_i}{\sum f_i} = \frac{146}{20} = 7.3$$

(3) **Mean of Grouped Frequency distribution: Let us consider the following** grouped frequency distribution:

Table 2.13

Daily wages (in ₹)	Number of workers
150-160	5
160-170	8
170-180	15
178-190	10
190-200	2

What we can infer from this table is that there are 5 workers earning daily somewhere from ₹150 to ₹160 (not included 160). We do not know what exactly the earnings of each of these 5 workers are.

Therefore, to find mean of the grasped frequency distribution, we make the following assumptions:

Frequency in any class is centred at its class mark or mid point: Now, we can say that there are 5 workers earning a daily wage of ₹$\frac{150+160}{2}$ = ₹155 each, 8 workers earning a daily wage of ₹$\frac{160+170}{2}$ = ₹165, 15 workers earning a daily wage of ₹ $\frac{170+180}{2}$ = ₹ 175 and so on.

Table 2.14

Daily wages (in ₹)	Number of workers (f_i)	Class marks (x_i)	$f_i x_i$
150-160	5	155	775
160-170	8	165	1320
170-180	15	175	2625
180-190	10	185	1850
190-200	2	195	390
	$\Sigma f_i = 40$		$\Sigma f_i x_i = 6960$

$$\text{Mean} = \frac{\sum f_i x_i}{\sum f_i} = \frac{6960}{40} = 174$$

So, the mean daily wage = ₹ 174

Q103. Write the method for determining Median for ungrouped and grouped data with the help of an example giving its definition.

Ans. The **median** is that value of the given number of observations, which divides it into exactly two parts. So, when the data is arranged in ascending (or descending) order the median is denoted by M_e.

(1) Median of Ungrouped Data:

(i) When the number of observations (n) is odd, the median is the value of the $\left(\frac{n+1}{2}\right)^{th}$ observation. For example, if $n = 13$, the value of the $\left(\frac{13+1}{2}\right)^{th}$, i.e., the 7th observation will be the median.

(ii) When the number of observations (n) is even, the median is the mean of the $\left(\frac{n}{2}\right)^{th}$ and the $\left(\frac{n}{2}+1\right)^{th}$ observations.

Example: The heights (in cm) of 9 students of a class are as follows:

155 160 145 149 150 147 152
144 148

Find the median of this data.

Solution: First of all, we arrange the data in ascending order, as follows:

144 145 147 148 149 150 152
155 160

Since the number of students is 9, an odd number, we find out the median by finding the height of the $\left(\frac{n+1}{2}\right)$th = $\left(\frac{9+1}{2}\right)$th = the 5th student, which is 149 cm.

So, the median, i.e., the median height is 149 cm.

Example: The points scored by a Kabaddi team in a series of matches are as follows:

17, 2, 7, 27, 15, 5, 14, 8, 10, 24, 48, 10, 8, 7, 18, 28

Find the median of the points scored by the team.

Solution: Arranging the points scored by the team in ascending order, we get

2, 5, 7, 7, 8, 8, 10, 10, 14, 15, 17, 18, 24, 27, 28, 48

There are 16 terms. So there are two middle terms, i.e. the $\frac{16}{2}$th and $\left(\frac{16}{2}+1\right)$th, i.e., the 8th and 9th terms.

So, the median is the mean of the values of the 8th and 9th terms.

i.e., the median = $\frac{10+14}{2} = 12$

So, the medial point scored by the Kabaddi team is 12.

(2) **Median of Ungrouped Frequency Distribution:** We illustrate calculation of the median of ungrouped data through examples.

Example: Find the median of the following data, which gives the marks, out of 15, obtained by 35 students in a mathematics test.

Table 2.15

Marks obtained	3	5	6	11	15	14	13	7	12	10
Number of Students	4	6	5	7	1	3	2	3	3	1

Solution: First arrange marks in ascending order and prepare a frequency table as follows:

Table 2.16

Marks obtained	3	5	6	7	10	11	12	13	14	15
Number of Students (frequency)	4	6	5	3	1	7	3	2	3	1

Here, $n = 35$, which is odd. So, the median will be $\left(\frac{n+1}{2}\right)$th,

i.e., $\left(\frac{35+1}{2}\right)$th ,i.e., 18th observation.

To find value of 18th observation, we prepare cumulative frequency table as follows:

Table 2.17

Marks obtained	Number of students	Cumulative frequency
3	4	4
5	6	10
6	5	15
7	3	18
10	1	19
11	7	26
12	3	29
13	2	31
14	3	34
15	1	35

From the table above, we see that 18th observation is 7

So, Median = 7

(3) Median for Grouped Data: In grouped data, the median is in the class where the cumulative frequency reaches half the sum of the absolute frequencies.

That is to say, the median is within the class $\frac{N}{2}$.

$$M_e = L_i + \frac{\frac{N}{2} - F_{i-1}}{f_i} \cdot a_i$$

L_i is the lower limit of the median class.

$\frac{N}{2}$ is half the sum of the absolute frequency.

F_{i-1} is the absolute frequency immediately below the median class.

a_i is the width of the class containing the median class.

The median is independent of the widths of the classes.

Example: The grouped data in Table given below represent the number of children from birth through the end of the teenage years in a large apartment complex. Find the median.

Table 2.18

Class	0-3	4-7	8-11	12-15	16-19
Frequency	7	4	19	12	8

Solution: For simplicity of calculation, we create a Table:

Table 2.19

Class	f_i	**Cumulative** F_i
0 – 3	7	7
4 – 7	4	11
8 – 11	19	30
12 – 15	12	42
16 – 19	8	50
	$N = \sum f_i = 50$	

The first interval for which the cumulative relative frequency exceeds 0.5 is the interval that contains the median. Hence, the interval 8 to 11 contains the median. Therefore, $L_i = 8, f_i = 19, N = 50, a_i = 3$ and $F_{i-1} = 11$. Then, the median is

$$M_e = L_i + \frac{\frac{N}{2} - F_{i-1}}{f_i} a_i$$

$$= 8 + \frac{\frac{50}{2} - 11}{19} \times 3 = 8 + \frac{14}{19} \times 3 = 10.21$$

There are following steps of calculating median in grouped distribution:

(i) Calculate the Cum. F_i and locate the C.I. in which the median lies.

(ii) Determine the exact lowest limit of the C.I. (L_i) in which the median lies.

(iii) From the calculations of the Cum. F_{i-1}, determine the total frequency below the exact lower limit of the C.I. (F_{i-1}) in which the median lies.

(iv) Find the difference $N/2 - F_{i-1}$, divide the difference with the frequency of the scores within the C.I. in which the median lies and multiply it with the length of the C.I.

(v) Add the result in 4 with the exact lower limit L_i to get the median.

Q104. What do you understand by Mode? Describe the method of finding mode giving a suitable example.

Ans. The **mode** is that value of the observation which occurs most frequently, i.e., an observation with the maximum frequency is called the mode.

The readymade garment and shoe industries make great use of this measure of central tendency. Using the knowledge of mode, these industries decide which size of the product should be produced in large numbers.

Let us illustrate this with the help of an example.

Example: Find the mode of the following marks (out of 10) obtained by 20 students:

4, 6, 5, 9, 3, 2, 7, 7, 6, 5, 4, 9, 10, 10, 3, 4, 7, 6, 9, 9

Solution: We arrange this data in the following form:

2, 3, 3, 4, 4, 4, 5, 5, 6, 6, 6, 7, 7, 7, 9, 9, 9, 9, 10, 10

Here 9 occurs most frequently, i.e., four times. So, the mode is 9.

The mode is simply the number, which appears **most often.**

To find the mode or modal value, there is a need to put the given numbers in order.

For example, look at these numbers:

3, 7, 5, 13, 20, 23, 39, 23, 40, 23, 14, 12, 56, 23, 29

In order these numbers are:

3, 5, 7, 12, 13, 14, 20, 23, 23, 23, 23, 29, 39, 40, 56

This makes it easy to see which numbers appear the most.

In this case, the mode or modal value is 23.

To calculate an approximate value of mode in a perfectly symmetrical distribution, the formula is: **Mode = 3 × median – 2 × mean** Mode is used when we wish to know what the most typical case is. Mode is most unstable measure of central tendency. Mode is a score of the distribution and not a frequency.

Q105. What are the two types of measures of variability or dispersion? Discuss them in detail.

Or

Write procedure for calculating average deviation for ungrouped and grouped data giving suitable examples.

Ans. There are two types of measures of dispersion; distance measures and measures of average deviation.

(1) Distance measures: These describe the variation in the data in terms of the distance between selected measurements. The most frequently used distance measures are Range and Inter-Quartile Range.

(i) **Range:** Range is the difference between the highest and the lowest values in a frequency distribution.

Example: To find the range in 3, 5, 7, 3, 11

Step 1: Arrange the numbers in ascending order.

3, 3, 5, 7, 11

Step 2: In the above distribution,

The largest number is 11

The smallest value is 3

Formula = largest number - smallest number

Range = 11-3 = 8

This type of range is called ***'Exclusive Range'***.

For grouped data, we define range = difference between the class marks of the first and the last class.

Or when we determine the range through the difference between the *upper real limit* (URL) of the highest score and the *lower real limit* (LRL) of the lowest score, we call it ***'Inclusive Range'***.

Here, Inclusive Range = 11.5 – 2.5 = 9

In the above example, the URL of the highest score 11 is 15.5 and the LRL of the lowest score 3 is 2.5 (Every observation in social science is not absolute and fixed. Rather it is assumed to be stretched over an interval of 0.5 before and after the score. Therefore, the score 11 is any value in the interval of 10.5 - 11.5, the extreme points of the interval determines the upper and lower real values of 11).

Significant measures of average deviations are mean deviation, standard deviation and variance. All of these tell us an average distance of any observation in the data set from the mean of the distribution.

(ii) **Interquartile Range:** Quartile deviation or semi-interquartile range is the dispersion which shows the degree of spread around the middle of a set of data. It depends on the lower quartile Q_1 and the upper quartile Q_3. The difference $Q_3 - Q_1$ is called the inter quartile range. The difference $Q_3 - Q_1$ is divided by 2 is called semi-inter quartile range or the quartile deviation. For both grouped and ungrouped data, quartile deviation can be calculated by using the formula:

$$\text{Quartile Deviation} = \frac{\text{Third Quartile} - \text{First Quartile}}{2}$$

$$\text{Quartile Deviation (Q.D.)} = \frac{Q_3 - Q_1}{2}$$

Example: Following are the runs scored by a batsman in last 20 test matches: 96, 70, 100, 96, 81, 84, 90, 89, 63, 90, 34, 75, 39, 82, 85, 86, 76, 64, 67 and 88. We have to calculate the Quartile Deviation.

Solution: On arranging data in ascending order:

34, 39, 63, 64, 67, 70, 75, 76, 81, 82, 84, 85, 86, 88, 89, 90, 90, 96, 96, 100

First Quartile (Q_1): The calculation of First quartile is given below:

$$Q_i = \frac{i(n+1)}{4}\text{th observation}$$

$$Q_1 = \frac{1(20+1)}{4}\text{th observation}$$

$$Q_1 = 5.25\text{th observation}$$

Since 5.25th observations lies between 5th and 6th value in the ordered group, or midway between 67 and 70 therefore

$$Q_1 = 67 + 0.25(70 - 67)$$

$$Q_1 = 67 + 0.75$$

$$Q_1 = 67.75$$

Here,

67 = Lower Value

70 = Higher Value

0.25 = 5.25 – 5

Third Quartile (Q_3): The formula for the calculation of third quartile is given as:

$$Q_i = \frac{i(n+1)}{4}\text{th observation}$$

$$Q_3 = \frac{3(20+1)}{4} \text{th observation}$$

$$Q_3 = 15.75\text{th observation}$$

15.75th observation lies between 15th and 16th value in the ordered group

15th observation = 89

16th observation = 90

$$Q_3 = 89 + 0.75(90 - 89)$$

$$Q_3 = 89 + 0.75$$

$$Q_3 = 89.75$$

By putting the values into the formulas of quartile deviation and coefficient of quartile deviation, we get:

$$\text{Quartile Deviation (Q.D.)} = \frac{Q_3 - Q_1}{2} = \frac{89.75 - 67.75}{2} = 11$$

The quartile deviation is a slightly better measure of absolute dispersion than the range, but it ignores the observations on the tails. If we take difference samples from a population and calculate their quartile deviations, their values are quite likely to be sufficiently different. This is called sampling fluctuation, and it is not a popular measure of dispersion. The quartile deviation calculated from the sample data does not help us to draw any conclusion (inference) about the quartile deviation in the population.

(2) Measures of Average Deviation: Distance from the mean of score is called its deviation. When the average of such deviation scores are taken into consideration, the measure of variability becomes more accurate and reliable.

The scores nearer to the mean show that the measure of average deviations would be small and vice versa. This helps us to understand the nature of distribution. For example, in a class examination, the mean of scores in Mathematics test was 65 and the standard deviation was 10, while the mean of Language test scores was 60 and the standard deviation was 5. We find majority of students scored nearer to 60 in Language. But in Mathematics the score are spread much wider than that of the scores on Language. There would be quite a number of students securing lower marks in Mathematics; below the minimum score in Language. Valid conclusions from the measures of central tendency alone cannot be drawn without the measure of average deviations.

Average deviation (also called mean deviation) is computed by subtracting the mean from each individual observation, summing all the deviations (ignoring the sign of the deviations), the then dividing by the total number of observations. The signs (+, -) of the deviation are ignored because otherwise the sum of the deviations from the mean will be zero.

Thus, the mean deviation for an **ungrouped data** consisting of n observations $x_1, x_2, \ldots, x_n$ is computed as

$$MD = \frac{\sum | x_i - \bar{x} |}{n}$$

In the case of **grouped data** with $\sum f_i = n$, we have

$$MD = \frac{\sum f_i |x_i - \bar{x}|}{\sum f_i}$$

Average or mean deviation is the mean of deviations of all scores from the mean of the scores in the distribution.

Deviation score (x) = Score – Mean = $x - \bar{x}$

If in a distribution the mean is 50, the deviation of the score 55 is given by

$$x - \bar{x} = 55 - 50 = 5,$$

And the deviation of the score 45 = 45 – 50 = –5.

Example of Average Deviation for Ungrouped Data:

If we have to find the mean deviation about the mean for the following data: 6, 7, 10, 12, 13, 4, 8, 12

Solution: We proceed step-wise and get the following:

Step 1: Mean of the given data is

$$\bar{x} = \frac{6+7+10+12+13+4+8+12}{8} = \frac{72}{8} = 9$$

Step 2: The deviations of the respective observations from the mean $\bar{x}$, i.e., $x_i - \bar{x}$ are

6 – 9, 7 – 9, 10 – 9, 12 – 9, 13 – 9, 4 – 9, 8 – 9, 12 – 9,

or –3, –2, 1, 3, 4, –5, –1, 3

Step 3: The absolute values of the deviations, i.e., $|x_i - \bar{x}|$ are

3, 2, 1, 3, 4, 5, 1, 3

Step 4: The required mean deviation about the mean is

$$M.D.(\bar{x}) = \frac{\sum_{i=1}^{8} |x_i - \bar{x}|}{8}$$

$$= \frac{3+2+1+3+4+5+1+3}{8} = \frac{22}{8} = 2.75$$

Example of Average Deviation for Grouped Data:

Example: Computation of Mean Deviation of the earnings of 80 salesmen

Table 2.20

L_i-L_a	f_i	x_i	$\lvert x_i - x \rvert$	$f_i \lvert x_i - x \rvert$
50-59	6	54.5	28.875	173.25
60-69	9	64.5	18.875	169.875
70-79	15	74.5	8.875	133.125
80-89	25	84.5	1.125	28.125
90-99	13	94.5	11.125	144.625
100-109	7	104.5	21.125	147.875
110-119	5	114.5	31.125	155.625
	$\sum f_i = 80$			$\sum f_i \lvert x_i - \bar{x} \rvert = 952.5$

Here, $\sum f_i = 80$, and Mean $(\bar{x})$=83.375 and $\sum f_i \lvert x_i - \bar{x} \rvert = 952.5$

$$MD = \frac{\sum f_i \lvert x_i - \bar{x} \rvert}{\sum f_i} = \frac{952.5}{80} = 11.9$$

Q106. Write the steps of computation of standard deviation. Compute standard deviation for ungrouped and grouped data taking examples of your choice.

Or

Write the formula of standard deviation.

Ans. The proper measure of dispersion about the mean of a set of observations is expressed as positive square-root of the variance and is called *standard deviation.* Therefore, the standard deviation for ungrouped data, usually denoted by σ, is given by

$$\sigma = \sqrt{\frac{1}{n}\sum_{i=1}^{n}(x_i - \bar{x})^2}$$

and *standard deviation of a frequency distribution* is given by

In this case standard deviation $(\sigma) = \sqrt{\frac{1}{N}\sum_{i=1}^{n} f_i (x_i - \bar{x})^2}$

where $N = \sum_{i=1}^{n} f_i$

Here's a quick preview of the steps we're about to follow:

Step 1: Find the mean.

Step 2: For each data point, find the square of its distance to the mean.

Step 3: Sum the values from Step 2.

Step 4: Divide by the number of data points.

Step 5: Take the square root.

Standard deviation for Ungrouped Data:

Example: Find the Variance of the following data:

6, 8, 10, 12, 14, 16, 18, 20, 22, 24

Solution: From the given data, we can form the following Table. $\bar{x} = \frac{\sum x_i}{n} = \frac{150}{10} = 15$

Table 2.21

x_i	Deviations from mean $(x_i - \bar{x})$	$(x_i - \bar{x})^2$
6	–9	81
8	–7	49
10	–5	25
12	–3	9
14	–1	1
16	1	1
18	3	9
20	5	25
22	7	49
24	9	81
		330

Variance $\left(\sigma^2\right) = \frac{1}{n}\sum_{i=1}^{10}\left(x_i - \bar{x}\right)^2 = \frac{1}{10} \times 330 = 33$

Thus, Standard deviation $\left(\sigma\right) = \sqrt{33} = 5.74$

Standard deviation of ungrouped data:

Example: Calculate the mean and standard deviation for the following distribution:

Class	**30-40**	**40-50**	**50-60**	**60-70**	**70-80**	**80-90**	**90-100**
Frequency	**3**	**7**	**12**	**15**	**8**	**3**	**2**

Solution: From the given data, we construct the following Table:

Table 2.22

Class	Frequency (f_i)	Mid-point (x_i)	$f_i x_i$	$(x_i - \bar{x})^2$	$f_i(x_i - \bar{x})^2$
30-40	3	35	105	729	2187
40-50	7	45	315	289	2023
50-60	12	55	660	49	588
60-70	15	65	975	9	135
70-80	8	75	600	169	1352
80-90	3	85	255	529	1587
90-100	2	95	190	1089	2178
	50		**3100**		**10050**

Thus, Mean $\overline{x} = \frac{1}{N}\sum_{i=1}^{7} f_i x_i = \frac{3100}{50} = 62$

$$\text{Variance } (\sigma^2) = \frac{1}{N}\sum_{i=1}^{7} f_i (x_i - \overline{x})^2$$

$$= \frac{1}{50} \times 10050 = 201$$

And, Standard deviation $(\sigma) = \sqrt{201} = 14.18$

Q107. Write the uses of Measures of Variability.

Ans. When we want a quick estimate of the spread of scores which are very small in number and there are no extreme scores, we use range.

When there are some extreme scores in a distribution and median is the measure of central tendency, semi-interquartile range is preferred.

When the scores are too scattered which would influence SD unduly, average deviation is used to give us a reasonable estimate of the spread of scores.

SD is most stable and accurate, among all the measures of variability.

Q108. What are Expressions and what are Algebraic Expressions? Explain with examples.

Ans. In arithmetic, we have come across expressions like $(3 \times 8) + 2; (10 \div 5) + (3 \times 20) - 7$ etc.

In these examples, we can observe:

(i) Expressions are formed from numbers.

(ii) All the four fundamental operations such as addition, subtraction, multiplication and division or some of them are used in an expression

Algebraic Expressions: The expressions formed by using variables are called 'Algebraic expressions'.

Example: Raju is in Class-VI. In his class, there are *'m'* girl students. Number of boys is 7 less than the girls. Calculate the total no. of students in his class.

No. of girl students = m

No. of boy students = m – 7

Total no. of students = m + (m – 7) = 2m – 7

Here 2m – 7 is an expression which is formed using variable *m* and constant 2 and 7.

Subtraction and multiplication operations are used here.

So, a combination of constants and variables connected by some or all of the four fundamental operations +, -, × and ÷ is called an **algebraic expression**.

Classification of Expressions: An algebraic expression is classified into different categories depending upon the no. of terms contained in it.

(1) Monomial: An expression, which contains only one term is called a monomial.

For example: 7xy, 2x, -4n and $3a^2b$ are all monomials as they contain only one term.

(2) Binomial: An expression which contains two unlike terms is called a binomial.

For example: x + y , 2p – 3q, z + 1 and 3xy + 2x because of having two terms, they are all binomials.

(3) Trinomial: Expression having 3 unlike term is called a trinomial.

For example: 2a– 5b + 3c, x + y – 3 and pq + p – 2q are all trinomials.

(4) Polynomial: An expression with one or more terms is known as a polynomial in general. For example: 5x, 2a + 3b, m + n – 3 are all polynomials. A polynomial can be a monomial, a binomial or a trinomial.

Q109. Define the Terms of an Algebraic Expression.

Ans. We know that an algebraic expression consists of one or more terms. For example, xy +3z –5 is an expression.

To form this expression we first formed xy separately as a product of x and y. Then we formed 3z separately as a product of 3 and z. We then added them (xy and 3z) and then added (–5) to it to get the expression.

In the above example xy, 3z and 5 are terms.

Definition: The different parts of an algebraic expression separated from each other by the sign '+' or '–' are called the **terms** of the expression.

Q110. What is difference between Variables and Constants?

Ans. Here, we take a mathematical statement P = 4s

Here, when s = 1, then p = 4 × 1 = 4

when s = 2, then p = 4 × 2 = 8

when s = 3, then p = 4 × 3 = 12

Now, we can conclude that for different values taken for *'s'*, the value of *'p'* changes. I.e. *P* varies with the change in the value of s. We say that *'s'* and *'p'* both are changeable or variable. Hence, we can say:

A symbol which does not have any fixed value for it, but may be assigned any numerical value according to the requirement is known as a ***variable****.*

A symbol having a fixed numerical value is called a ***constant****.*

In the statement $P = 4s$, 's' and 'P' are called variables and '4' is a constant.

Conclusions: A variable has no fixed value.

The letters x, y, z, p, q, r are usually taken to represent variables.

All real nos. are constant.

Algebraic expressions are formed from variables and constants.

Q111. Differentiate between Product, Factor and Coefficient and also clarify how two variables are multiplied.

Ans. In the given multiplication $2 \times 5 = 10$, 10 is the product and 2 and 5 are the factors of 10.

In the multiplication of two variables 3 and z the product of 3 and z $= 3 \times z = 3z$

If we multiply x, y and z, the product of x, y and z $= x \times y \times z = xyz$

Thus, an expression consist of one or more terms. For example, expression $2ab - 3$ has 2 terms namely 2ab and –3. Here 2ab is the product of 2, a and b. We say that 2, a and b are the factors of the term 2ab.

A constant factor is called a **numeric** factor. A variable factor is called is a **literal (algebraic)** factor.

The expression 3xy-5y has two terms 3xy and -5y. The numerical factor of a term calls it numerical coefficient or simply coefficient. 3 is the coefficient of 3xy and -5 is the coefficient of -5y.

Q112. Write the definitions of Like and Unlike Terms.

Ans. The terms having the same algebraic factors are known as **similar or like terms**. When the terms do not have the same algebraic factors are called **unlike terms**.

For example, in the expression $2a + 5ab - 3a - b$, the terms $2a$ *and* $-3a$ have same algebraic factor a. So they are like terms. But the terms 2a, 5ab have different algebraic factors, they are unlike terms. Similarly, the terms $5ab$ and $-b$ are unlike terms.

Q113. Explain basic operations on algebraic expressions with example.

Ans. There are four fundamental operations – addition, subtraction, multiplication and division on numbers. Since letters represent nos. in Algebra, they follow all the rules and properties of addition, subtraction, multiplication and division of number.

Different operations in algebra are performed in two phases:

(i) Operations on letters

(ii) Operations on expression

(1) Addition: There are a number of real life problems in which we need to use algebraic expressions and apply arithmetic operations on them.

(i) Addition of letters/monomials:

We know that $2 + 2 + 2 = 2 \times 3 = 3 \times 2$

Similarly, we can have $x + x + x = x \times 3 = 3 \times x = 3x$

and $x + x + x + x + x = 5 \times x = 5x$

Now sum of 3x and $5x = 3x + 5x$

$= (x + x + x) + (x + x + x + x + x)$

$= x + x + x + x + x + x + x + x = 8x$

Also $3x + 5x = (3 \times x) + (5 \times x)$

$= (3 + 5) \times x$ (distributive law)

$= 8 \times x = 8x$

(ii) Addition of Algebraic Expressions:

Example: Find the sum of $5a + 7$ and $2a - 5$.

Solution: The sum $= 5a + 7 + 2a - 5$

$= (5a + 2a) + (7 - 5)$ (putting the like terms together)

$= 7a + 2$

(2) Subtraction: We know how to subtract integers. The same principle also works with algebraic expressions.

(i) Subtraction of Monomials: Let us subtract $2x$ from $5x$

$5x - 2x = (x + x + x + x + x) - (x + x)$

$= x + x + x + x + x - x - x$

$= x + (-x) + x + (-x) + x + x + x$ [As x and $-x$ are additive inverse of each other]

$= 0 + 0 + x + x + x$

$= 0 + 3x = 3x$

In brief, we can also do the work as follows:

$5x - 2x = (5 \times x) - (2 \times x)$

$= (5 - 2) \times x = 3 \times x = 3x$

(ii) Subtraction of Algebraic Expressions: The process of subtraction is similar to that of addition. Let us observe the following examples.

Example: Subtract $3a + 2b$ from $4a + 5b - 2$

Solution: $(4a + 5b - 2) - (3a + 2b)$

$= 4a + 5b - 2 - 3a - 2b$

$= (4a - 3a) + (5b - 2b) - 2$ (Putting the like terms together)

$= a + 3b - 2$

Alternative method : We have to write the expressions one below the other with the like terms remaining in one column and perform subtraction on each of the terms separately as shown below:

$$\begin{array}{r} 4a + 5b - 2 \\ -3a - 2b \\ \hline a + 3b - 2 \end{array}$$

After changing the signs we get

(3) Multiplication:

(i) ***Multiplication of monomials:*** $a \times a = a^2$ where 2 is the number that represents the number of a's.

The number 2 in a^2 is known as **index** or **exponent** or **power** of a and 'a' is the **base**.

The product of a and b, that is a × b can briefly be written as *'ab'*

Similarly, $a \times a \times b = a^2b$

$a \times a \times b \times b = a^2b^2$ and so on.

(ii) ***Multiplication of a monomial with a polynomial:*** for this multiplication, commutative, associative and distributive properties are used as and when required.

Example: Multiply $3a$ with $(5a - 2b + 4)$

Product $= 3a \times (5a - 2b + 4)$

$= 3a \times 5a + 3a \times (-2b) + 3a \times 4$ (distributive Law)

$= 3 \times a \times 5 \times a + 3 \times a \times (-2) \times b + 3 \times a \times 4$

$= 3 \times 5 \times a \times a + 3 \times (-2) \times a \times b + 3 \times 4 \times a$

$= 15a^2 - 6ab + 12a$

(iii) ***Multiplication of a polynomial by a polynomial:*** Here also, we use distributive property.

Example: Multiply $(2x + 5)$ by $(x^2 - 3x + 2)$

Solution : $(2x + 5) \times (x^2 - 3x + 2)$

$= 2x \times (x^2 - 3x + 2) + 5\,(x^2 - 3x + 2)$ (distributive Law)

$= 2x \times x^2 + 2x \times (-3x) + 2x \times 2 + 5 \times x^2 + 5 \times (-3x) + 5 \times 2$

$= 2x^3 - 6x^2 + 5x^2 + 4x - 15x + 10$

$= 2x^3 + (-6 + 5)\,x^2 + (4 - 15)\,x + 10$

$= 2x^3 - x^2 - 11x + 10$

(4) Division: We know the procedure for division of numbers. Similar procedure is also followed while dividing an algebraic expression by another

(i) ***Division of monomial by a monomial:***

Algorithm:

(a) Write the dividend as numerator and divisor as denominator.

(b) Express the numerator and denominator both as the product of factors.

(c) Simplify the fraction by cancelling the common factors from the numerator and denominator.

Example:

- Division of 15mn by 5m $= \frac{15mn}{5m} = \frac{3 \times 5 \times m \times n}{5 \times m} = 3n$
- $18x^2y^2 \div (-6xy) = \frac{18x^2y^2}{-6xy} = \frac{3 \times 6 \times x \times x \times y \times y}{-6 \times x \times y} = -3xy$

(ii) ***Division of polynomial by a monomial:*** Here, the dividend is a polynomial and the divisor is a monomial. The working rule for division is:

Divide each term of the dividend by the divisor.

Simplify each fraction as earlier.

Example: Divide $9x^2 - 15xy$ by $3x$

Now, $(9x^2 - 15xy) \div (3x) = \frac{9x^2 - 15xy}{3x} = \frac{9x^2}{3x} - \frac{15xy}{3x} = 3x - 5y$

(iii) ***Division of Polynomial by a Polynomial:***

Example: Divide $11x + 15x^2 - 12$ by $5x - 3$

Step 1: Arrange the terms of the dividend and divisor in descending order of powers of a certain variable contained in the polynomials.

$5x - 3\overline{)15x^2 + 11x - 12}$

Step 2: Divide the 1st term of the dividend by the 1st term of divisor and get the 1st term of the quotient.

Here $\frac{15x^2}{5x} = 3x$

Step 3: Multiply 3x with each term of the divisor and write the result below the dividend. Then subtract it from the dividend.

$$
\begin{array}{r|l}
 & 3x \\
\hline
 & 15x^2 + 11x - 12 \\
5x - 3 & 15x^2 - 9x \\
 & - \quad + \\
\hline
 & \quad 20x - 12
\end{array}
$$

Step 4: Repeat the process from step 2 to 3 considering 20x – 12 as the new dividend.

Here the 2nd term of the quotient $= \frac{20x}{5x} = 4$

$$\begin{array}{r|l} & \quad 3x+4 \\ \hline & 15x^2+11x-12 \\ 5x-3 & 15x^2-9x \\ & - \quad + \\ \hline & \qquad 20x-12 \\ & \qquad 20x-12 \\ & \qquad - \quad + \\ \hline & \qquad\quad 0 \end{array}$$

Product of 2nd term of the quotient and the divisor is now to be subtracted from the new dividend. Result is '0'.

Hence, the quotient = 3x + 4 and the remainder = 0

$\therefore \left(15x^2 + 11x - 12\right) \div \left(5x - 3\right) = 3x + 4$

This process of division is known as the long division process.

Q114. What is an equation?

Ans. An equation can be compared with a balance in equilibrium. The two sides of the balance being compared with the two sides i.e. LHS and RHS of an equation. An Algebraic Expression is said to be an equation if L.H.S. and R.H.S. of the equation are equal or balanced. The two sides of an equation are separated by the equality sign (=). For example, in the equation 3x – 5 = 16, the LHS 3x – 5 is in the left pan and RHS 16 is in the right pan of the balance. Also the balance is in equilibrium as the values of the two sides of the equation are equal. x in the equation is known as the unknown.

Fig. 2.106: Picture of Balance

Q115. What is a Linear Algebraic Equation?

Ans. An equation involving only a linear polynomial is called a **linear equation**. A linear equation in one variable generally is of the form ax + b = 0 where a, b are numbers and x is unknown.

Linear equations are also known as **first degree** equations.

For example, $y + 9 = 15$ is a linear equation. As two sides LHS and RHS of this equation are separated by equality sign (=) and its degree (exponent) is 1.

Q116. Explain different processes of solving a Linear Equation.

Ans. Different processes of solving a linear equation are as follows:

(1) Process of Trial: Complete the table and by inspection of the table find the solution to the equation $x + 7 = 16$.

Table 2.23

X	1	2	3	4	5	6	7	8	9	10
x + 7	8	9	10	11	12	13	14	15	**16**	

Here we go on trying with the integers for 'x' till the equation holds good. In this way, we can obtain the value of the unknown. We say this process as the **process of trial**. Here, after so many unsuccessful trials we got the value of the unknown which satisfies the equation. In this example, $x = 9$.

(2) Process of Adding or Subtracting: An equation can be compared to a balance in equilibrium. The two sides of the equation are like the two pans and the equality sign indicates that the pans are balanced. Doing an arithmetic operation on an equation is like adding weights or removing weights from the pans of the balance. If we add the same weights to both the pans, the beam of the balance remains horizontal. Similarly, if we remove equal weights from the pans, the beam also remains horizontal. On the other hand, if we add or remove different weights, the balance is tilted, that is the beam of the balance does not remain horizontal. We use this principle for solving an equation.

Supposing 'x' represents the weight of packet of rice kept on the left pan and a weight 'w' kept on the right pan and the balance remains in equilibrium, then we say : $x = w$.

Case I: If we add a weight *'c'* on both the pans, surely it will remain horizontal.

Thus, we get, $x + c = w + c$

Case II: If we remove weight *'c'* from both of the pans, the beam remains horizontal.

Thus, we get $x - c = w - c$

Case III: Similarly, if we make the weights on both the pans *'c'* times, the beam would still remain horizontal.

The mathematical representation of this situation is $xc = wc$

Case IV: Also if we make the weights on both the pans '$\frac{1}{c}$',

(where $c \neq o$) times then the beam would remain balanced.

Thus, we get, $\frac{x}{c} = \frac{w}{c}$ (when $c \neq 0$)

From the above properties of weighing with a balance, we got four rules of equality for solving an equation. Those rules help in solving linear equations in precise manner. The rules state as follows:

(i) The same quantity can be added to both sides of an equation and it does not change the equality.

(ii) The same quantity can be subtracted from both sides of an equation and it does not change the equality.

(iii) Both sides of an equation may be multiplied by the same number and it does not change equality.

(iv) Both sides of an equation may be divided by a non-zero number and it does not change the quality.

Example: Solve: $y - 5 = 11$

Solution : Solving an equation means finding the value of the unknown.

So, $y - 5 = 11$

$\Rightarrow (y - 5) + 5 = 11 + 5$ (Adding 5 on both the sides)

$\Rightarrow y + (-5 + 5) = 16$ (Associativity)

$\Rightarrow y + 0 = 16$ (Additive inverse)

$\Rightarrow y = 16$ (Additive identity)

(3) Process of Transposition: While solving a linear equation, we can transpose a number from LHS to RHS or vice versa instead of adding or subtracting it from both sides of the equation. In doing so, the operation that connects the number on one side of the equation changes as it is removed to the other side. That is on transposing a term from one side to the other the operation of:

(i) Addition changes to subtraction

(ii) Subtraction changes to addition

(iii) Multiplication changes to division

(iv) Division changes to multiplication

These are called the Rules of Transposition.

Let us apply these rules in solving the following equations:

Example: Solve: $2x - 7 = 5$

Solution: $2x - 7 = 5$

$\Rightarrow 2x = 5 + 7$ (Transposing 7 to RHS)

$\Rightarrow 2x = 12$

$\Rightarrow x = \frac{12}{2}$ (Transposing 2 to RHS)

$\Rightarrow x = 6$

(4) Rule of Cross Multiplication: If the equation involves a fraction, let us learn an easier method to remove the fraction without disturbing the equality.

Suppose the equation is of the form $\frac{a}{b} = \frac{c}{d}$

$\Rightarrow a = \frac{c}{d} \times b$ (Transposing 'b' to RHS)

$\Rightarrow a = \frac{c \times b}{d}$

$\Rightarrow a \times d = c \times b$ (Transposing 'c' to LHS)

Thus, we find: $\frac{a}{b} = \frac{c}{d} \Rightarrow a \times d = c \times b$

Otherwise $\frac{a}{b} = \frac{c}{d}$

$\Rightarrow \frac{a}{b} \times bd = \frac{c}{d} \times bd$ (Multiplying 'bd' on both side)

$\Rightarrow ad = cb$

This is known as Rule of Cross Multiplication.

Example: Solve : $\frac{3x+1}{2} = \frac{x+7}{4}$

Solution: $\frac{3x+1}{2} = \frac{x+7}{4}$

$\Rightarrow (3x+1) \times 4 = (x+7) \times 2$ (By cross multiplying)

$\Rightarrow 12x + 4 = 2x + 14$ (Distribute law)

$\Rightarrow 12x - 2x = 14 - 4$ (Bringing unknown terms to LHS and Constants to RHS)

$\Rightarrow 10x = 10$

$\Rightarrow x = \frac{10}{10}$ (Transposing 10 to RHS)

$\Rightarrow x = 1$

Q117. How can the word problems be solved with the help of Algebraic Expressions? Explain with examples.

Ans. A mathematical statement can be converted into a simple equation. Then we can solve it as a simple equation. The algorithm (method) involved in solving real life problems is to:

(i) Understand the situation expressed in the word problem.

(ii) Choose a symbol and substitute it for the unknown to be determined.

(iii) Write an equation from the given relation in the problem.

(iv) Solve the equation and find the value of the unknown.

(v) Verify the correctness of the solution.

The following example is given as a word problem:

Example: Sita thinks of a number. She gets the result 17. If she multiplies the number by 4 and subtracts 7 from the product. What is the number?

Solution : Suppose Sita thinks of the number x.

Multiply the number by 4 = $x \times 4$ or $4x$

After taking away 7 from 4x, Sita has $4x - 7$.

According to the problem, $4x - 7 = 17$

Hence, we got the equation for x.

Now solve the equation $4x - 7 = 17$

$\Rightarrow 4x = 17 + 7 \Rightarrow 4x = 24$

$\Rightarrow x = \frac{24}{4}$

$\Rightarrow x = 6$

So, the required number is 6

Q118. Write the expression for the following:

(i) One third of the sum of numbers p and q.

(ii) Sum of the numbers a and b subtracted from their product.

(iii) 8 added to 2 times the product of x & y.

Ans. (i) The given nos. are p and q.

Sum of the numbers = $p + q$

$\frac{1}{3}$ of the sum of these numbers $= \frac{1}{3} \times (p + q)$

$= \frac{p+q}{3}$

(ii) The given nos. are a and b.

Sum of the numbers = $a+b$

Product of the numbers = $a \times b = ab$

The sum subtracted from their product = $ab - (a+b)$

(iii) 8 added to 2 times the product of x & y.

Product of x & y = xy

2 times the product = 2 × xy = 2xy

8 added to the product = 2xy +8

Q119. Solve the following equations:

(i) $\frac{8x}{6+3x}=\frac{-4}{3}$

(ii) $\frac{z}{3}+\frac{z}{5}=40$

Ans. (i) $\frac{8x}{6+3x}=\frac{-4}{3}$

By cross multiplication we get;

$3\times 8x=-4(6+3x)$

$24x=-24-12x$

Using the method of transposition, we get;

$24x+12x=-24$

$36x=-24$

$x=-\frac{24/12}{36/12}$

$x=-\frac{2}{3}$

(ii) $\frac{z}{3}+\frac{z}{5}=40$ or $\frac{z}{3}+\frac{z}{5}=\frac{40}{1}$

Taking LCM 15 as common denominator of LHS we get -

$\frac{(z)15\div 3+(z)15\div 5}{15}=\frac{40}{1}$

$\Rightarrow 5z+3z=15\times 40$

$\Rightarrow (5+3)\times z=600$

$\Rightarrow 8z=600$

$\Rightarrow z=\frac{600}{8}=75$

The book you can most believe—GPH book.

Objective Type Questions

Q1. How many integers lie between –10 and + 10?

(a) 21

(b) 20

(c) 19

(d) 18

Ans. (c) 19

Q2. $0.\overline{25}$ can be written as a $\frac{p}{q}$ in the following manner:

(a) $\frac{1}{4}$

(b) $\frac{25}{99}$

(c) $\frac{250}{99}$

(d) $\frac{252}{99}$

Ans. (b) $\frac{25}{99}$

Q3. A sum of money at simple interest amounts to 815 in 3 years and to 854 in 4 years. The sum is:

(a) 650

(b) 690

(c) 698

(d) 700

Ans. (c) 698

Q4. Formula for volume of pyramid is:

(a) $\frac{1}{3}\times$ base area × height

(b) 3 × base area × height

(c) $\frac{1}{2}\times$ base area × height

(d) 2 × base area × height

Ans. (a) $\frac{1}{3}\times$ base area × height

Q5. What is the sequence of rotation symmetry of the equilateral triangle?

(a) four

(b) six

(c) Three

(d) Five

Ans. (c) Three

Q6. One litre is equal to

(a) $\frac{1}{10}$ decalitre

(b) $\frac{1}{10}$ decilitre

(c) $\frac{1}{100}$ decilitre

(d) $\frac{1}{100}$ decalitre

Ans. (a) $\frac{1}{10}$ decalitre

Q7. What is the smallest unit of measurement?

(a) C-G-S

(b) M-K-S

(c) F-P-S

(d) SI

Ans. (c) F-P-S

Q8. What is the British method of measurement?

(a) Millimetre

(b) Centimetre

(c) Decimetre

(d) Metre

Ans. (d) Metre

Q9. In drawing a pie chart, students use:

(a) central angle

(b) straight angle

(c) right angle

(d) circle

Ans. (d) circle

Q10. Cumulative frequency is required to calculate:

(a) median

(b) mode

(c) mean

(d) standard deviation

Ans. (a) median

Q11. Product of (a–b) and (5a+3b) is:

(a) $5a^2 - 3b^2$

(b) $5a^2 + 2ab - 3b^2$

(c) $5a^2 - 2ab - 3b^2$

(d) $5a^2 - 2ab + 3b^2$

Ans. (c) $5a^2 - 2ab - 3b^2$

Q12. The HCF and LCM of two numbers are 12 and 36 respectively. If one of the numbers is 12, what is the other number?

(a) 36

(b) 6

(c) 12

(d) 20

Ans. (a) 36

Q13. How many lines can you draw passing through a given point?

(a) 1

(b) 2

(c) 3

(d) many

Ans. (d) many

Q14. Which of the following statement is incorrect?

(a) A right angle is greater than a straight angle.

(b) An obtuse angle is greater than 90°.

(c) An acute angle is less than 90°

(d) A complete angle equals 360°

Ans. (a) A right angle is greater than a straight angle.

Q15. The measure of a complete angle is:

(a) 90°

(b) 180°

(c) 360°

(d) none of these

Ans. (c) 360°

Q16. Which of these angles cannot be constructed using a ruler and compass?

(a) 60°

(b) 120°

(c) 115°

(d) 150°

Ans. (c) 115°

Q17. The number of times of times a particular observation occurs is called its:

(a) Tally mark

(b) Frequency

(c) Class size

(d) Class interval

Ans. (b) frequency

Q18. The representation of an information through pictures is called:

(a) Histogram

(b) Bar graph

(c) Pie chart

(d) Pictograph

Ans. (d) Pictograph

Q19. The perimeter of a rectangle is 90 m. It is 30 m long. Its breadth is:

(a) 3m

(b) 60m

(c) 15m

(d) 150 m

Ans. (c) 15m

Q20. The value of a variable is:

(a) fixed

(b) not fixed

(c) zero

(d) none of these

Ans. (b) not fixed

3 Learner Assessment in Mathematics

INTRODUCTION

Assessment for learning is an important tool for increasing the level of learning in mathematics classrooms. Mathematics is an important school subject in developing mathematical thinking and reasoning as well as in developing critical thinking among the learners. Uninteresting classroom transaction as well as stressful assessment procedure create phobia towards mathematics learning. Assessment can play a key role in exemplifying the new types of mathematics learning students must achieve. Assessments indicate to students what they should learn. They specify and give concrete meaning to valued learning goals. Mathematics assessments can help both students and teachers to improve the work that students are doing in mathematics. Students need to learn to monitor and evaluate their progress. When students are encouraged to assess their own learning, they become more aware of what they know, how they learn, and what resources they are using when they do mathematics.

Q1. Briefly discuss the nature of mathematics learning at the early stage of schooling.

Ans. Nature of mathematics learning at the early stage of schooling is given below:

(1) Mathematical thinking is developed by children through active interaction with the world around them (rural children are rich in oral mathematical tradition) utilising the cognitive resources available in the environment. At the early stage, every object and event in the immediate environment of the child can be used for learning mathematics.

(2) Initial understanding of children about mathematics is 'concrete' and 'contextual'.

(3) With concrete elements, active manipulation leads children to construct mathematical concepts and processes.

(4) Learning of mathematics appropriates the developmental (intellectual/cognitive) concerns required to design learning continuum from concrete to abstract concepts.

Q2. What are the three principles of assessment of 'mathematics learning'? Also discuss any two criteria of a good assessment.

[October-2016, Q.No.-42]

Or

What are the principles of assessment of mathematics learning? Explain.

Ans. In the USA, the National Research Council Mathematical Sciences Education Board (1993) published a conceptual guide for assessment which emphasised that assessment should make the important measurable rather than making the measurable important. To this end, they proposed the following three principles for the assessment of mathematics that are relevant at the personal, class and system level.

(1) The Content Principle: Applying the content principle to a mathematics assessment means judging how well it reflects the mathematics that is most important for students to learn. The judgments are similar to early notions of content validity that were limited to asking about the representativeness and relevance of test content. The difference lies in a greater concern today for the quality of the mathematics reflected in the assessment tasks and in the responsed to them.

(2) The Learning Principle: Learning Principle, which is closely related to the Teaching Principle, calls for students to "learn mathematics with understanding, actively building new knowledge from experience and prior knowledge" (NCTM, 2000, p. 20). Presenting students with alternative approaches to learning the content of mathematics provides valuable opportunities to build upon those that are most closely related to students thinking and previous experiences .

(3) **The Equity Principle:** The Equity Principle states, "excellence in mathematics education requires equity–high expectations and strong support for all students" (NCTM, 2000, p.11). Equity "demands that reasonable and appropriate accommodations be made as needed to promote access and attainment" (NCTM, 2000, p. 12)

A good assessment of mathematics learning needs to satisfy the following three criteria besides these three principles:

(1) In order for a student assessment to reform a student's mathematics learning, and give feedback to lessons, the assessment must be open. In terms of the **openness** of an assessment, factors such as the openness of information related to the assessment, openness of assessment participation, and changes and reforms can be thought about.

(2) About mathematics learning, assessment should promote valid **inferences**. A valid inference is based on evidence that is adequate and relevant. The amount and type of evidence that is needed depends upon the consequences of the inference. For example, a teacher may judge students' progress in understanding place value through informal interviews and use this information to plan future classroom activities. However, much more evidence and a more formal analysis of that evidence is required by a large scale, high quality assessment.

(3) Assessment should be a **coherent** process. In assessment, three types of coherence are involved:

- The phases of assessment must fit together.
- The assessment must match the purpose for which it is being conducted.
- The assessment must be aligned with the curriculum and with instruction.

Q3. Discuss the nature of assessment of mathematics learning.

Ans. Assessment should enhance mathematics learning and support good instructional practice. The nature of assessment in mathematics approximates the nature of learning process of mathematics very closely. Therefore, assessment of mathematics is as follows:

(1) **Experiential and contextual:** Through direct interaction, mathematics concepts can be learnt with the objects and events in the immediate environment of the child, assessment can also utilize those or similar materials and processes that the child experiences in the environment. Again, since mathematics concepts at the early stage are learnt effectively being embedded in a context familiar to the child, assessment is also effective if it is also conducted in a similar context.

(2) **Combinatorial:** Since, there is more than one way of learning a mathematical concept; therefore, assessment of learning that concept, requires more than one mode of assessment. Further, learning a concept not only enhances achievement, it also brings about the change in several aspects of learner's socio-personal characteristics. That is why assessment of mathematics learning has to take recourse to several modes and approaches separately or in combination.

(3) **Orality to performance-activity to written:** Even process of assessment should begin with oral assessment and then proceed to the performance tasks and then to written tests which use comparatively more of formal mathematical symbols and procedures and seem abstract to the children in the elementary schools.

(4) **Appropriate to sequence of mathematics learning:** Since, mathematics contents follow a logical and sequential order and as such assessment process which follows the learning sequence must be in that order.

(5) **Concrete-contextual to abstract:** assessment of mathematics learning need to begin with manipulation of concrete materials and experiences to methods and processes dealing with abstract concepts.

Q4. What dimensions are included in the process of assessment in mathematics?

Or

Elucidate the dimensions of assessment of mathematics learning.

Or

Mention different aspects of mathematics learning to be assessed. **[April-2016, Q.No.-37]**

Ans. Following dimensions of mathematical learning are included in the process of assessment:

(1) Concepts and procedures: A great deal is known through research about the nature and development of mathematical concepts and procedures. It is possible and also desirable that through assessment teachers should explore the nature of children's learning of both concepts and procedures systematically, as this would enable teachers to plan their own instruction more effectively. We have identified about broad areas under which we have delineated concepts and procedures, which are learnt by children:

- Number (including number representation and decimal system)
- Number operations- addition, subtraction, multiplication and division
- Fractions
- Shapes and spatial thinking
- Measurement
- Problem solving
- Patterns
- Data handling
- Basic algebraic processes (only in upper primary stage)
- Simple equations (only in upper primary stage)

At this stage, for ensuring comprehensive assessment of mathematics learning, appropriate tools and methods for assessing the concepts, skills, procedural knowledge, thinking skills, vocabulary and arguments included in each of above areas have to properly planned.

(2) Mathematical reasoning: Even from the earliest stage of learning, mathematics is distinguished by its strong logical order. Inductive and Deductive reasoning, is dominantly employed in the mathematics learning at the elementary stage. The emphasis on reasoning in mathematics learning not only influences the ways of solving and presenting the solutions of mathematical problems, it also impacts learners' language, ways of presenting communications logically, and even different activities conducted by the learners in their daily life. Therefore, assessment of mathematics learning cannot exclude this important aspect. Several methods including the tests, both oral, written, and performance, observation of learners' activities, etc. are included in assessing mathematical reasoning.

(3) **Dispositions towards mathematics:** Teachers' dispositions and attitudes towards mathematics are closely related to the quality of their teaching and the students' learning of mathematics. Mathematics learning is influenced by learner's perception, interest, attitude and personality characteristics. The learners can enjoy learning mathematics and can get rid of the anxiety and phobia associated with mathematics learning at the early stage of schooling when taught and assessed properly in a learner-friendly environment.

(4) **Using mathematical knowledge and techniques to solve problems:** Mathematics learning in schools means solving the problems given in the textbooks or some other problems similar to the textual problems. And in the course of solving the problems, the students acquire skills in using new techniques and methods. The traditional trend of assessment of mathematics learning has focused on assessing the textual problems. But the real test of mathematics learning is the extent of use of mathematical knowledge and techniques learnt in the classroom in solving the day-to-day real life problems. This aspect cannot be afforded by comprehensive assessment.

(5) **Communication:** Development of the way of communication is one of the important outcomes of mathematics learning, which is typically precise, logical, relevant and disciplined. These characteristics can be observed in both oral and written communications. Furthermore, use of symbols, figures, graphs and charts makes the written communications more precise, and orderly. These aspects of mathematical communication have to be included in both formal and informal modes of assessment.

Following are the different dimensions of assessment of learning mathematics from another consideration:

(1) **Scholastic/Curricular:** As most of the instructional objectives are written in scholastic/curricular assessment, so we are more concerned with this form. These objectives are assessed through written, oral and performance. These objects also deal with recall, recognition and identification, etc. of

knowledge, understanding and application. This type of assessment is mainly related with curriculum.

(2) **Co-scholastic/Co-curricular/other curricular areas:** We need to assess performance of learner in various other areas where s/he uses the knowledge of mathematics acquired in the classroom like the participation and performance in mathematics quizzes, debates, competitions, Mathematics Olympiad, modeling, exhibitions, developing TLMs in mathematics, etc. besides assessing scholastic or curricular aspects. We need to encourage our students to participate in as many activities and to adopt various methods for assessing their participation and performance in these activities.

(3) **Interest and attitude:** Interest and attitude of learner towards mathematics is considered crucial for effective learning which we can assess by observing their classroom activities, their mode of questioning and their participation in different co-curricular activities.

(4) **Creative ability:** In mathematics, creative abilities of learner are indicated by his/her ability to solve problems in novel ways, framing unusual and yet important questions, developing innovative learning materials, writing interesting articles on mathematics, drawing unique graphs, diagrams and pictorial representations of mathematical data and processes, creating materials and activities for fun in mathematics and such other unusual activities. As indicators, we can assess our students' creative abilities in mathematics, by using these activities.

(5) **Recreational activities:** Mathematical puzzles, contests, games, reading mathematics fun books and history of mathematics, preparing charts, preparing different designs, these all are recreational activities which help to create interest and zest for mathematics learning. We can assess our students in these areas through their involvement in the programmes and activities.

(6) **Socio-personal qualities:** Some exemplars of socio-personal qualities associated with mathematics learning are – exactness, precise expression, logical approach to all activities, higher order thinking. By sharp observation, interaction with students individually or in groups, evaluation of students' products like writings, and materials

are some of the methods of assessing socio-personal qualities associated with mathematics learning can be assessed.

Q5. What are the characteristics of the learning-centered approach and characteristics of assessment in this approach?

Ans. A learning-centered approach does not necessarily mean that student activity is is the focus of the teaching strategy. This approach is mainly based on the tenants of constructivism whose basic belief is that the learner constructs his/her own knowledge. Following are the major characteristics of the learning-centered approach:

- The process, techniques and strategies of learning are emphasised. If the process of learning is better, then acquisition of knowledge and competencies would be easier.
- In a natural and contextual situation, learning takes place.
- Learner dominantly controls learning. Consequently, the learner learns at the pace s/he desires. In that sense, learning is quite flexible and democratic.
- Learner is active and the teacher facilitates for active learning. The major role of the teacher is facilitating and supporting learning.
- Activity-based methods activate the learner for learning.

The characteristics of assessment in the learning-centered approach are as follows:

- The major objective in this approach is to assess the process and techniques of learning rather than the product and competencies supposed to be acquired.
- Assessment is done while the learner is engaged in learning process not necessarily at the end of the unit of content.
- Assessment is done in the context of learning and is related to the authentic learning experience in the real world situation. It is done while the learner is engaged in solving a real life problem.
- Preferable methods of assessment in this approach are – cooperative, collaborative, portfolio, rubric and problem solving methods of assessment. Any method that leads to a sense of success is the preferred method of assessment in this approach.
- Flexibility in terms of timing and place of assess are provided for the learners to feel a sense of freedom while participating in such assessment process.

Q6. How the transformation is changing the assessment of mathematics learning?

Ans. With emphasis on the continuous and comprehensive evaluation (CCE) in the RTE Act, 2009, traditional practice of conducting periodic examinations is undergoing total transformation. Following is the discussion of how the transformation is changing the assessment of mathematics learning:

(1) The frequency of assessment in mathematics like in other subjects has increased and is being conducted at regular intervals in the form of unit testing, observation of performances in different activities.

(2) Assessment of attainment of mathematical concepts is no more confined only to the textbook questions. Different tools and techniques are being liked and used outside the purview of the textbook.

(3) The acquisition of mathematical concepts is not only assessed, but several other characteristics that are expected to develop as a result of mathematics learning are also being assessed. Change in interest and attitude towards learning mathematics, development of creative ideas in mathematics, solving problems in different ways are some of the examples of such dimensions of assessment that are being increasingly included in assessment programmes.

(4) There has been a distinct shift towards using real life problems in the context of the child's immediate environment. The objects, animals, trees, persons, land forms around the child can be used for natural learning of mathematical concepts at the elementary level. These elements and the real world problems perceived by children can also be used to assess the mathematics learning. NCF, 2005 has advocated such authentic assessment and included in the CCE programme in the elementary schools.

Q7. Define self-assessment. What are the basic beliefs of self-assessment in mathematics learning?

Ans. Self-assessment involves students in evaluating their own work and learning progress. Self-assessment helps students to:

- Reflect on their own learning;
- Identify their strengths and areas where they need to improve using clear criteria related to the expectations and achievement levels;

- Set goals and identify next steps for learning;
- Develop skills in meta-cognition;
- Become independent, self-directed students;
- Select work for their portfolios that represent their progress and best efforts over time.

Self-assessment is based on some basic beliefs that are as follows:

- Students' involvement in assessment tasks increase by involving them in the assessment of their work, especially giving them opportunities to contribute to the criteria on which that work will be judged.
- Closely related is the argument that self-assessment contributes to variety in assessment methods, a key factor in maintaining student interest and attention.
- Students get information by self-assessment that is not easily determined, such as how much effort students spent in preparing for the task.
- Besides other techniques self-assessment is a more cost-effective.
- When students know that they will share responsibility for the assessment of what they have learned, they take interest in learning more.

In mathematics, self-assessment will improve learning because, it:

- Motivate the students.
- Construct their own understandings.
- Focus student attention on the objectives measured.
- Know how to use assessment information and improve performance.
- Learn how to think about their learning and how to self-assess.

Q8. Enumerate the techniques and benefits of self-assessment in mathematics learning.

Ans. Following are the techniques of self-assessment in mathematics learning:

(1) **Scrutiny:** After completing a task or developing a model, a learner has to minutely scrutinise the outcome after each step followed to complete the task and the final outcome against the expected outcomes.

(2) **Comparison:** After scrutinise, the learner then compares his/her own performance (in class work, home assignments, project work, participation in teaching learning process, etc.) with those of other learners in the class.

(3) **Self-analysis:** In terms of the steps, formula, principle and techniques followed to solve the problems with own answer, the learner analyses his own response/result/solution. S/he tries to detect omissions, repetitions, mistakes, etc. in his/her performance in course of such analysis.

(4) **Reflection:** The learner reflects on the quality of the totality of his/her performance and tries to estimate it after the analysis of his/her own performance. And while reflecting on the performance s/he draws a mental balance sheet of his mistakes, limitations and excellence in the performance and accordingly estimates the results.

Benefits of Self-assessment: Self-assessment is an important skill to develop for lifelong learning (Race, 2001). Once students enter the workforce it is imperative that they are able to critically evaluate their own performance. In mathematics, self-assessment helps in becoming conscious of the formulae, steps and procedure of solving a mathematics problem in a correct way, discriminating correct way from the incorrect ones, recognising the mistakes and thereby knowing the ways to correct the mistakes. Learners get intrinsic motivation through self-assessment and it also enhances self esteem and self-confidence to attempt challenging problems.

Despite its proven benefits, it is not easy for any learner to assess himself/herself as it is very difficult to develop the abilities like self-analysis and reflection. Without these abilities, one cannot conduct self-assessment without being biased. Sometimes, the fear of mathematics disables the learner for correct scrutiny and analysis. Thus, to develop the ability for carrying out self-assessment we can help the learner.

Q9. Define peer assessment. Also discuss the assessment of tasks performed by peers/group by nature.

Or

What are the socio-personal skills that can be assessed in per/group assessment.

Ans. Peer assessment is a practice existing in the conventional system of education. The students share their experiences and learn better from each other in a group. The students sharing each other's experiences and assessment can be more objective when the assessment is based on a shared set of assessment schedule.

Peer assessment occurs when other students in the class evaluate a students work. Often, these strategies are already at work in the primary mathematics classroom. Students are afforded multiple opportunities to practice peer and self-assessment strategies. A variety of checklists are available to help students gain facility applying this double-sided strategy. Some schools set up math buddies so that students can routinely solve problems and share their problem-solving solutions.

In groups, solving mathematical problems encourages peer learning and develops among the group members several social skills like sharing, fellow feeling, helping each other which can also be assessed by the group.

Assessment of tasks performed by peers/group by nature:

- **Open, candid and trustworthy:** In the peer group, since the interaction is free, frank and friendly, the assessment is done in an open manner in an environment without any external restriction. Again, the result of assessment is arrived at through the involvement of all, hence for each member in the group, it is more meaning and trust worthy.
- **Enhances effective sharing and communication:** Sharing and communication skills are developed and strengthened, while during group work those are also utilised effectively during the group assessment. In course of assessing mathematics learning and the socio-personal skills associated with it, the communication among the members of the group and also with the teacher is free and yet more systematic and disciplined than any other subject. This is due to the nature of the problems and methodical approach of solving mathematical problems.
- **Develops a range of thinking skills:** As solving mathematics problem requires reasoning of varied complexity, assessment of those abilities also requires all those skills, which are being assessed by the group.

Ensuring levels of contribution of each of the group members is the trickiest matter in the group assessment. It is natural that in a group all the members might not be contributing in equal degree, and as such the assessment of the members would vary. But in extreme cases, a few members would be dominating while some would remain totally passive. Peer assessment would not have uniform and valid conclusions regarding the aspects of a learner being assessed by the group in such cases.

Peer assessment cannot be totally valid when considered separately. Although, it can supplement and enrich your assessment of the students This is because of the fact that the perception of the young students might not be that mature as yours. But nonetheless, the peer assessment can bring out some interesting aspects of mathematics learning which would be difficult for an adult (teacher or parents) to perceive.

Following are the socio-personal skills that can be assessed in peer/group assessment:

- Listening and accepting others ideas
- Sharing of experiences/ideas
- Taking Leadership
- Participation in the group work
- Sharing the workload
- Helping peers
- Doing self correction

Q10. Discuss the assessment through assignment in mathematics learning.

Ans. Assignments are widely used to assess students learning. An assignment is a task or work allotment. In this technique, the learners are provided with the responsibility for his/her own learning. The teacher acts as an advisor and guide in case of any difficulty encountered.

While for assessment and for learning, the role of home assignments in mathematics is recognised by most of the teachers and parents, most of them want specific answers to the two crucial questions, "How much time should students spend doing homework?" and "What kinds of homework assignments are most effective?" Research studies conducted on the assignment in mathematics in answering the two questions are varied. However, the few consistent findings are, discussed as follows:

- Homework assignments that included both (a) Practice of previously covered material and (b) introduced new, preparatory material for the next related topics along with content to be taught on the same day are superior to assignments that included only same-day content. Assignments including same-day-only content are less effective then practice of past material and introducing future material.
- Mixing hard and easy material throughout the assignment has a positive effect on measures of homework accuracy and completion rates. Also, students rate these assignments as being less difficult, requiring less effort, and requiring less time than the assignments that did not use the mixing up the difficult and easy items.

- So far as duration and frequency of home assignment in mathematics are concerned, these studies hint at the possibility that shorter (duration of responding), but more frequent homework assignments may be most effective.
- In the achievement of students, no consistent improvement was observed when classes in which students were assigned individualised homework were compared with classes in which all students did the same assignment. The results also suggest that students who are struggling in school require more time to complete homework that are not individualised. By contrast, more time is spent by teachers in constructing and monitoring individualised assignments.
- Distributing the content of mathematics homework assignments so that it includes material meant to practice past lessons or prepare for future lessons, or both, can be more effective than assignments that include only same-day content.
- There is improvement in students interest, motivation, and, ultimately, achievement when the students are offered choices for selecting their homework assignments. This is probably because children do things without the presence of obvious external demands, or that include expressions of autonomy, they are more likely to internalize positive sentiments about the activity.

It is very common to give home assignments in the form of some problems from the exercises in the mathematics textbook to solve. So times, problems on the concepts taught are also given from outside the textbook. Several other types of tasks can also be given as home assignments besides the problems, textual or non-textual, which may include:

- Development of models for teaching and learning mathematics concepts.
- Framing of non-textual and real life problems on the mathematical concepts taught.
- Projects in mathematics (depending on the grade level several projects can be given as both long and short duration projects).
- Developing decorative designs using common geometrical figures.
- Preparation of graphs and figures based on some local data like occupation of community members (in %), Expenditure of

family in days of a week, proportion of boys and girls in different classes of the school etc.

- Solving given problems using more than one method of solution.

Assignments are essentially meant to strengthen the learning of concepts taught in the classroom. Hence, assessment of assignments are formative in nature. Scoring or marking the home assignments serves very little purpose. Feedback in the form of errors committed and highlighting the points of excellent performance are better forms of reporting assessment results. By rating the components of the responses, we can assess a long assignment as shown in the following table:

Table 3.1: Proforma for Assessment of Home Assignment in Mathematics

Sl. No	**Aspects to be assessed**	**Ratings of the Aspects**		
		Good	**Average**	**Poor**
(1)	Understanding on the concept			
(2)	Style of presentation			
(3)	Logical steps for solution			
(4)	Use of own language			
(5)	Use of appropriate formula			
(6)	Use of proper mathematical symbols			
(7)	Length of the answer			
(8)	Correlation with previous knowledge and experiences			

Q11. Describe participation in different activities in mathematics learning. Also, give strategies to assess student's participation in different activities.

Ans. All activities that teachers and students undertake to get information are broadly included in assessment of learning mathematics, and it can be used diagnostically to improve teaching and learning. Assessments are based on teacher observation, classroom discussion, participation in activities employed in the classroom, analysis of student work, homework and tests. Students participated in discussion, question answer session, individual activities, group activities, mathematics quizzes, mathematics funs, mathematics projects, preparation of TLMs, put questions etc. in classroom.

For example, in school, an official market is arranged by a teacher, distributed assignments among the students. After the completion of the work, a discussion was made. The teacher assessed performance of the students how they have employed mathematical skills in their assigned works. During the discussion, the teacher ensured participation of the students in: (i) preparation for the work, (ii) co-operation with their peers, (iii) organizing the task, (iv) presentation of the assigned work in a systematic way, (v) discussion with their peers, (vi) innovation in work, etc.

Strategies to assess Students' participation in different activities: Following strategies are included to assess students' participation in different activities:

- Present several possible answers to a question, then ask students to discuss on it.
- Interview students individually or in groups, about the reasoning they are employed for solving problems.
- Assess students from the questions they ask during a lesson.
- Invite students to discuss their thinking about a question in pairs or small groups and then ask a representative to share the thinking with the larger group (think-pair- share).
- Assess student's interest by their participation in exhibition, quizzes and puzzles or in mathematical activities like solving mathematical problems, working out challenging problems from other books.
- Ask all students to write down an answer and then read a selected few out loud.
- Ask students to point out the formula (if any) used for solving the problem.

Q12. Define and discuss continuous and comprehensive assessment in mathematics.

Ans. Continuous assessment of learners' work not only facilitates their learning of Mathematics, but also enhances their confidence in application of learning in Mathematics. This view changes the focus of assessment from summative evaluation, where learners are evaluated at the end of unit and provided grades, to the formative evaluation where learners are evaluated in the pursuit of learning. So, the approach of evaluation solely for the purposes of grading and ranking has been changed to approach of integrating evaluation with learning activities that support learners' construction of knowledge.

By comprehensive assessment, we mean that assessment should not concern itself only with knowledge but it shall also take into account the factors that are inherent in students' growth such as skills, understanding, appreciation, interest, attitude and habits. In other words, assessment should cover all the learning experiences of the learner in curricular as well as non-cognitive areas.

Assessment in mathematics is linked with the aims of teaching mathematics. The aim of school mathematics is to develop useful capabilities and also to develop the ability to think and reason mathematically in the primary schools years. Useful 'capabilities' include conceptual and spatial understanding, problem solving and mathematical modeling. While learning mathematics children develop and express self confidence, creativity, ability to communicate and use mathematical concepts and symbols. Following are the focusing points of learning assessment in mathematics at primary level are related to understanding:

- how children learn mathematics,
- the mathematical concepts included in primary school curriculum, and
- child understanding of mathematics.

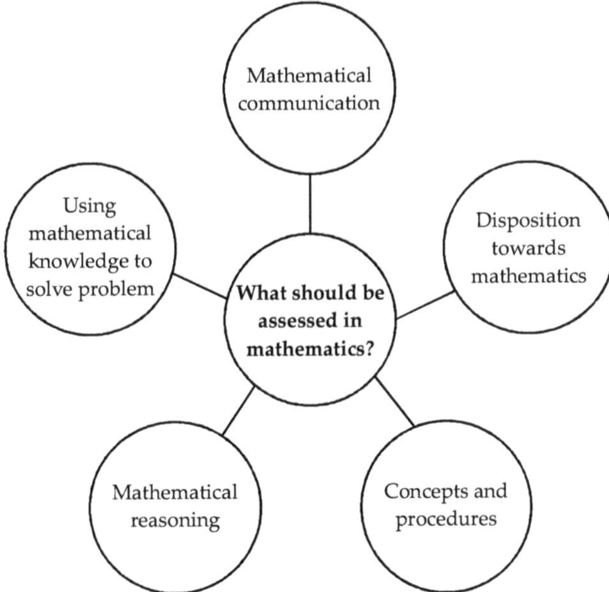

Fig. 3.1: Aspects of Assessment of Mathematics Learning at Primary Level

The teacher can use a wide choice of methods or *tools and techniques* to assess different dimensions of child's learning in mathematics. Besides the traditional paper pencil test and oral tests, the teacher can use other modes of observation, assignments, projects, portfolio, checklists, rating scales, anecdotal records etc. Use of multiple tools are required to enable us to assess the learners in a more comprehensive and objective manner.

Every day, a simple test should be record the number of questions asked by distinct students in a maths class/activity more the number of questions, more the learning.

Q13. Explain objective-based items test in mathematics with examples.

Or

Mention four behavioural specifications related to 'comprehension objective' in Mathematics learning.

[October-2016, Q.No.-34]

Ans. First, we read the following items:

1. Find the value of 7 +6 -3.

2. Who was the first Prime Minister of Independent India?

3. India got independence in the year _____.

We are very familiar with such type of items. These types of items are normally used in most of the tests. The answers to such items are definite and unique and hence can be scored objectively. Because such an item can be scored objectively (not influenced by any subjective personal criteria of the respondent or examiners), it is called an ***objective item***.

The objective based test item is supposed to measure a specific objective of instruction (learning outcomes). Learners' achievement are described more accurately by such types of items. The items are based on the specific objectives of a particular concept. Following are some objectives along with items in mathematics.

Table 3.2: Examples of Specific Objectives of Mathematics Learning

Objectives	**Behavioural specifications**
Knowledge	• Recalls facts, rules, theorems, definitions, principles and terms. • Recognises facts, relations, definitions, formulae, etc.
Comprehension	• Detects errors in figures, statements and rectifies these. • Interprets the principle in his/her own term. • Converts words into symbols and vice versa. • Classifies on the basis of certain criteria. • Provides more example on a principle/rule. • Verifies the mathematical conclusions. • Discriminate between similar things.
Application	• Suggests alternative plan or method for

	solution of a mathematical problem. • Makes generalisation on the basis of given facts. • Takes decision about sufficiency of the given facts. • Makes predictions and verifies them.
Skills	• Uses geometrical instruments correctly. • Represents a given data diagrammatically. • Draws geometrical figures with accuracy and speed.

Objective tests present students with a highly structured task that limits their response to supply a word, a number, a symbol or to select the answer from among the given number of alternatives. In general, objective type of items take less time to answer and easier to score uniquely than the extended or restricted response types of items

Some examples of objective type of items are given below:

(1) Which is the smallest prime number?

(2) What is the sum of the measures of the interior angles of a rectangle (in degree)?

(a) 90 (b) 180 (c) 270 (d) 360

(3) The number 9 is an odd number, because

(a) It is the biggest one digit number.

(b) It is not divisible by 2.

(c) It has three factors.

(d) It is the square of 3.

(4) In which of the following conditions a triangle ABC *CANNOT* be constructed?

(a) AB = 5cm, BC = 4cm, CA = 3cm

(b) AB = 6cm, BC = 5cm, CA = 3cm

(c) AB = 5cm, BC = 4cm, CA = 1cm

(d) AB = 7.5cm, BC = 4cm, CA = 3.9cm

All the four items given above are objective type of items.

We can observe that, the item in (a) demands the learner's ability in recalling specific facts. If we will observe the table given above, we will definitely mark that this item is a knowledge based item. This type of items is known as knowledge based item. Following are some examples of knowledge based objective type items:

- What is the formula to find out the perimeter of a rectangle?
- What is the definition of rational number?
- An equilateral triangle has
  (a) three equal sides
  (b) two equal sides with an angle of 90 degree
  (c) three unequal sides
  (d) one obtuse angle
- What is the sum of the measure of the interior angles of a quadrilateral?

After observing all the four items, we will definitely mark that all the items demand either *recall* of facts, principles, rules, formula etc or *recognition* of facts, relations etc. The learner has to recall the facts or information s/he has acquired earlier to answer such type of items.

We consider the item in (2), this item does not require mere recalling the facts directly from the text, rather allows the learner to restate the problem and respond logically. Such type of items are termed as understanding/comprehension based items.

Some examples are as follows:

(1) The three angles of a triangle can be respectively-
(a) Obtuse angle, Acute angle, Obtuse angle
(b) Right angle, Obtuse angle, Acute angle
(c) Acute angle, Acute angle, Acute angle
(d) Right angle, Right angle, Acute angle

(2) A triangle cannot be constructed with three angles measuring
(a) 75°, 55°, 60° (b) 60°, 35°, 85°
(c) 90°, 40°, 50° (d) 5°, 10°, 165°

(3) Which of the following represent a set of parallel straight lines?
(a) Spokes of a cycle wheel
(b) Opposite edges of a book
(c) Concentric circles
(d) Minute hand and hour hand of a clock at 12 noon

The learner can answer these questions if s/he has understood the mathematical concepts and processes. Simple cramming the principles will not help the learner to answer these questions.

Q14. Give brief description on the application-based items in mathematics.

Ans. The learner has to apply the acquired knowledge and comprehension in a new situation in the application-based items. Responding to such type of questions requires higher mental functioning than the knowledge and understanding based questions. Following are some examples of application-based questions:

(1) In which of the following cases the principle of inverse variation can be used?

   (a) 10 boys get 3 chocolate each. Calculate the total numbers of chocolates required for 10 boys.

   (b) One child is given 2 toffees. How many children will get 10 toffees?

   (c) One pen costs 8 rupees. Find out the price of 10 pens.

   (d) 10 persons complete a work in 8 days. In how many days 5 persons will complete that work?

(2) Using the property of a triangle regarding the sum of the measures of its angles, find out the sum of the measures of the angles of a quadrilateral.

(3) If the length and breadth of a rectangle are increased by two times, then the area of the rectangle will be:

   (a) Decrease by 2 times

   (b) Increase by 4 times

   (c) Increase by 2 times

   (d) Decrease by 4 times

Q15. What do you know about open-ended items in mathematics? Give comparison of close-ended and open-ended items.

Ans. The objective type of test item has a definite and unique answer that helps scoring the response easily and objectively. Such types of items are described as closed-ended items. But there are test items which allow a variety of correct responses and elicit different kind of students thinking. Such types of items are known as open-ended items.

The differences between open-ended and closed-ended items can be understood from the examples given in the following table:

Table 3.3

Closed ended items	Open ended items
(1) Fill up the blank in 5+— — = 9	(1) Which numbers when added give 9?
(2) Write the word by suffixing 'ing' to play.	(2) Write down as many words adding 'ing' like playing, looking etc.
(3) Draw a triangle with two adjacent sides of 5cm and 9cm with measure of included angle to be 600.	(3) How many ways can you draw a triangle?
(4) Which is the main material used in building pucca houses besides cement and mortar?	(4) How many ways can you use a brick?
(5) Who controls the teachers and students in a school?	(5) If you were the headmaster what would you do to improve your school?

Following are the characteristics/features of the open ended items in mathematics:

- Solved in different ways and on different levels. Students of different abilities can be able to give at least one correct answer.
- Provide teachers with valuable information regarding individual student way of thinking and way of solving mathematical problems.
- Develop student's reasoning and communication skill when those are discussed in the classroom.
- No fixed answer i.e. many possible answers
- Develop self-confidence if student for higher achievement. Since, such items have several possible correct responses, every student, even the poor performers; can provide at least one correct response. The better performing students can give several correct responses. All categories of students can aspire to perform in the subsequent occasions.
- Open to student's creativity and imagination when relates to real life context of their experience.
- Offer students scope for own decision-making and natural mathematical way of thinking. Each child can think according to his own experience.

Q16. State utilities of question banks in mathematics.

Or

What is the purpose of question bank in mathematics?

Or

Mention two purposes fulfilled by a question bank.

[April-2016, Q.No.-30]

Ans. In mathematics, preparing objective based test items of different types are quite important on the part of a teacher and at the same time, it is also not an easy task. But if we have a stock of quite a large number of items (questions) at our hand, we will have little difficulty in using appropriate test for our students at different times.

Following are the sources from which we can get variety of questions other than those available in the textbooks:

- We can prepare questions by ourselves,
- We can collect the questions prepared by the students during the course of teaching,
- We can bring some questions from different reference materials and
- Collect questions developed by other teachers of our schools or teachers in other schools.

Purposes of question bank: For the teachers, the question bank is useful in bringing reform in the traditional evaluation system. It was rightly observed by the National Curriculum Framework (2005) that, the present evaluation system can be described as "one-exam fits-all", as one question paper is employed to all students during the examination. This is because the teacher has no other options but to use some questions, which are available with him. But, if the teacher has a variety of questions in the question bank then he can prepare different question papers and use them for different learners as per their requirement. Following are some other purposes of question bank:

- Though the test items in a question bank are objective based, those are helpful for the teachers to evaluate the learning progress with respect to learning objectives.
- The learners can also self-evaluate themselves by using the question bank.
- Question bank is useful to prepare a test for instant testing of the learners
- Questions not only help in assessment of learning, but also aid in classroom transactions for helping the students to learn

better. Therefore, variety of items on different learning outcomes should be available to teachers and their students in the classroom. Question bank in the classroom serves this purpose effectively.

- The learners can prepare themselves in the questions available in the question bank.

Question banks should be prepared by every school on their own. This brings ownership of the materials by the teachers and students of that school (why?). Following points should be taken into consideration while preparing question bank in mathematics and their proper use:

- Test items from knowledge, understanding, application and skill objectives may be developed in each chapter. Besides, project activities and practical activities should be there.
- Instead of a register, it is better to write one or two questions on an item card - a post card size paper. Cards have several advantages in developing, sorting, using and storing. Sometimes different cards containing questions may be supplied to different students in the class to engage everyone in learning. (If a register will be maintained. then what will be the consequences?)
- On each chapter, both oral and written items should be prepared. Oral items in mathematics are quite useful in measuring the skills of speed and accurate calculation. Those oral items can be used in assessing the child's ability in mental arithmetic.
- For questions, different colour cards may be used on different objectives and subjects. It will help the teachers to select and use the questions as per the purpose.
- Experts should edit question after their preparation and collection. Teachers from different schools or a cluster may sit and discuss on each item and finalise them.

For example, red colour cards may be used for knowledge type of items while blue and yellow colour cards may be used for comprehension and application objectives. The teacher may use different colour of cards for different purposes, like – different color of cards may be used for extended response type of items (essay type of items), restricted response type of items (short answer type and objective type) and open-ended items.

Class V | Type of Task : Performance
Topic : Fraction | Difficulty Level : Medium
Objective : Demonstrates fractions
As part of a figure (Understanding)
Problem: Shade 2/3 of the square given below

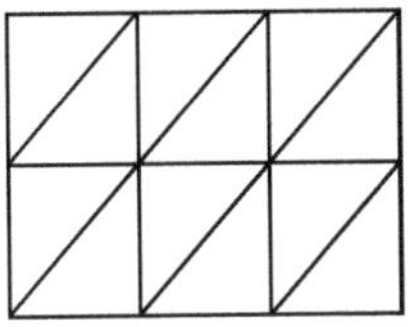

Answer on the overleaf

Fig. 3.2: Sample of an Item Card

Q17. Briefly discuss 'project' as a technique of assessment in mathematics learning.

Ans. A project is a motivated problem, solution of which requires thought and collection of data and its completion results in the production of something of value to the learners.

Project enables learners to conduct real inquiry in an interdisciplinary manner. It promotes problem-solving in Mathematics and connects it to real life application.

Projects in mathematics provide opportunity to observe, collect data, analyse, organise and interpret data and data and draw generalisation.

A project could be individual or group project and could be presented in the form of a document, report and/or a multimedia presentation.

In mathematics, projects can be used as an effective tools and techniques of assessment. Here the assessment becomes an integral part of the routine classroom activities and the teaching learning process. The teacher has to observe the behaviour of the child during the execution of the project, his interest towards the work, process of collection, recording, interpreting the data. Therefore, the teacher can assist the learner and helps in improving the learning.

Q18. Elucidate portfolio for assessment of learning mathematical concepts or skills.

Ans. Portfolio is a collection of learner's work. It can be designed to represent many things in relation to children's Mathematics learning experiences. It compiles academic work and other forms of educational evidence assembled for the purpose of evaluating the curriculum quality, learning progress, academic achievement, etc. It also helps in determining whether the learners have met learning standards, helping the learners to reflect on their academic goals and progress as learners. It provides a means for managing and evaluating multiple assessments for each learner. It includes a variety of entries including test reports, projects reports, essays, lab reports, assignments, problem solving tasks, a book review, photos, self-assessments, peer assessment, teacher assessment, parents' assessment, etc. From the following case study, we can understand better about 'Portfolio' for assessment of learning mathematics:

Anita, teaching in primary classes uses different ways of learner assessment. She also uses portfolio as one of the way. While teaching the concept of "percentage" in the class, she discussed with the students different activities to be conducted collaboratively. Once the students and Anita decided to collect and store different products prepared by the individual learner. The students were encouraged to write or collect essays, poems, stories, collect paper cutting and giving their own remarks on the articles/issues, narrative or descriptive piece communicating a significant experience, riddles, mathematical puzzles, teaching-learning materials, etc. involving the concept of percentage. The students were engaged in creating and collecting different products. They were given a period of 10 days to complete the task. After 10 days, all the students along with their teacher sat. The students displayed their creations and described them in detail. The creations (portfolio) of some students are given below.

- Sapna discussed with her father who is a bank employee and collected the interest rates given by various banks on fixed deposits and saving deposits. She also prepared a chart on this.
- Shashank collected some news from the newspaper and pasted on a chart paper. He also wrote his own views on some of the articles.
- Ashish wrote a story involving the concept of percentage.
- Rohit visited some of the households in his habitation, collected data on number of school going age children in each family. Calculated the percentage of the school going children to the number of persons and prepared a chart etc.
- Kavita has gone through textbooks and reference books of other schools of their locality and collected 10 different types of examples to understand the concept of percentage.

The activity was enjoyed by all the students.

Portfolio is a purposeful collection of students work that exhibit the students' efforts, progress, or achievement in given area. This collection must include:

- Students participation in selection of portfolio content,
- The criteria of selection,
- The criteria of judging merit, and
- The evidence of student self-reflection.

Thus, portfolios encourage teachers and schools to focus on important student outcomes, provide parents and the community with credible evidence of student achievement. Portfolio provides a cumulative record of growth and development of a skill or competence in an area over a period of time. It also enables a student to demonstrate to others, his/her learning and progress. Care should be taken that only selected works having specific purpose need to be put into the portfolio.

Q19. Write the usefulness of an exhibition in mathematics for the learners.

Or

How do you organise exhibition in mathematics for the learners?

Ans. In mathematics, we can also use exhibitions to share and assess student's learning. Mathematics exhibition creates opportunities for the learners to show their talent in mathematics outside the formal classroom activities. Such type of activity helps in skill building, developing positive attitudes among the learners and also fosters mathematical awareness among learners.

The students learn certain concepts using concrete objects and verify many mathematical facts and properties using models, measurements and other activities in the mathematics exhibition. Thus, Spenser and Angus (1998) point out that student exhibition involve complex cognitive skills as they must "collaboratively synthesise and evaluate information, and effectively communicate their ideas to others."

How to organise exhibition: The teacher should discuss the time and venue of the mathematical exhibition before organising it. The children should be intimated well in advance the exhibition so that they will get sufficient time to share among themselves, teachers and their guardians regarding their materials to be demonstrated in the exhibition. The children may prepare different models, materials, charts and interesting facts, puzzles etc. in the exhibition the parents may also give scope to participate. During the exhibition, different types of activities may be organised, which are as follows:

- Photo exhibition (photograph of mathematicians reflecting their contribution).
- Activities for parents to show their talents and participate in different activities.
- Demonstration of models, charts by the students and teachers.
- Different recreational activities in mathematics for the students.
- Demonstration of reference books in mathematics.
- Popular talk on different mathematical concepts by the teacher or invited experts.
- Teaching-learning material (TLM) preparation.

Exhibition can helpful in formative assessment as well as in assessing the learner's ability to apply the acquired knowledge in different situations. Observing the nature of learners, participation during different activities of the exhibition the teacher can assess the learner's understanding on a particular concept, his/her attitude towards mathematical learning. In addition, the teacher has to plan for further learning of the individual learner on the basis of the assessment findings. In addition, it creates scope for learning from each other in an informal situation as well as peer assessment.

Q20. How a teacher can assess the student's performance through quizzes and games?

Or

How do students learn mathematics from quizzes and games?

Ans. When students engage themselves in meaningful mathematical tasks then they learn mathematics more enthusiastically. Learners think mathematically by such tasks. Tasks like mathematical quizzes, puzzles and games provide situations to learn mathematics without fear and anxiety. While participating in those activities, the teacher should observe the learners and assess their performance. On the basis of the observation, the teacher should find out the areas where further inputs can be provided to the learners. The procedures of assessment through these activities are given below:

Quiz: A quiz is a brief assessment used in education and similar fields to measure growth in knowledge, abilities, and/or skills. Normally in the quiz progamme, oral questions are asked to the participants and those are responded orally. But sometimes the respondents are allowed to use paper-pencil to get the answer. The question may be asked to an individual participant or to a group of participants (preferably 2 or 3). Such techniques may be applied to conduct mathematical quizzes. The following points may be kept in mind while conducting mathematical quiz:

- Questions based on real life situations may be asked to the learners.
- Questions prepared by the learners during the course of teaching-learning process may also be used during quiz programme.
- All the children may be allowed to participate in the quiz programme.
- Questions based on audio-visual support may be used to arouse interest among the learners.
- Different round of answering like – answering using paper pencil, answering without paper-pencil, answering with clue and quick answer round may be conducted.

The teacher gets enabled by quiz programme to understand the student's progress in learning. It helps the teacher to know the learners interest towards mathematics learning. The teacher will observe how the students choose the answer and how they respond to the questions.

Games: Using games is one of the most important ways to teach efficiently. Games mean the world to children. Nothing is more fun than playing games for them because they feel happy and free while playing. In games, they participate naturally without any fear. Normally mathematics is associated with fear and failure. But participation of the child in different types of games and interesting puzzles removes the fear from the child. Such games and puzzles enable the child to understand the basic mathematical process without memorizing the facts and formulae. Also, the teacher creates situation to link the bookish knowledge to the real life situations.

Implicitly, the mathematical games create interest among the learners than the traditional teaching inside the classroom. But the teacher should plan carefully how the mathematical understanding is developed among the children through the game. Observing the children during the game (i.e. how they are planning & performing, communicating with each other, building strategies) helps the teacher to assess whether they are able to apply the mathematical ideas in other situations.

Q21. How observing children during mathematics activities will be beneficial for teachers in assessment process?

Ans. By observation, we mean directly observing student and class progress on particular mathematics activities. It is a technique of assessment for learning or formative assessment.

Some observations can be done in course of teaching from the behaviours like: how the child is answering the questions asked to him/

her, how he is describing the facts, how he is responding to the answers of other children, what type of questions he is asking the teacher, how he is presenting the group reports, how he is participating in the discussions, etc. During the activity, the teacher could record number of questions asked by distinct students. Various aspects of the child's personality development can be assessed. It can be used to assess individuals and groups. If a task is assigned to different groups then teacher can assess the performance of a group. Through observation, the teacher can get evidence of child's performance based 'on-the-spot' record. Over time, detailed observations of behaviour as well as interests, challenges-patterns/trends emerge which allow teachers to create a comprehensive picture/view of the child. So observations are to be made by the teacher over a period of time, across different activities and settings. When the child is engaged in a number of tasks/activities, it will be easier on the part of the teacher to observe the child and assess him. So teaching based on the *lecture method* cannot create scope for the child to do much works. Therefore, the child may be engaged in a lot of activities (individual/group) which will help the teacher to assess the child's learning as well as enable the child to identify his own weaknesses and rectify them.

Teacher can observe the children from a very close quarter without disturbing their attention on the activity. This would provide information on the children's style of learning and their learning difficulties.

- In the classroom, teacher can observe the level of participation of students in the activities. Many students are afraid of mathematics and do not like to get involved in group activities in mathematics. Detecting their reservations, teacher can take appropriate actions to improve their participation in mathematics activities.
- Better opportunity is provided by observation to detect the degree of involvement of each child in the activities, several personality characteristics, the strengths and weaknesses of students on the topics of concern.
- Teacher may gain insight into several aspects about students, learning of mathematical concepts like interest for mathematics activity, aesthetic sense of mathematics, symptoms of mathematical anxiety and phobia, typical errors committed, alternative methods applied for solution of problems, specific points of difficulty, etc. by observing them in mathematics class.

Q22. What points should be kept in mind while collecting assessment information regarding the child? Briefly list the kinds of information generated by evaluation.

Ans. The teacher can be helped to collect data regarding the learner's performance in mathematics by tools and techniques like written and oral tests, observation, interviewing the learner, portfolio analysis.

Every child is unique and s/he learns differently from others. His/her learning mathematics does not take place only in the school or classroom. S/he learns the mathematical concepts from the immediate environment. For example, while purchasing articles from the market the child uses the mathematical calculations in his/ her own way. Similarly, the community is the storehouse of a variety of mathematical knowledge and the child learns those in an informal way. So, teacher has to keep the following points in his/her mind while collecting assessment information regarding the child.

- What are the sources to collect information while assessing the child?
- What kind of information should be collected?
- In what way the information can be collected?

On assessment, different literatures suggest that a wide range of information should be collected regarding the assessment objects. According to Guba and Lincoln (1981), evaluation generates five kinds of information:

- descriptive information regarding the evaluation objectives,
- information about relevant issues,
- information responsive to concerns of relevant audiences(here the parents and the teachers),
- information about values,
- information about standards to merits,

Q23. What dimensions of mathematical learning are included in the process of assessment? Briefly discuss tools and techniques to assess them.

Or

Enumerate tools and techniques of assessment of mathematics learning.

Ans. Teacher has to know the evaluation objectives while assessing the learner's performance in mathematics, and these objectives are essentially associated with the expected learning outcomes. In elementary school years, the learning outcomes are focused on developing *useful* capabilities and also on developing the ability to think and reason mathematically. Conceptual understanding and ability to understand and solve problems in the areas of numbers, number operations, fractions, shapes and spatial thinking, measurement, problem solving, patterns and data handling are some useful capabilities.

Based on these capabilities, the process of assessment in mathematics includes five major dimensions of mathematical learning for which the probable tools and techniques are given in below table:

Table 3.4: Tools and techniques of assessment of mathematical learning

Aspects to be assessed	Tools and techniques
Concepts and procedures	• Written, oral and performance tests and tasks. • Observation of interactions in classroom and elsewhere.
Mathematical reasoning	• Tests and/or tasks (written or oral) • Oral description of the process of solving any problem • Observation of interactions in the groups. • Observation of orderly approach to normal tasks.
Disposition towards mathematics	• Observing the participation of the child in different mathematical activities like mathematics exhibition, puzzles, games • Observation of learner's interest in collecting and preparing TLMs, reading articles relating to mathematics, Portfolios. • Child's participation in performing mathematical tasks.
Using mathematical knowledge to solve problems	• Written and oral tests. • Projects and assignments. • Observing learner in co-curricular activities.

Mathematical Communication	• Content analysis of communications (written articles, diagrams, pictures, and recorded interactions, portfolios) • Observation, interviews and interaction in the classroom and elsewhere.

Q24. Why is recording of assessment results necessary?

Ans. To monitor the learner's progress in different dimensions of development is the main purpose of recording the assessment results. These areas are achievement in scholastic areas, physical, cognitive, social, emotional, creativity and personality, and such other areas indicative of a holistic growth and development. The requirements of different stakeholders are served by the record of assessment:

- It provides information to teachers on the recent and the earlier results to estimate the trend of progress/development of the learner so as to make appropriate decisions regarding the management of teaching-learning activities for improvement and enrichment of students' learning.
- It is a permanent source for the administrators and planners of education basing on which the school effectiveness is evaluated and appropriate planning can be made for enhancement of quality of learning in the school.
- It provides feedback to learner regarding his/ her progress along with the areas of his/her strength and weakness which in turn motivates for improving his/her learning.
- It intimates the parents regarding the status of learning growth of their child making them aware of the care to be taken in specific areas in which the child has problem and requires help and attention from the family.

In addition to these, reporting helps to present several attributes of each learner in the class, which ordinarily is not possible to capture for a teacher on a single occasion. About each learner small incidents recorded in different times when reviewed afterwards presents a holistic picture of the learners' learning progress.

Q25. Give structure of the individual progress card to record the learner performance in mathematics suggested by the NCERT. Also, discuss the aspects from which teachers have to be cautious while recording the learner's progress.

Ans. Across the country, different types of report cards are being used in different schools. Following is the individual progress card to record the learner performance in mathematics suggested by the National Council for Educational Research &Training, New Delhi:

Table 3.5: Record of Progress

Child's Name: **Class:**	**Recording results of**		
	Item-1	**Item-2**	**Item-3**
Conceptual Area (1) counting & concept of numbers (2) recognition of numerals and knowledge of number names (3) writing numerals (4) grouping round tens and ones **Mathematical reasoning** Is able to appreciate alternate ways of solving problem Is able to invent his own new problem Is able to help others at solving problems Is able to appreciate source of others. Is able to use mathematical reasoning in other curricular area **Mathematical Communication** is able to explain why she did and why/ how she solved the problem Is able to listen and follow explanations and solutions given by others **Attitudes and Dispositions** Is confident and willing to attempt new problems Is willing to persist with problems and does not give up too easily Seeks out and solves new problems. Enjoys doing mathematical problems			

We have to be cautious while recording the learner's progress in this progress card:

- Recording has to be done individually.
- Recording format would vary depending on the type of data and the way it is generated.
- Recording has to be done with positive and helping mindset to enhance learning level of student. Recording should not be an exercise of fault finding.
- We have to finalise the specific conceptual areas in which we want to assess the learner's performance.
- We have to conduct activities on that conceptual area, so that during the process of working we can assess the learner's performance.
- Acquisition of knowledge, understanding and skills in conceptual areas can be reflected in the progress card in the form of marks or grades. Task based assessments is emphasised, no assessment would be complete without paper pencil tasks on worksheets.
- Moreover, the common features on the specific content areas (aspects of mathematical reasoning, communication and attitudes) need to be observed objectively and recorded in appropriate form.

In this progress card, not only the recording will helpful for us to get a holistic picture on the child's performance and learning progress, but the collection of material like teacher's analytical notes, sample of child's work, special work sheets designed to teach as well as assess can help us. Formal notes in the form of written records may be kept by us for future reference, but ongoing classroom observation in the form of mental notes we make as we teach and while children work should be a part of assessment.

Q26. How to identify strengths and weaknesses from recorded data for assessment? How is it beneficial for teachers?

Ans. The purpose of assessment can be solved by only recording the performance, rather its utility to plan for further learning of individual child is very important. The next work of teacher is to analyse the data critically once the record is filled in and ready. Here the recording of the assessment results of two teachers are given.

Teacher-A

Suhana conducted an assessment on some selected conceptual areas of mathematics in class-V. She recorded the performance of the children as follows:

Table 3.6: Recording of assessment results

S.No.	Name of the child	Marks obtained by students			
		Oral (10)	Written (30)	Performance (10)	Total (50)
(1)	Riya	6	23	6	35
(2)	Ravi	9	24	8	41
(3)	Akash	3	12	5	20
(4)	Karan	5	19	9	26
(5)	Rohit	8	16	4	28

Teacher-B

Divya analysed the same assessment activity in different way. She recorded the performances of the children as given below:

Table 3.7

S. No.	Name of the child	Marks obtained by students					
		Fractions as part of a whole (10)	Fractions as part of a collection (10)	Fractions as division (10)	Understanding equivalence Of fractions (10)	Estimating fractional quantities	Total (50)
(1)	Riya	10	9	8	6	2	35
(2)	Ravi	10	10	7	10	4	41
(3)	Akash	7	6	5	2	0	20
(4)	Karan	7	7	6	4	2	26
(5)	Rohit	8	8	6	4	2	28

In the recording done by Mrs. Suhana, the strengths and weaknesses of individual learner with respect to mode of responses to the test item can be obtained. But in the second format, Mrs. Divya presented the assessment results with respect to conceptual areas given in the syllabus. In the second case, the teacher tries to analyze item wise, so that she can be able to identify the conceptual area which the child has not mastered. On the basis of the strengths and weaknesses of the child, plan for further learning can be made. So it is important on the part of the teacher to record the learning performances in such a way that S/he can get a comprehensive picture of each child's learning performances.

Identification of the strengths and weaknesses of individual learner are beneficial in following manner:

- Those children who have mastered a particular concept may be engaged in a variety of ways such as: helping other children to learn the concept, developing TLMs on the concept, assisting he teacher in other classroom activities.

- The learner can be motivated to learn those concepts which s/he has not mastered. Different learning experiences may be provided to the individual child to learn those concepts which he has not understood.
- Students with good mathematical communication skills and positive attitude towards mathematics learning may be engaged in leading learning of mathematics, in different types of mathematical activities like organisation of mathematics club, mathematics exhibition etc.

Q27. Identify and address typical problems in assessment of learning mathematics.

Ans. Some children face peculiar difficulties during learning mathematics in some situations. Those peculiar mistakes committed by the children cannot be reflected in marks and grades. We can understand it better by the case study given below:

Naksh is a class III student in a primary school. While learning the concept of 'number name and writing the numbers', he commits some mistakes frequently. Once the teacher calls a number name and asked Naksh to write the number like 103, 210 123. In response Naksh wrote the numbers like 1003, 20010 and 10023 respectively. The teacher gave Naksh zero mark and recorded the mark in his progress card.

We have observed that Naksh was unable to write the three digit numbers correctly. But the peculiar problems can not be identified from the marks or the progress report card.

Across the education sector, teachers are discovering the work of Newman (1977), who suggests five prompts to assist in determining students' errors with attempting to solve word problems (White 2005). These errors are discussed as follows:

- **Reading Errors (R):** If a student could not read a key word of symbol that prevented him/her from proceeding further.
- **Comprehension Errors (C):** The student read all the word or symbol correctly but had not understood the overall meaning and thus unable to proceed further.
- **Transformation Errors (T):** The student is unable to identify the operation, or series of operation.
- **Process Errors (P):** The student was able to identify the appropriate operation, or series of operations, but did not know the necessary measures to carry out these operations perfectly.

- **Encoding Errors (E):** The student worked out a solution to a problem but could not express the solution in an acceptable written form.

Above problems committed by the learners should be identified at the right time and appropriate interventions may be given to rectify them. Therefore, teacher should observe each child during the teaching-learning process. When teacher suspects that some children are committing typical errors over a period of time, teacher has to use further diagnostic processes to identify the errors. Teacher may record these results using codes or descriptive sentences.

Q28. Discuss the process of providing feedback on assessment to learners, parents and other stakeholders.

Or

What is the significance of providing feedback to learners, parents and stakeholders? [April-2016, Q.No.-38]

Or

Why is feedback to parents necessary in teaching-learning process? [October-2016, Q.No.-22]

Ans. On the basis of learning outcome, helping the students and parents to take the decision is a part of the school evaluation system. A particular decision may depend upon specific information. So a viable reporting system should be in place to help the learner, his/ her parents and other stakeholders to use the assessment outcomes. Following discussion is about who needs information and how these people use it:

(1) Feedback to the learners: In education, there has been increased emphasis on the importance of feedback to learners. The feedback to the learner is basically of two folds: to which level s/he has achieved the educational objectives and the way of communication of this information to them.

The children may be empowered to take decisions on the basis of the assessment outcomes for their learnings in mathematics. They may be guided to take right decisions in the following areas:

- It should be informed to the learner that in which conceptual areas s/he has specific learning difficulties. If the learner is doing mistakes in the division of fractional number, s/he need not be once again oriented on all the concepts of fractional number, rather s/he may be provided with additional instruction to perform division operations only.

- Though the results of the formative assessment provide periodical feedback to the learner to identify his/her problems and eradicate the problems, on the other hand summative assessment helps the learner to take long-term plan for improving the performance in mathematics.
- The knowledge of learning achievement improves subsequent learning. The learner may be guided to take decision on the nature of curricular preparation.
- On the basis of the learning outcomes, the teacher may identify specific learning difficulties of individual learner. On the basis of that, daily interaction between the teacher and the student may be done. This will help the learner to be motivated to learn.

The children are subjected to demonstrate very high level performance in the school subject mathematics by the parents and teachers irrespective of their levels of capacity to learn. Therefore, while providing feedback on mathematics to the young learners, the teacher needs to be extremely careful on the following aspects:

- The teacher should provide the results of assessment correctly and accurately without any change.
- The teacher should convey the feedback to the learner individually and not in groups as far as possible.
- No disparaging comment should be given on poor performance by the learner.
- The teacher should discuss with the learner in a very cordial and encouraging manner as to the ways of improving his/her further performance.
- The teacher should be honest with the learners and should not adopt any pretension while providing feedback.

(2) Feedback to the parents: Section 24(d) & 24(e) of the Right of Children to Free and Compulsory Education Act, 2009 states:

A teacher appointed under sub-section (1) of section 23 will perform the following duties, namely:

(d) Assess the learning ability of each child and accordingly supplement additional instructions, if any, as required;

(e) Hold regular meetings with parents and guardians and appraise them about the regularity in attendance, ability to learn, progress made in learning and other relevant information about the child.

Regarding the progress of the child in learning, the teacher has to appraise the parents in the meetings. On the other hand, parents also need to know how their children are doing in school and good reporting practices should result in improved relations between home and school. Reporting to parents on learning progress in mathematics can enable them:

- to take care of the study at home,
- to discuss with the teachers on student's learning and development,
- to know to what extent the child has learned,
- to help the child by providing with other reference books and supporting materials,
- to monitor whether the child is doing the mathematical projects activities, homework given to him by the school.

The progress card (written communication) can help the parents to get an information regarding child's learning and progress. But a comprehensive reporting system covers a variety of ways. Convening parent-teacher meetings, meeting of the Mother-Teacher Association (MTA) to discuss and share the learning outcome is very helpful. The parent-teacher meeting can act as an important supplement to the written report of student's progress.

Fig. 3.3: Parents-teacher meeting

Following points may be kept in mind while preparing and conducting the parents meeting to appraise them about the child's progress in learning mathematics:

Table 3.8: Considerations for parent-teacher meeting

What to do in the meeting?	Description
Teacher has to make plan for the meeting	• the venue and timing of the meeting, • what type of information regarding the child to be communicated.

	• Organizing information well in advance what you are going to present before them. • arrangement of written assignments and portfolio of the child that to be shown to the parents
Begin the meeting in a positive manner	• welcome them to the meeting so that they will feel comfortable • make positive comment on the child's performance
Presenting the student's strong points first	• give appropriate examples on the student's strength • show the parents evidence of students performance e.g. portfolio, pictures, projects, written assignments • comparison of the improvement in two assessment event
Encourage parents to participate and share	• listening the parents carefully • noting down what are their expectations • get information about the child's activities at home
Plan a course of action cooperatively	• appraise them what they will do at their home • say them how they can support their child
Using good human skills during the meeting	• explaining in understandable words, try to avoid technical terms • willing to accept their feelings, do not reject their suggestions • do not compare one child's performance with another

(3) **Feedback to other stakeholders:** The recorded results need to be shared with different stakeholders like, administrators, teachers, monitoring personnel, as feedback so that each stakeholder can contribute to learner's progress in his own way.

- The teacher of mathematics needs to evaluate his/her own strengths and weaknesses which might have some impact on the performance of the learner. If the learners are doing well in some aspects of a conceptual area, but poorly in others, teacher needs to examine his/her instructional procedure.

- The effectiveness of the school and teacher is indicated by the summative assessment outcomes. On the basis of the results, planning for teacher capacity building in mathematics may be made. In which areas of the content the teachers need content upgradation programme and what type of pedagogical skills they required.
- In mathematics, performances of learner provide useful feedback to take decisions regarding types of materials required for the teachers and learners in mathematics. The learner's behaviour gives insight to review the vision of mathematics learning, the nature of textbook, the instructional strategies and the assessment procedure to be adopted by the school and the state authorities.
- The planning for monitoring of the teacher's activity and providing need based on-site support to the teacher can be obtained from the assessment outcomes of the learners.

In the learning of the child, parents, teachers and administrators should work as partners. The assessment outcomes provide feedback to all the partners. They should jointly plan for a better mathematics education in the schools on the basis of the outcomes.

Q29. What are the essential steps to follow up measures of assessment in mathematics?

Or

What remedial activities are adopted by the teacher to overcome the learning difficulties after diagnosis of the specific learning difficulties of the learner?

Or

Enumerate enrichment activities in mathematics.

Or

Give one difference between remedial activities and enrichment activities in mathematics. [October-2016, Q.No.-23]

Ans. There are two levels of evaluation in diagnosing students learning difficulties. First, students who need some form of remediation must be identified. Consistently poor performance in mathematics implies the need to intervene and modify student behaviour. Second, the specific areas of weakness must be determined. One example of a class may be taken:

In a class during the teaching of division of fractions, the following weaknesses were observed. Some children faced problem to divide a proper fraction with another proper fraction. Three/four students performed the operation correctly, but cannot communicate the operation correctly while some children found problem in dividing a proper fraction by 1.

The teacher can go for extensive diagnostic testing after careful observation of problems of the learners. Then the specific learning difficulties of individual learner may be identified and noted in his personal profile. To overcome learner's difficulties the teacher may plan for providing remedial activities to him/her.

In mathematics, item analysis data can also provide a basis for remedial work. Though the test results in a class can clarify and correct many specific points, item analysis frequently brings to light general areas of weakness requiring more focused attention.

The teacher may revisit particular concept on the basis of the specific learning difficulties of the learner. Item analysis may indicate a general weakness, in understanding principles or in the ability to interpret the data in a word problem in mathematics. Such information makes it possible to focus remedial work directly on the particular areas of weakness.

Nature of the remedial activities: The teacher has to plan for remedial activities to overcome the learning difficulties and help him/her in learning after diagnosis of the specific learning difficulties of the learner. The remedial activities could focus on the following:

- More interesting and provides alternate learning experience to the child, i.e. different learning experience from the earlier one.
- More material intensive.
- Individualised in nature.
- Presented in step wise. The task may be broken into smaller steps, where after each step the learning progress can be assessed.
- Based on the experience of the child.

Enrichment activities in mathematics: There are the children who face learning difficulties; on the other hand, there are some children who are doing well. The teacher should help those children to enrich their potential. A conducive and enriched environment may be provided to those children so they can learn to optimize their ability. The nature of enrichment activities are as follows:

- The activities involve higher order thinking.
- As far as possible open-ended items may be given as enriched activities for them.
- While performing mathematical calculations, the time may be delimited for those children. Sometimes within a specific time period, they may be asked to solve more problems.
- The children may be encouraged to find alternate solutions to a given problem and formulate more mathematical problems as a part of enrichment activity.

In mathematics, this is how the recording and reporting of learning outcomes can be done and used in our schools. A well designed recording and reporting practice can be helpful in creating a conducive learning environment in the school. The assessment results can be best utilised with a scientific recording and reporting system. On the basis of the outcomes, the teacher can plan for optimising the learning of individual learner. Read GPH books and score excellent marks.

Objective Type Questions

Q1. Which characteristic is not involved in Continuous and Comprehensive Evaluation?

(a) It increases the workload on students by taking multiple tests.

(b) It replaces marks with grades.

(c) It evaluates every aspect of the student.

(d) It helps in reducing examination phobia.

Ans. (a) It increases the workload on students by taking multiple tests.

Q2. A teacher who is not able to draw the attention of his students should

(a) Evaluate his teaching method and improve it

(b) Resign from the post

(c) Find fault in his pupils

(d) Start dictating

Ans. (a) Evaluate his teaching method and improve it

Q3. Which aspect of mathematics learning makes its assessment a systematic process?

(a) Interest and attitude

(b) Mathematical learning

(c) **Logical and hierarchical structure**

(d) **Mathematical reasoning**

Ans. (c) Logical and hierarchical structure

Q4. What is the sum of the measure of the interior angles of a quadrilateral?

(a) **180**

(b) **90**

(c) **120**

(d) **360**

Ans. (d) 360

Q5. What are the aspects would you focus for assessing the student's participation in the learning activity in the classroom?

(a) **Style of presentation, use of appropriate formula, use of own language**

(b) **Sharing, active involvement, asking and answering questions**

(c) **Taking leadership, doing self correction, participation in the group work**

(d) **Comparison, self analysis, reflection**

Ans. (b) Sharing, active involvement, asking and answering questions

Q6. The number 9 is an odd number, because

(a) **It is the biggest one digit number**

(b) **It is not divisible by 2**

(c) **It has three factor**

(d) **It is the square of 3**

Ans. (b) It is not divisible by 2

Q7. What is the sum of the measures of the interior angles of a triangle (in degree)?

(a) **90**

(b) **180**

(c) **270**

(d) **360**

Ans. (b) 180

Q8. What is the formula to find out the perimeter of a rectangle?

(a) **P=2(l+w)**

(b) **P=a+b+c**

(c) **P=4a**

(d) $C=2\pi r$

Ans. (a) P=2(l+w)

Q9. By which source(s) you can get variety of questions other than those available in the textbooks.

(a) You can prepare questions by yourself

(b) You can bring some questions from different reference materials

(c) You can collect the questions prepared by the students during the course of teaching

(d) All of the above

Ans. (d) All of the above

Q10. Projects can be used as_______of assessment in mathematics.

(a) Opportunities to explore

(b) curricular areas

(c) effective tools and techniques

(d) interest towards the work

Ans. (c) effective tools and techniques

Q11. What is to be observed during the exhibition for assessing a learner?

(a) Are the activities showed variety, flexibility, creativity and innovation?

(b) Different recreational activities in mathematics for the students

(c) Teaching-learning material (TLM) preparation

(d) Demonstration of reference books in mathematics

Ans. (a) Are the activities showed variety, flexibility, creativity and innovation?

Q12. An equilateral triangle has:

(a) Three equal sides

(b) Two equal sides with an angle of 90 degree

(c) Three unequal sides

(d) One obtuse angle

Ans. (a)Three equal sides

Q13. While conducting mathematical quiz which of the following point may be kept in mind:

(a) Students participation in selection of portfolio content

(b) The evidence of student self-reflection

(c) All the children may be allowed to participate in the quiz programme

(d) Preparing the report

Ans. (c) All the children may be allowed to participate in the quiz programme.

Q14. Newman(1977) suggested a diagnostic process of structured interview to identify:

(a) Typical mistakes in mathematics learning

(b) Strengths and weaknesses

(c) Performance of the children

(d) Learning of individual child

Ans. (a) Typical mistakes in mathematics learning

Q15. How many principles are there in assessment of mathematics learning?

(a) 5

(b) 3

(c) 8

(d) 4

Ans. (b) 3

Q16. Project creates scope for:

(a) Preparing the report

(b) oral and written items

(c) Keeping record

(d) Learning mathematical concepts

Ans. (d) Learning mathematical concepts

Q17. Different color cards may be used for:

(a) Questions on different objectives and subjects

(b) project activities

(c) Develop student's self-confidence

(d) practical activities

Ans. (a) Questions on different objectives and subjects

Q18. By which which medium teacher can get evidence of child's performance based 'on-the-spot' record:

(a) Project

(b) Learning

(c) Observation

(d) Search

Ans. (c) Observation

Q19. Participation of the learners in activities like project, portfolio, mathematical exhibition, quiz, mathematical games helps the learner to learn in:

(a) An informal way

(b) A formal way

(c) An interview

(d) None of the above

Ans. (a) An informal way

Q20. In order to overcome specific learning difficulties, teacher plans for:

(a) enrichment activities

(b) remedial activities

(c) feedback

(d) record of progress

Ans. (b) remedial activities

Q21. For doing comprehension assessment, it is required to use:

(a) only multiple-choice questions

(b) only projects

(c) only skill-based tests

(d) variety of tools and techniques

Ans. (d) variety of tools and techniques

Q22. The average of three numbers is 84. Find the numbers. This is:

(a) an open-ended item

(b) a closed-ended item

(c) a comprehension item

(d) impossible

Ans. (a) an open-ended item

Q23. Providing more examples, converting words into symbols and vice versa, verifying conclusions, etc., are related to:

(a) knowledge objective

(b) comprehension objective

(c) application objective

(d) skill objective

Ans. (b) comprehension objective

Q24. Which of the following is not a measure of central tendency?

(a) Median

(b) Range

(c) Mode

(d) Mean

Ans. (b) Range

Q25. Choose a tool or technique for assessment among the following:

(a) Projects and activities

(b) Concepts and procedure

(c) Mathematical reasoning

(d) Mathematical communication

Ans. (a) Projects and activities

☺☺☺

Question Papers

Diploma in Elementary Education (D.El.Ed.)
Learning Mathematics at Elementary Level
(504)
April, 2016

Note : (i) Attempt **all** the questions.
(ii) Marks are indicated against each question.

निर्देश : (i) **सभी** प्रश्न हल कीजिए।
(ii) प्रत्येक प्रश्न के सामने अंक दिए गए हैं।

Note : Question Nos. **1** to **15** are multiple-choice questions. Choose the correct alternative from (A), (B), (C) and (D) and write it in the answer-book:

निर्देश : प्रश्न संख्या 1 से 15 बहु-विकल्पीय प्रश्न हैं। दिए गए विकल्पों (A), (B), (C) एवं (D) में से सही विकल्प चुनकर उत्तर-पुस्तिका में लिखिए:

Q1. "The students will be able to differentiate between prime and composite numbers." This is a:

(A) broader aim

(B) narrower aim

(C) general aim

(D) instructional objective

"छात्र भाज्य तथा अभाज्य संख्याओं में अंतर करना सीखेंगे।" यह है एक:

(A) विस्तृत उद्देश्य

(B) संक्षिप्त उद्देश्य

(C) सामान्य उद्देश्य

(D) अनुदेशात्मक उद्देश्य

Ans. (D) instructional objective

Q2. Optimisation means:

(A) utilisation of available conditions and resources to the fullest extent

(B) increase the availability of resources

(C) demand for good conditions and resources

(D) form good conditions and construct good resources

समुचित उपयोगिता का अर्थ है:

(A) उपलब्ध संसाधनों एवं परिस्थितियों का पूर्णतम उपयोग

(B) संसाधनों की उपलब्धता को बढ़ाना

(C) अच्छी परिस्थितियों एवं संसाधनों की माँग करना

(D) अच्छी परिस्थितियाँ तैयार करना एवं अच्छे संसाधनों की रचना करना

Ans. (A) utilisation of available conditions and resources to the fullest extent

Q3. Providing mathematics learning beyond classroom is:

(A) dull

(B) difficult

(C) boring

(D) joyful

कक्षा से बाहर गणित शिक्षा होती है:

(A) नीरस

(B) कठिन

(C) उबाऊ

(D) आनंददायक

Ans. (D) joyful

Q4. Nature of mathematics is:

(A) good

(B) positive

(C) exact

(D) problem solving

गणित की प्रकृति है:

(A) अच्छी

(B) सकारात्मक

(C) सटीक

(D) समस्या का समाधान

Ans. (C) exact

Q5. Matching, sorting, comparing, ordering are:

(A) number concepts

(B) pre-number concepts

(C) counting process

(D) measurement concepts

मिलान, छाँटना, तुलना करना, क्रमबद्धता है:

(A) संख्या अवधारणाएँ

(B) पूर्व-संख्या अवधारणाएँ

(C) गिनती प्रक्रिया

(D) मापन अवधारणाएँ

Ans. (B) pre-number concepts

Q6. How many integers lie between –10 and +10?

(A) 21

(B) 20

(C) 19

(D) 18

–10 तथा +10 के मध्य कितने पूर्णांक आते हैं?

(A) 21

(B) 20

(C) 19

(D) 18

Ans. (C) 19

Q7. In cyclic quadrilateral *PQRS*, if $\angle P = 50^\circ$ and $\angle Q = 110^\circ$, then

(A) $\angle R = 50^\circ$ **and** $\angle S = 110^\circ$

(B) $\angle R = 130^\circ$ **and** $\angle S = 70^\circ$

(C) $\angle R = 110^\circ$ **and** $\angle S = 50^\circ$

(D) $\angle R = 70^\circ$ **and** $\angle S = 130^\circ$

चक्रीय चतुर्भुज *PQRS* में, यदि $\angle P = 50^\circ$ तथा $\angle Q = 110^\circ$, हैं, तो

(A) $\angle R = 50^\circ$ तथा $\angle S = 110^\circ$

(B) $\angle R = 130^\circ$ तथा $\angle S = 70^\circ$

(C) $\angle R = 110^\circ$ तथा $\angle S = 50^\circ$

(D) $\angle R = 70^\circ$ तथा $\angle S = 130^\circ$

Ans. (B) $\angle R = 130^\circ$ and $\angle S = 70^\circ$

Q8. In drawing a pie chart, students use:

(A) central angle

(B) straight angle

(C) right angle

(D) circle

पाई-चार्ट बनाने में विद्यार्थी प्रयोग करते हैं:

(A) केंद्रीय कोण

(B) सरल कोण/रेखीय कोण

(C) समकोण

(D) वृत्त

Ans. (D) circle

Q9. Identify binomial among the following:

(A) Three times a number

(B) *m* divided by 12

(C) Twice a number multiplied by 8

(D) 15 subtracted from a number

निम्न में से द्विपदीय पद की पहचान करें:

(A) एक संख्या का तीन गुना

(B) m को 12 से भाग दिया

(C) किसी संख्या के दुगुने की 8 से गुना

(D) किसी संख्या में से 15 घटाना

Ans. (D) 15 subtracted from a number

Q10. Providing more examples, converting words into symbols and vice versa, verifying conclusions, etc. are related to:

(A) knowledge objective

(B) comprehension objective

(C) application objective

(D) skill objective

अधिक उदाहरण देना, शब्दों को संकेतों व संकेतों को शब्दों में बदलना, निष्कर्षों को जाँचना आदि संबंधित हैं:

(A) ज्ञान उद्देश्य से

(B) समझ उद्देश्य से

(C) अनुप्रयोग उद्देश्य से

(D) कौशल उद्देश्य से

Ans. (B) comprehension objective

Q11. In order to overcome specific learning difficulties, teacher plans for:

(A) enrichment activities

(B) remedial activities

(C) feedback

(D) record of progress

विशिष्ट अधिगम कठिनाइयों को दूर करने हेतु अध्यापक नियोजित करते हैं:

(A) समृद्धिकरण गतिविधियाँ

(B) सुधारात्मक गतिविधियाँ

(C) पृष्ठपोषण

(D) प्रगति का रिकॉर्ड

Ans. (B) remedial activities

Q12. Choose a tool or technique for assessment among the following:

(A) Projects and activities

(B) Concepts and procedures

(C) Mathematical reasoning

(D) Mathematical communication

निम्नलिखित में से आकलन के उपकरण अथवा तकनीक का चयन करें:

(A) परियोजनाएँ तथा गतिविधियाँ

(B) अवधारणाएँ तथा प्रक्रियाएँ

(C) गणितीय तार्किकता

(D) गणितीय संप्रेषण

Ans. (A) Projects and activities

Q13. Place, where new innovations in mathematics with hands on experience can be done, is:

(A) Mathematics classroom

(B) Mathematics library

(C) Mathematics laboratory

(D) Mathematics teacher's room

गणितीय क्रियाकलाप करके नई गणितीय खोज करने का स्थान है:

(A) गणित की कक्षा

(B) गणितीय पुस्तकालय

(C) गणितीय प्रयोगशाला

(D) गणित शिक्षक का कक्ष

Ans. (C) Mathematics laboratory

Q14. Which natural number is neither prime nor composite?

(A) 0 **(B) 100**

(C) –1 **(D) 1**

निम्नलिखित में से कौन-सी प्राकृत संख्या न तो भाज्य है, न ही अभाज्य?

(A) 0 (B) 100

(C) –1 (D) 1

Ans. (D) 1

Q15. Numbers 10 and 33 form a pair of:

(A) prime numbers

(B) composite numbers

(C) co-prime numbers

(D) twin primes

संख्याएँ 10 तथा 33 युग्म बनाती हैं:

(A) अभाज्य संख्याओं का

(B) भाज्य संख्याओं का

(C) असहभाज्य संख्याओं का

(D) यमज अभाज्य का

Ans. (C) co-prime numbers

Note : Question Nos. **16** to **30** are very short answer-type questions. Answer each question in few words or one/two sentence(s):

निर्देश : प्रश्न संख्या 16 से 30 अति लघु-उत्तरीय प्रश्न हैं। प्रत्येक प्रश्न का उत्तर कुछ शब्दों या एक वाक्य/दो वाक्यों में दीजिए:

Q16. Mention two reasons for developing fear for mathematics in the classroom.

कक्षा-कक्ष में गणित के प्रति भय के दो कारण लिखें।

Ans. Refer to Chapter-1, Q.No.-5

Q17. Which method focuses on application or use of formula directly on problem?

कौन-सी विधि समस्याओं के हल में सूत्रों के प्रत्यक्ष उपयोग पर केंद्रित है?

Ans. Deductive method focuses on application or use of formula directly on problem.

Q18. What is meant by conservation of length?

लंबाई के संरक्षण से क्या तात्पर्य है?

Ans. Conservation of length is attained when the child realises that the length of an object remains unchanged irrespective of the position of the object.

Q19. Differentiate between cardinal aspect and ordinal aspect of numbers.

संख्याओं के गणनात्मक पहलू तथा क्रमबद्ध पहलू में अंतर स्पष्ट करें।

Ans. Refer to Chapter-1, Q.No.-2

Q20. Mention two visions for school mathematics as stated in NCF, 2005.

राष्ट्रीय पाठ्यचर्या रूपरेखा, 2005 में कथित विद्यालयी गणित के दो परिप्रेक्ष्यों का उल्लेख करें।

Ans. Refer to Chapter-1, Q.No.-16

Q21. Find the mean of data given below:

10, 11, 12, 13, 14, 15, 16, 17, 18, 19

नीचे दिए गए आँकड़ों का माध्य ज्ञात करें–

10, 11, 12, 13, 14, 15, 16, 17, 18, 19

Ans. $\text{Mean} = \frac{\text{Sum of Observations}}{\text{No. of Observations}}$

$$= \frac{10+11+12+13+14+15+16+17+18+19}{10}$$

$$= \frac{145}{10} = 14.5$$

Q22. 0.001 m³ water is poured into a container that already contains 1000 cm³ water. Find total volume of water in litres.

1000 घन से.मी. पानी भरे बर्तन में 0.001 घन मीटर पानी डाला गया है। पानी का कुल आयतन लीटर में ज्ञात करें।

Ans. We know that $1000\ cm^3 = 1\ l$

and $1 m = 100\ cm$

$0.001 m^3 = 0.001 \times 100 \times 100 \times 100\ cm^3$

$= 1000\ cm^3$

$= 1\ l$

So, the total volume of water = Already contained water + Poured water

$= (1 + 1)\ l$

$= 2\ l$

Q23. Name any two non-standard units of length using body parts.

शरीर के अंगों के प्रयोग से लंबाई की कोई दो अमानक इकाइयों के नाम बताएँ।

Ans. Refer to Chapter-2, Q.No.-73

Q24. To construct an angle of measure 82.5° using ruler and compass, what should be the break-up of angle?

रूलर और परकार के प्रयोग से 82.5° माप के कोण की रचना करने के लिए कोण का विभाजन किस प्रकार होना चाहिए?

Ans. Refer to Chapter-2, Q.No.-61

Q25. Define complementary angles.

पूरक कोण को परिभाषित करें।

Ans. Refer to Chapter-2, Q.No.-30 (2)

Q26. Define 'solar year'.

'सूर्य वर्ष' को परिभाषित करें।

Ans. Refer to Chapter-2, Q.No.-89

Q27. Give two characteristics of a bar diagram.

दंड आलेख की दो विशेषताएँ बताएँ।

Ans. Refer to Chapter-2, Q.No.-99

Q28. Convert the following to open-ended item:

"Find average of 412, 115 and 133."

निम्न को मुक्त पद में परिवर्तित करें:

"412, 115 तथा 133 का औसत ज्ञात करें।"

Ans. Open ended item for the given item is :

"The average of three numbers is 220. What are those numbers"?

Q29. Which characteristics of student may be observed to assess attitudes and dispositions towards mathematics?

गणित के प्रति रुख एवं मनोवृत्ति जानने के लिए छात्र के किन गुणों का अवलोकन किया जाना चाहिए?

Ans. To assess attitudes and dispositions of students towards mathematics, we have to observe their classroom activities, their mode of questioning and their participation in different co-curricular activities.

Q30. Mention two purposes fulfilled by a question bank.

प्रश्न बैंक द्वारा पूर्ण होते दो उद्देश्य लिखें।

Ans. Refer to Chapter-3, Q.No.-16

Note : Question Nos. 31 to 40 are short answer-type questions. Answer the questions briefly in not more than 50 words each:

निर्देश : प्रश्न संख्या **31** से **40** लघु-उत्तरीय प्रश्न हैं। प्रत्येक प्रश्न का संक्षिप्त उत्तर अधिकतम 50 शब्दों में दीजिए:

Q31. What are the benefits of 'problem posing' for learning?

अधिगम में 'समस्या निर्माण' के क्या लाभ हैं?

Ans. Refer to Chapter-1, Q.No.-25

Q32. Write basic unit for measure of mass. Relate it to three higher units.

द्रव्यमान के माप की मूल इकाई बताएँ। तीन उच्च इकाइयों से इसका संबंध बताएँ।

Ans. Refer to Chapter-2, Q.No.-86

Q33. Define and explain concept map with example.

अवधारणा का खाका को परिभाषित करें एवं उदाहरण सहित समझाएँ।

Ans. Refer to Chapter-1, Q.No.-28

Q34. What is the broader aim of mathematics education? Discuss.

गणित शिक्षा का विस्तृत उद्देश्य क्या है? चर्चा करें।

Ans. Refer to Chapter-1, Q.No.-14

Q35. Name few subjects to which you can relate 'mathematics'. Discuss relation of mathematics with any two of these subjects.

कुछ ऐसे विषयों के नाम लिखें जिनसे आप गणित को संबंधित कर सकते हैं। इनमें से किन्हीं दो विषयों की गणित से संबंध की चर्चा करें।

Ans. Refer to Chapter-1, Q.No.-11

Q36. What is the process of mathematical thinking for problem posing and problem solving?

समस्या निर्माण तथा समस्या समाधान में गणितीय सोच की क्या प्रक्रिया है?

Ans. Refer to Chapter-1, Q.No.-13

Q37. Mention different aspects of mathematics learning to be assessed.

गणित अधिगम में आकलन करने वाले के विभिन्न पक्षों की चर्चा करें।

Ans. Refer to Chapter-3, Q.No.-4

Q38. What is the significance of providing feedback to learners, parents and stakeholders?

विद्यार्थियों, अभिभावकों एवं संबंधितों को पृष्ठपोषण उपलब्ध कराने का क्या महत्त्व है?

Ans. Refer to Chapter-3, Q.No.-28

Q39. The length of a rectangular plot exceeds its breadth by 3 metres. Perimeter of the plot is 154 metres. Find the length of the plot.

किसी आयताकार भूखंड की लंबाई उसकी चौड़ाई से 3 मीटर अधिक है। भूखंड का परिमाप 154 मीटर है। भूखंड की लंबाई ज्ञात करें।

Ans. Let breadth of the plot = x m

then length = x + 3 m

and Perimeter = 154 m (given)

Now, Perimeter of the plot = $2(l+b)$

Hence, $2(l+b) = 154$

$\Rightarrow \quad 2(x+x+3) = 154$

$\Rightarrow \quad 2(2x+3) = 154$

$\Rightarrow \quad 4x + 6 = 154$

$\Rightarrow \quad 4x = 148$

$\Rightarrow \quad x = \frac{148}{4} = 37$

Hence, breadth of the plot = 37 m

and length = 37 + 3

= 40 m

Thus, the length of the plot is 40 m.

Q40. Write properties of 'addition in rational numbers'.

'परिमेय संख्याओं में योग' के गुणधर्म लिखें।

Ans. Refer to Chapter-2, Q.No.-7

Note : Question Nos. 41 and 42 are long answer-type questions. Answer each question elaborately in not more than 500 words:

निर्देश : प्रश्न संख्या **41** और **42** दीर्घ-उत्तरीय प्रश्न हैं। प्रत्येक प्रश्न का उत्तर विस्तारपूर्वक अधिकतम 500 शब्दों में दीजिए:

Q41. What must be the nature of assessment of mathematics learning? What types of errors are committed in mathematics learning at the early school level?

गणित अधिगम के आकलन की प्रकृति कैसी होनी चाहिए? गणित अधिगम के दौरान, प्रारंभिक विद्यालय स्तर पर विद्यार्थी किस प्रकार की गलतियाँ करते हैं?

Ans. Refer to Chapter-3, Q.No.-3 and Q.No.-27

Q42. Name the stages of cognitive development according to Piaget. Discuss the main features of each stage.

पियाजे के अनुसार संज्ञानात्मक विकास की अवस्थाओं के नाम लिखें। प्रत्येक अवस्था के मुख्य लक्षणों की चर्चा करें।

Ans. Refer to Chapter-1, Q.No.-1

Diploma in Elementary Education (D.El.Ed.)
Learning Mathematics at Elementary Level
(504)
October, 2016

Note : (i) Attempt **all** the questions.
(ii) Marks are indicated against each question.

निर्देश : (i) **सभी** प्रश्न हल कीजिए।
(ii) प्रत्येक प्रश्न के सामने अंक दिए गए हैं।

Note : **Question Nos. 1 to 15 are multiple-choice questions. Choose the correct alternative from (A), (B), (C) and (D) and write it in the answer-book:**

निर्देश: प्रश्न संख्या 1 से 15 बहु-विकल्पीय प्रश्न हैं। दिए गए विकल्पों (A), (B), (C) एवं (D) में से सही विकल्प चुनकर उत्तर-पुस्तिका में लिखें:

Q1. Cumulative frequency is required to calculate:

(A) median
(B) mode
(C) mean
(D) standard deviation

निम्नलिखित में से किसकी गणना के लिए संचयी बारंबारता की आवश्यकता रहती है?

(A) माध्यक
(B) बहुलक
(C) माध्य
(D) मानक विचलन

Ans. (A) median

Q2. Product of $(a - b)$ and $(5a + 3b)$ is:

(A) $5a^2 - 3b^2$
(B) $5a^2 + 2ab - 3b^2$
(C) $5a^2 - 2ab - 3b^2$
(D) $5a^2 - 2ab + 3b^2$

$(a - b)$ तथा $(5a + 3b)$ का गुणनफल है:

(A) $5a^2 - 3b^2$
(B) $5a^2 + 2ab - 3b^2$

(C) $5a^2 - 2ab - 3b^2$

(D) $5a^2 - 2ab + 3b^2$

Ans. (C) $5a^2 - 2ab - 3b^2$

Q3. Which of the following is not a measure of central tendency?

(A) Median

(B) Range

(C) Mode

(D) Mean

निम्नलिखित में से कौन-सा केंद्रीय प्रवृत्ति का मापक नहीं है?

(A) माध्यक

(B) परिसर

(C) बहुलक

(D) माध्य

Ans. (B) Range

Q4. Sum of two numbers is 64. One number is thrice the other. The two numbers are:

(A) 30 and 34

(B) 14 and 42

C) 16 and 48

(D) 24 and 40

दो संख्याओं का योग 64 है। एक संख्या दूसरी संख्या की तीन गुनी है। दो संख्याएँ हैं:

(A) 30 तथा 34

(B) 14 तथा 42

(C) 16 तथा 48

(D) 24 तथा 40

Ans. (C) 16 and 48

Q5. One litre is equal to:

(A) $\frac{1}{10}$ **decalitre**

(B) $\frac{1}{10}$ **decilitre**

(C) $\frac{1}{100}$ **deciliter**

(D) $\frac{1}{100}$ **decalitre**

एक लीटर के बराबर है:

(A) डेकालीटर

(B) डेसीलीटर

(C) डेसीलीटर

(D) डेकालीटर

Ans. (A) $\frac{1}{10}$ decalitre

Q6. Formula for volume of pyramid is:

(A) $\frac{1}{3} \times$ base area $\times$ height

(B) $3 \times$ base area $\times$ height

(C) $\frac{1}{2} \times$ base area $\times$ height

(D) $2 \times$ base area $\times$ height

पिरामिड के आयतन का सूत्र है:

(A) $\frac{1}{3} \times$ आधार का क्षेत्रफल $\times$ ऊँचाई

(B) $3 \times$ आधार का क्षेत्रफल $\times$ ऊँचाई

(C) $\frac{1}{2} \times$ आधार का क्षेत्रफल $\times$ ऊँचाई

(D) $2 \times$ आधार का क्षेत्रफल $\times$ ऊँचाई

Ans. (A) $\frac{1}{3} \times$ base area $\times$ height

Q7. In a cyclic quadrilateral *KLMN*:

(A) $KL = LM = MN = NL$

(B) $m\angle K = m\angle L = m\angle M = m\angle N$

(C) $m\angle K + m\angle L = m\angle M + m\angle N = 180°$

(D) $m\angle L + m\angle N = m\angle K + m\angle M = 180°$

चक्रीय चतुर्भुज *KLMN* में:

(A) $KL = LM = MN = NL$

(B) $m\angle K = m\angle L = m\angle M = m\angle N$

(C) $m\angle K + m\angle L = m\angle M + m\angle N = 180°$

(D) $m\angle L + m\angle N = m\angle K + m\angle M = 180°$

Ans. (D) $m\angle L + m\angle N = m\angle K + m\angle M = 180°$

Q8. For doing comprehensive assessment, it is required to use:

(A) only multiple-choice questions

(B) only projects

(C) only skill-based tests

(D) variety of tools and techniques

व्यापक आकलन करने के लिए किसका प्रयोग किया जाना चाहिए?

(A) केवल बहुविकल्पीय प्रश्न

(B) केवल परियोजना

(C) केवल कौशल-आधारित प्रश्न

(D) विभिन्न प्रकार के उपकरण एवं तकनीक

Ans. (D) variety of tools and techniques

Q9. The average of three numbers is 84. Find the numbers. This is:

(A) an open-ended item

(B) a closed-ended item

(C) a comprehensive item

(D) impossible

तीन संख्याओं का औसत 84 है। संख्याएँ ज्ञात करें। यह:

(A) एक मुक्त पद है

(B) एक बंद पद है

(C) एक व्यापक पद है

(D) असंभव है

Ans. (A) an open-ended item

Q10. The record of assessment is important, because:

(A) it provides feedback to learner

(B) it provides information to teachers for planning of activities

(C) it intimates the parents the areas in which child requires attention and help

(D) All of the above

आकलन का रिकॉर्ड महत्त्वपूर्ण है, क्योंकि:

(A) यह विद्यार्थी को पृष्ठपोषण प्रदान करता है

(B) यह शिक्षकों को गतिविधियों की योजना हेतु सूचनाएँ देता है

(C) यह अभिभावकों को सूचित करता है कि किस क्षेत्र में बच्चे की ओर ध्यान देने और उसे सहायता की आवश्यकता है

(D) उपर्युक्त सभी

Ans. (D) All of the above

Q11. Choose the incorrect statement.

(A) Mathematics is precise

(B) Mathematics is problem

(C) Mathematics is symbolic

(D) Mathematics is logical

असत्य कथन का चयन करें।

(A) गणित सटीक है।

(B) गणित समस्या है।

(C) गणित चिह्नात्मक है।

(D) गणित तार्किक है।

Ans. (B) Mathematics is problem

Q12. 'Problem-solving process' does not involve the process of:

(A) observing and inferrring

(B) comparison and classification of objects

(C) trial and error

(D) merely contemplating knowledge already gained

'समस्या-समाधान प्रक्रिया' में कौन-सी प्रक्रिया सम्मिलित नहीं है?

(A) अवलोकन तथा अनुमान लगाना

(B) तुलना करना तथा वस्तुओं का वर्गीकरण करना

(C) जाँच और त्रुटि

(D) केवल पहले से प्राप्त ज्ञान पर विचार करना

Ans. (D) merely contemplating knowledge already gained

Q13. Which of the following is an instructional objective of mathematics?

(A) To apply mathematics in other subjects

(B) To apply addition of two-digit numbers in solving problems of daily life

(C) To see aesthetics in mathematics

(D) To become familiar with mathematical language and symbolism

निम्नलिखित में से कौन-सा गणित का अनुदेशनात्मक उद्देश्य है?

(A) अन्य विषयों में गणित का उपयोग करना

(B) दैनिक जीवन की समस्याओं के हल में द्वि-अंकीय संख्याओं के जोड़ का प्रयोग करना

(C) गणित में कलात्मकता देखना

(D) गणितीय भाषा और चिह्नों से परिचित होना

Ans. (B) To apply addition of two-digit numbers in solving problems of daily life

Q14. 'From abstract to concrete' is related to:

(A) inductive method

(B) deductive method

(C) analytic method

(D) synthetic method

'अमूर्त से मूर्त' संबंधित है:

(A) आगमन विधि से

(B) निगमन विधि से

(C) विश्लेषणात्मक विधि से

(D) संश्लेषणात्मक विधि से

Ans. (B) deductive method

Q15. New innovations in mathematics with hands on experience can be done in:

(A) mathematics classroom

(B) mathematics library

(C) mathematics laboratory

(D) mathematics teacher's room

गणितीय क्रियाकलाप करके नई गणितीय खोज करने का स्थान है:

(A) गणित का कक्षा-कक्ष

(B) गणितीय पुस्तकालय

(C) गणितीय प्रयोगशाला

(D) गणित शिक्षक का कक्ष

Ans. (C) mathematics laboratory

Note : Question Nos. **16** to **30** are very short answer-type questions. Answer each question in few words or one/two sentence(s):

निर्देश : प्रश्न संख्या 16 से 30 अति लघु-उत्तरीय प्रश्न हैं। प्रत्येक प्रश्न का उत्तर कुछ शब्दों या एक वाक्य/दो वाक्यों में दें:

Q16. Write one major aim of mathematics education.

गणित शिक्षा का एक मुख्य उद्देश्य लिखें।

Ans. Refer to April-2016, Q.No.-34

Q17. Form a conjecture related to the following pattern:

3 + 2 = 5	5 + 2 = 7
3 + 4 = 7	5 + 4 = 9
3 + 6 = 9	5 + 6 = 11

निम्नलिखित प्रतिरूप से संबंधित एक अनुमान (कंजेक्चर) बताएँ:

3 + 2 = 5	5 + 2 = 7

3 + 4 = 7 5 + 4 = 9

3 + 6 = 9 5 + 6 = 11

Ans. From the given pattern, we can conclude that the sum of an even number and an odd number is always an odd number.

Q18. Give an example to show the relation between 'mathematics and science'.

'गणित तथा विज्ञान' के संबंध को दर्शाता एक उदाहरण दें।

Ans. Refer to Chapter-1, Q.No.-11

Q19. Which of the pre-number concepts are used for classification of objects?

वस्तुओं के वर्गीकरण के लिए कौन-सी पूर्व-संख्या अवधारणाओं का प्रयोग किया जाता है?

Ans. Matching and sorting

Q20. In which stage of cognitive development are the students of primary classes?

प्राथमिक कक्षाओं के विद्यार्थी ज्ञानात्मक विकास की किस अवस्था में होते हैं?

Ans. Concrete operational stage

Q21. During assessment for mathematics learning, one student wrote story involving the concept, other collected information from newspapers and another student went to relevant public place to gather information. Which assessment technique is being applied by the teacher?

गणित अधिगम के आकलन के मध्य, एक विद्यार्थी ने संबंधित अवधारणा पर कहानी लिखी, दूसरे ने समाचार-पत्रों से जानकारी एकत्रित की तथा एक अन्य विद्यार्थी जानकारी एकत्रित करने संबंधित सार्वजनिक स्थान पर गया। शिक्षक द्वारा कौन-सी आकलन तकनीक प्रयोग की गई?

Ans. Portfolio Technique

Q22. Why is feedback to parents necessary in teaching-learning process?

शिक्षण-अधिगम प्रक्रिया में अभिभावकों को पृष्ठपोषण उपलब्ध कराना आवश्यक क्यों है?

Ans. Refer to Chapter-3, Q.No.-28

Q23. Give one difference between remedial activities and enrichment activities in mathematics.

गणित में सुधारात्मक गतिविधियों व समृद्धिकरण गतिविधियों में एक अंतर लिखें।

Ans. Refer to Chapter-3, Q.No.-29

Q24. How many lines of symmetry are there in a square?

एक वर्ग की कितनी सममिति रेखाएँ होती हैं?

Ans. There are four lines of symmetry in a square.

Q25. Find the range of the given data:

10, 11, 12, 13, 14, 15, 16, 17, 18, 19

दिए गए आँकड़ों का परिसर ज्ञात करें:

10, 11, 12, 13, 14, 15, 16, 17, 18, 19

Ans. The range of the given data = 19 – 10 = 9

Q26. 1000 cm^3 water is poured into a container already containing 0.001 m^3 water. Find the total volume of water in litres.

0.001 m^3 पानी से भरे बर्तन में 1000 cm^3 पानी डाला गया। पानी का कुल आयतन लीटर में ज्ञात करें।

Ans. Refer to April-2016, Q.No.-22

Q27. Using body parts, name any two non-standard units of length.

शरीर के अंगों का प्रयोग कर लंबाई की किन्हीं दो अमानक इकाइयों के नाम लिखें।

Ans. Refer to April-2016, Q.No.-23

Q28. Write the number of terms and the terms in the expression $-\frac{2pq}{5}+7$.

बीजीय व्यंजक $-\frac{2pq}{5}+7$ में पदों की संख्या तथा पद बताएँ।

Ans. No. of terms = 2

Terms in the expression = $-\frac{2pq}{5}, 7$

Q29. What is the formula for perimeter of a rhombus?

समचतुर्भुज के परिमाप का सूत्र क्या है?

Ans. The formula for perimeter of a rhombus is,

$P = 4 \times a$, where P is perimeter and a is side of the rhombus.

Q30. Dates of birth of Kanak and Pritika are 29.06.2010 and 06.09.2012 respectively. What is the difference in their age?

कनक और प्रीतिका की जन्मतिथियाँ क्रमशः 29.06.2010 और 06.09.2012 हैं। उनकी आयु में क्या अंतर है?

Ans.

	Year	Month	Day
Pritika	2012	09	06
Kanak	2010	06	29
	02	02	07

On this basis, we can say that Pritika is older than Kanak by 2 years 2 months and 7 days but, 2012 is a leap year. So February has 29 days. Hence, we will add 1 day to the obtained result. And hence, it can be concluded that Pritika is older than Kanak by 2 years, 2 months and 8 days.

Note : Question Nos. **31** to **40** are short answer-type questions. Answer the questions briefly in not more than 50 words each:

निर्देश : प्रश्न संख्या **31** से **40** लघु-उत्तरीय प्रश्न हैं। प्रत्येक प्रश्न का संक्षिप्त उत्तर अधिकतम 50 शब्दों में दें:

Q31. Explain "additive identity in $\mathbb{W}$, $\mathbb{Z}$ and $\mathbb{Q}$ is zero whereas no additive identity exists in $\mathbb{N}$".

व्याख्या करें "*W, Z* तथा *Q* में शून्य योज्य-तत्समक है जबकि *N* में कोई योज्य-तत्समक नहीं है"।

Ans. The element zero, denoted 0, is an element of $\mathbb{W},\mathbb{Z},\mathbb{Q}$ and has the property that for every number $a \in (\mathbb{W},\mathbb{Z},\mathbb{Q})$, a + 0 = a = 0 + a. So we are not able to add zero to any natural number to get that natural number within the set $\mathbb{N}$ again because additive identity is not applicable like $\mathbb{W}$, $\mathbb{Z}$ and $\mathbb{Q}$.

Q32. Draw a flowchart showing the interrelation connecting different types of quadrilaterals.

भिन्न प्रकार के चतुर्भुजों का आपसी संबंध दर्शाता हुआ एक प्रवाह चार्ट बनाएँ।

Ans. Refer to Chapter-2, Q.No.-34

Q33. What is a 'solar year'? How will you relate 'solar year' to 'solar day'?

'सूर्य वर्ष' से क्या तात्पर्य है? आप 'सूर्य वर्ष' को 'सूर्य दिवस' से कैसे जोड़ेंगे?

Ans. Refer to Chapter-2, Q.No.-89

Q34. Mention four behavioural specifications related to 'comprehension objective' in Mathematics learning.

गणित अधिगम में 'समझ उद्देश्य' संबंधी चार व्यवहारगत विशेषताएँ बताएँ।

Ans. Refer to Chapter-3, Q.No.-13

Q35. Suggest a mathematical game/activity to teach single-digit subtraction to Class I students.

कक्षा I के विद्यार्थियों को एक-अंकीय व्यवकलन सिखाने के लिए कोई गणितीय खेल/गतिविधि सुझाएँ।

Ans. A mathematical activity to teach single-digit subtraction to Class-I students is as follows:

There are seven toys in a basket. Three of them are broken. Students are asked to tell the number of unbroken toys in the basket to teach them subtraction. To get the answer of this question, students will be asked to pop out broken toys from the basket and count the remaining unbroken toys. Students will count them and give the answer as 4 toys. Then they can learn single-digit subtraction with the help of this activity.

Q36. Give two measures to remove 'mathematics phobia' of a Class VIII student.

कक्षा VIII के एक विद्यार्थी का 'गणित से भय' मिटाने के लिए दो तरीके बताएँ।

Ans. Refer to Chapter-1, Q.No.-8

Q37. How would art education be affected, if there were no mathematics?

यदि गणित न होता, तो कला-शिक्षा किस प्रकार प्रभावित होती?

Ans. Refer to Chapter-1, Q.No.-11

Q38. Mention two points of vision for school mathematics as stated by NCF, 2005.

राष्ट्रीय पाठ्यचर्या रूपरेखा, 2005 के अनुसार विद्यालयी गणित के परिप्रेक्ष्य के कोई दो बिंदु लिखें।

Ans. Refer to Chapter-1, Q.No.-16

Q39. Mention the steps that a teacher follows in deductive approach for effective learning.

निगमन प्रणाली द्वारा प्रभावशाली शिक्षण के लिए शिक्षक द्वारा अनुसरण किए जाने वाले चरण बताएँ।

Ans. Refer to Chapter-1, Q.No.-21

Q40. Discuss 'exploration phase' of 5E's learning model.

पाँच अधिगम प्रतिमान के 'अन्वेषण चरण' की चर्चा करें।

Ans. Refer to Chapter-1, Q.No.-26

Note : Question Nos. **41** and **42** are long answer-type questions. Answer each question elaborately in not more than 500 words:

निर्देश : प्रश्न संख्या **41** और **42** दीर्घ-उत्तरीय प्रश्न हैं। प्रत्येक प्रश्न का उत्तर विस्तारपूर्वक अधिकतम 500 शब्दों में दें:

Q41. What are the problems in teaching and learning of mathematics? How do 'mathematics education beyond classroom' is helpful in overcoming these problems? Give examples.

गणित शिक्षण एवं अधिगम की समस्याएँ क्या हैं? इन समस्याओं के निवारण में 'कक्षा से बाहर गणित' किस प्रकार सहायक हो सकता है? उदाहरण दें।

Ans. Refer to Chapter-1, Q.No.-17 and Q.No.-18

Q42. What are the three principles of assessment of 'mathematics learning'? Also discuss any two criteria of a good assessment.

'गणित अधिगम' के आकलन के तीन सिद्धांत क्या हैं? एक अच्छे आकलन की किन्हीं दो कसौटियों की भी चर्चा करें।

Ans. Refer to Chapter-3, Q.No.-2

A teacher who is attempting to teach without inspiring the pupil with a desire to learn, is hammering on a cold iron.

-Horace Mann

Gullybaba Publishing House (P) Ltd.

Feedback

Although, we make every effort to ensure that there are no errors in GPH books. However, if you want to point out and suggest any error or want any improvement in any of our books, please let us know so that we could rectify as soon as possible. Your feedback may save hours of frustration for other readers and at the same time you will be helping students to get even higher quality study materials. Your criticisms/suggestions are highly welcomed.

feedback@gullybaba.com

Why Name Gullybaba?

® Gullybaba is a combination of two significant words '**Gully**' & '**Baba**'. The word 'Gully' comes from the ancient game played in Rural India–**Tip cat**. In Hindi, we call it **Gully Danda** (**गुल्ली डंडा**) which is a great **symbol of Focus & Force**. The word 'Baba' stands for **Respect & Honour**. And these are the fundamental parameters for achieving success. **Focus & Force** are required to help one go a long way in life. This is all about achieving excellence in education and giving respect & honour to everyone, and thus, the name 'Gullybaba'.

To know more about why name GullyBaba visit: **GullyBaba.com/why-name-gullybaba.html**

www.ingramcontent.com/pod-product-compliance
Ingram Content Group UK Ltd.
Pitfield, Milton Keynes, MK11 3LW, UK
UKHW021706190726
13853UKWH00001B/437

9 789386 276513